"The IRS 1031 exchange is one of the most powerful tools a real estate investor can use. Gary Gorman has succeeded in making this complicated subject very understandable."

Martin Stone, Buckingham Investments, author of <u>The Unofficial Guide to Real Estate Investing</u> and <u>Secure Your Financial Future Investing in Real Estate</u>

"Gary's depth of knowledge places him at the top of experts in the 1031 Tax Deferred Exchange. Coupled with this knowledge, Gary's ability to explain complicated nuances in very understandable pieces is brilliant. This book has my highest recommendation. My copy is at the ready for reference on my office bookshelf."

Bob Behrens, CCIM, 2004 CCIM Institute President and Founding Director RE/MAX C/I Division

"This is an outstanding book for everyone involved in any type of real estate activity."

Christy Gillespie, realtor, Sotheby's International Realty

"Exchanging Up! is an excellent book on key tax-saving strategies that every real estate investor should know and utilize."

Trevor Stapleton, Esq., LLM (Taxation)

"Gary Gorman has produced a clearly written book on one of the most important real estate strategies available today."

Kathy Spitzer, Esq., author of <u>The Wyoming Corporate Handbook</u>

D0189117

|

Exchanging Up!

How to Build a Real Estate Empire Without Paying Taxes

by

Gary Gorman

A SuccessDNA Nonfiction Book

Page design by ImageSupport.com, llc
Cover design by Mesh Creative, Inc.

SuccessDNA, Inc.
COPYRIGHT © 2005, Gary Gorman
All rights reserved
Printed in the United States of America
10 9 8 7 6 5 4 3 2 1

Library of Congress Catalog Card Number: in progress
ISBN# 0-9746844-6-5

 SUCCESS **DNA** is a trademark of SuccessDNA, Inc.

Forward

The ideas you are about to read have made it possible for the average working person to become incredibly wealthy investing in real estate. Rather than working long hours and paying much of what you earn in taxes, by following the simple guidelines of exchanging, you can have something that seems impossible.

You can make a fortune investing in real estate and either delay or perhaps never pay taxes.

The reason I know this is because starting out as a former auto mechanic, with just one deal, I turned $3,500 into over $350,000 using the magic of tax-free exchanging. I say "magic" because until I had the opportunity to read this book that you have in your hands, I never fully understood how it all worked.

I had to hire Gary Gorman numerous times as an expert advisor to make sure that the deals I was doing met the IRS requirements. So as helpful as this guide will be to you, please realize that thousands of others like myself have invested 40 to 50 times the price of this book to achieve the same results you will get. And even at 50 times the price of this book, it has been worth every penny.

So take this book home and read it now. Don't wait to begin using the money that you thought you had to pay in taxes to help explode the growth of your investing empire.

Peter Conti
Co-Author of <u>Making Big Money Investing in Foreclosures without Cash or Credit</u>

Dedication

There are a large number of people, without whose encouragement and prodding, this book would never have happened. But, in the end, the people who played the biggest and most important role were my staff. God has blessed me with the opportunity to work with the greatest people in the world, so, to them I dedicate this book. I couldn't be more proud of them. Each truly is a 1031 Exchange Expert:

Ginger Barnhart, Kelly Berard, Stephani Beslin, Kristin Cancilla, Jimmie Chew, Nace Cohen, Dan Conte, Nick Dooher, Mike Eloranto, Jim Forrester, Debby Gorman, Ramon Guerra, Warren Hill, Robert Hinkston, Tere Johnson (who died tragically in the middle of the writing of this book – we miss her humor every day), Cindy Larsen, Curtis Moore, Sarah Morgan, Ann Padilla, Bridget Quandt, James Schuler, JonAnn Shackford, Carla Tartivita, Nancy Thompson, Cody Walkup, Tracey Wilson, Kristy Woodyard and Sonny Zayas.

And I have to single out two of the staff for special recognition:

Mark Houston – who first conceived of this book, and then continued to gently prod me to do it. Without him, this book wouldn't be.

And

Debby – my wife and head of our Trust department. She keeps the morale up, and the emotional seas in the office as smooth as glass. She is the sun around which all of us planets revolve. Without her I couldn't do it and wouldn't want to anyway.

Thanks, gang!

Table of Contents

Chapter 1   **Introduction**   **1**
What is an Exchange? Why would you want to do one?
How did these transactions come to be?

Chapter 2   **Held for Investment**   **9**
Property held for investment qualifies for an Exchange,
while property held for resale does not. The chapter
explains the difference.

Chapter 3   **45-Day Identification Requirement**   **21**
You have to submit a list of property that you might
purchase. Who do you submit the list to, and in what
format? What if you miss the deadline?

Chapter 4   **180-Day Purchase Deadline**   **33**
You have 180 days to purchase your replacement
property, and whatever you buy must be on your 45-Day
List.

Chapter 5   **Qualified Intermediary Requirement**   **39**
You have to use an independent third party – called a
Qualified Intermediary – to handle your Exchange. Who
can be an Intermediary? What do Intermediaries do?
How do they hold your money? How do you pick a
good one?

Chapter 6   **You Cannot Touch the Money**   **53**
You cannot touch the money in between the sale of
your Old Property and the purchase of your New. What
if you don't spend all the money – when can you get the
balance? What if you decide not to complete the
Exchange?

Chapter 7   **Ownership Issues**   **61**
However you hold title to the Old Property is how you
have to take title to the New.

Chapter 8   **Equal or Up**   **73**
You must buy equal or up. How do you calculate your
target price? What happens if you don't meet it?

Chapter 9   **Reinvest All the Cash**   **79**
You must reinvest the net cash from your Exchange.
How do you calculate the net cash? What happens if
you don't reinvest all of it? When can you get the
excess?

Chapter 10   **Related Pary Transactions**   **87**
With one exception, you cannot sell your Old Property
to, or buy your New Property from, a related party.

Chapter 11   **Seller Financing**   **91**
What if the buyer wants you to carry-back part of the
sales price? How does this affect your Exchange? How
do you make this tax-free?

Chapter 12   **What Documents Are Part of an Exchange**   **97**
What documents will you be required to sign? What do
they mean? Who prepares them, and when do you sign
them?

Chapter 13   **Reverse Exchanges**   **107**
You cannot take title to the New Property before you've
closed the sale of your Old Property. The IRS-approved
method for getting around this rule is called a "Reverse
Exchange," and this chapter explains how they are
structured, along with the two major speed bumps that
could impact you.

Chapter 14   **Construction Exchanges**   **119**
A Construction Exchange happens when you sell your
Old Property and use part of the money to buy a piece
of bare land and the balance of the money to build a
structure on the land.

Chapter 15   **Build-to-Suit Transactions**   **127**
The IRS has issued a couple of rulings that provide
guidance for taxpayers who want to sell their Old
Property and use the funds to build a structure on land
that they already own.

Chapter 16   **Improvement Exchanges**   **131**
An Improvement Exchange happens when you sell your
Old Property and use part of the money to buy a
replacement property and the balance of the money to
fix it up.

Chapter 17   **Tenants-in-Common (TIC) Transactions**   **137**
The IRS has special rules for TIC (rhymes with "stick")
transactions – groups of people whose Exchanges are
combined by a sponsor who is paid to organize the
group.

Chapter 18   **Personal Property Exchanges**   **145**
Personal Property is what the IRS calls property that can
be moved (furniture, fixtures, planes, boats, cars, etc.).
The rules governing 1031 Exchanges on personal
property are completely different from that for real
estate.

Chapter 19   **Mixed Use Exchanges**   **157**
Mixed Use Exchanges involve property that is either
part real estate and part personal property (like
restaurants and hotels) or involves only a partial 1031
Exchange (such as with an office in the home).

Chapter 20   **Exchanges of U.S. Real Estate by Nonresidents**   **163**
You do not have to be a United States citizen to own
real estate in this country. Nonresidents can also do
Exchanges, but are subject to special rules.

Chapter 21   **How to Turn Exchange Property Into Cash With
Little or No Tax**   **167**
You've built this real estate empire, and now you want
to turn it into cash, but you want to pay little or no tax.
This chapter will give you some ideas on how to
accomplish this.

Chapter 22   **Conclusion**   **175**

Appendix A   **Complete Copy of IRS Section 1031**

Appendix B   **Complete Copy of the Regulations for Section 1031**

About the Author

About the 1031 Exchange Experts, LLC

Chapter 1:
Introduction

What Does an Exchange Do?

In simple terms, a 1031 Exchange rolls the gain from the sale of an Old Property to a New Property. For example, Sue Jones sells her purple duplex (her "Old Property") and buys a different property, using the steps and following the requirements set out by the IRS in Section 1031, established specifically for exchanging property.

If Sue's gain on the sale of her purple duplex is $40,000, and she follows the requirements of Section 1031, this gain is transferred to her New Property. If Sue's New Property appreciates by $20,000, and she sells it, she can do another Exchange and roll the combined gain of $60,000 into the third property.

There is no limit to the number of times you can do an Exchange and continue to roll over the gains – all the while continuing to build your financial empire.

This book will teach you the steps you have to follow to successfully navigate the IRS rules for exchanging so that you too can "trade up" to wealth and financial security. Exchanging is one of the last tax loopholes left and is used daily by thousands of taxpayers to avoid paying tax. People with gains as small as $5,000 or $10,000 are successfully exchanging their property and building wealth.

Common Misconceptions About Exchanges

There are several common misconceptions about the Exchange process. First, people are confused about the proper protocol of an

Exchange. Second, they have misunderstandings about the type of property they must acquire. And third, some are misinformed about how they have to acquire the New Property.

Protocol. Section 1031 is all about form. If you sell your Old Property then turn around and fairly quickly buy a New Property, the transaction will be taxable. It may seem like that's what happens in an Exchange, but it will be taxable because you didn't follow the proper format required by Section 1031. If you don't want to pay tax, you have to follow the exact letter of the law.

Type of Property. Another old misconception is that what you buy has to be essentially the same as what you sold. If you sell a purple duplex, many think that you have to buy a purple duplex. Not true. As you will learn in this book, you can acquire any type of investment property, or trade and business property. (Trade and business property is property that you use in your business.)

Swapping Deeds. There are still people around who believe that if, for example, you have a purple duplex, you have to find someone who also has a purple duplex and then swap deeds simultaneously. Not true. If you follow the rules, you can sell your Old Property and then go out and find the New Property of your dreams.

Why Do An Exchange?

There are probably as many reasons why people do Exchanges as there are Exchanges being done. Nonetheless, we see some classic patterns when people Exchange property.

Increase Cash Flow. By moving from one property to another, a person can create or increase monthly cash flow. For example, if Fred sells a piece of bare land, with negative cash flow because of property taxes and insurance, he could Exchange into a piece of income-producing property (like an office building) that provides net rental income from the rents minus expenses. Fred can use an Exchange to create positive cash flow.

If Sue sells her purple duplex, which provides her with positive monthly cash flow of $500, and Exchanges into a different property that will give her positive monthly cash flow of $750, Sue's cash flow will increase by 50 percent (or $250) by doing an Exchange.

Job Relocation. If Sue takes a job transfer from California to the company headquarters in Connecticut, Sue can move her rental property with her by selling her purple duplex in Los Angeles and buying a replacement rental property in Connecticut.

Using the Tax Monies to Leverage Up. By doing an Exchange and not paying the tax, the funds that would have gone to the tax payments are now available for you to acquire larger replacement property without taking on additional debt. For example, if Sue's gain on the sale of her purple duplex is $100,000, her combined federal and state tax will run between $25,000 and $35,000 (or more) depending upon what state Sue lives in.

By doing an Exchange, rather than selling the duplex, paying the tax and using the net proceeds to buy the New Property, Sue can buy a larger New Property. For example, let's assume that the tax would only be $25,000, and let's assume that the lender will loan Sue 75 percent, if Sue puts down 25 percent. By doing an Exchange, Sue will have an extra $25,000 that would not be available to her if she paid the tax. The lender will loan Sue an additional $75,000 against this $25,000, allowing Sue to buy an additional $100,000 of property - more than she would be able to if she paid the tax.

If the value of her property doubles over the next ten years, Sue's additional property will grow to $200,000 in value. If she sells the property after ten years and pays back the $75,000 loan, the tax she didn't pay (of $25,000) will have created $100,000 of wealth for Sue (after paying back the loan of $75,000, she'll have $125,000 left, including the $25,000 of taxes deferred from the original sale). Sue used the tax money to leverage up.

You Must Prove an Exchange

As you read this book, you may come to the conclusion that what happens in an Exchange is that you sell your Old Property and within a certain timeframe you buy your New Property, and as a result you have an Exchange, and you don't have to pay tax on the gain (or at least not right now).

If this is the conclusion you come to, you've missed the real essence of an Exchange – the form of the transaction has to be exact. Not the substance, the form. This is one of those Code sections where you have to do everything exactly correctly, and even one tiny "foot fault" can end up in you paying substantial tax, if not tax on the entire transaction. Close enough is not good enough.

The place to start when you do an Exchange is to state that you intend to do an Exchange. Not that you intend to sell your Old Property and replace it with your New Property, but that you truly intend to

Exchange the Old Property for the New.

So how do you prove intent? The best way is to make that statement as part of the sale of your Old Property. Make it a clause, or an addendum, to your contract. The wording does not have to be complicated. Simply say that, as the seller, you intend to do an Exchange. (This is a good time to get the buyer's cooperation, so you may also want to include an addendum that the buyer agrees to cooperate with your Exchange). For the same reason, make it clear that your New Property is part of your Exchange by adding a clause, or addendum, that says, you, as the buyer, intend to do an Exchange, or intend to Exchange into, the property (and, of course, that the seller agrees to cooperate with you). Neither clause has to be complicated or fancy. You don't need an attorney to write it. You just want a clear statement, on the record (in the contracts), that ties the Old Property and the New Property together in an Exchange.

Types of Exchanges

There are actually a number of different kinds of Exchanges: Forward (or what I call "straight") Exchanges, Consolidation Exchanges, Diversification Exchanges, Reverse Exchanges, Construction Exchanges, and Improvement Exchanges.

Forward or Straight Exchanges. Typical Exchanges. You sell your Old Property and then you buy your New Property. For example, Sue sells her purple duplex and buys an office building. Pretty straightforward stuff. In this book when I talk about a straight exchange, this is what I'm talking about.

Consolidation Exchanges. When you sell a number of Old Properties and buy one or two New Properties. For example, Sue has built a real estate empire and now owns ten rental houses. In order to simplify her life, she wants to sell the ten properties and buy one large property with on-site management. She would do what we call a Consolidation Exchange.

Diversification Exchanges. The opposite of Consolidation Exchanges. You sell one Old Property and buy several New Properties. Every time there is a hurricane in Florida or an earthquake in California, we'll get a slew of calls from people who have decided it makes sense to sell their one investment property and buy several (maybe two or three) new properties in different parts of the country in order to spread their risk. They are diversifying – hence the name Diversification Exchange.

Reverse Exchanges. When you want to, or need to, buy the New Property before you've sold your Old Property. The IRS has rules that prevent you from owning both the Old Property and the New Property at the same time, and they now have rules that show you how to get around the first set of rules. I know it makes no sense – why didn't they just change the first rules? But they didn't, and these types of Exchanges are called Reverse Exchanges.

Construction Exchanges. When you sell your Old Property and use part of the proceeds to buy a piece of bare land and the balance of the proceeds to build a structure on it.

Improvement Exchanges. Similar to a Construction Exchange, an Improvement Exchange happens when you sell your Old Property and you use a portion to buy a structure that needs work and the balance of the proceeds to pay for the improvements.

The History of Exchanges

Much of tax law is "social legislation" – Congress creates tax law in order to create a desired result. So it was with Exchanges. The United States first imposed income taxes in 1918, and all dispositions of property were taxed under that first Internal Revenue Code. The first Code section allowing "like-kind" Exchanges was added to the Code in 1921.

While we've lost much of what those early legislators were thinking, it's clear that they felt it was in the best interest of the nation that taxpayers be encouraged to roll the gain from the sale of their Old Property to their New Property relatively tax-free. (I don't like the IRS terms of "relinquished property" and "replacement property" when I write. I feel that it takes too long for your brain to translate those terms, so I use the easy terms of Old Property and New Property).

From 1921 until the early 1970s the general interpretation of the requirements of a 1031 Exchange was that if you owned a purple duplex, you had to find someone who also owned a purple duplex and who wanted your purple duplex, and then the two of you would swap deeds. The two properties had to be relatively similar.

Since finding someone who had exactly what you wanted and who wanted your property, was difficult at best, we ended up with some very strange, multi-legged transactions. You had Property A, and wanted Property B, but the owner of B wanted C, who wanted D instead of C. The owner of Property D was willing to take your Property A, and in this way the Exchange circle was completed.

While this four legged transaction was complicated enough, I frequently saw ten, 15 or even 20-legged transactions. The real problem with Exchanges in those days was that if one of the legs collapsed, it usually meant that the whole transaction collapsed. It is still common today to run into people, especially older CPAs and attorneys who think that Exchanges are still done that way.

Starker Exchanges

In the late 1960s a wealthy Oregon landowner by the name of T.J. Starker, along with his son and daughter-in-law, sold several pieces of land. Mr. Starker was wealthy enough that he had excellent tax counsel, and these tax experts were convinced that you did not have to swap deeds to do an Exchange. So the Starkers sold their land and had the buyer hold the proceeds. Over the following five years the original buyers purchased a number of pieces of property, at the direction of the Starkers, and then transferred the title to them as their replacement property. As you might expect, the IRS attacked his Exchanges and the whole mess ended up in court.

In the end, the Starkers won, with the court ruling that it could find no requirement in Section 1031 for a Simultaneous Exchange. That opened the door, and for the next ten years or so people were running around doing their version of "Starker Exchanges." The IRS meanwhile was saying that only the Starkers could do a Starker Exchange. Needless to say, this was a real mess. So in 1991 Congress rewrote Section 1031 and added most of the elements that we have today.

T.J. Starker is truly the pioneer of modern 1031 Exchanges. Without his vision and the financial ability to push the cases through the court system, we wouldn't have the great exchanging opportunities we have today.

I still hear people call Exchanges "Starker Exchanges," but in truth it is an archaic term relating to Exchanges as they were done during the 1980s. Because of the Code section rewrites caused by Starker Exchanges, today's Exchanges are called "1031 Exchanges."

Real Estate vs. Personal Property Exchanges

In essence, Section 1031 has two parts: "real estate" and "personal property." Most of the Exchanges that we see are exchanges of real estate.

Real estate is dirt and everything that is attached to it, such as buildings, trees, rocks and water. Real estate also includes oil and gas as well as precious metals like gold and silver.

Personal property consists of things that move, such as planes, boats, construction equipment, professional sports contracts and even cattle.

Most of the Exchange rules are the same for both real estate and personal property. Since the vast majority of Exchanges are real estate Exchanges, that will be the topic of the vast majority of this book. Personal property rules are covered in a later section.

Section 1031 is an IRS Code Section

From time to time I hear concern that Exchanges are some type of gimmick, like the old butterfly straddle theories of the 1970s and 1980s. In fact, there is an IRS Code section, Section 1031, that says, in effect, that when you sell your Old Property and buy a New replacement Property within certain guidelines, the gain from the sale of the Old Property rolls into the New Property. In other words, the tax is deferred. The purpose of this book is to guide you through the mine field of Section 1031.

Section 1031 covers the sale of real estate and business personal property. Business personal property is stuff that can be moved: desks, restaurant equipment, hotel and motel furniture, boats, planes, cars, trucks and even horses.

The rules governing real estate and personal property are different. While there are certainly a substantial number of personal property Exchanges, the vast majority of 1031 Exchanges involve real estate, and I suspect real estate is the reason you bought this book. I'll cover real estate Exchanges first, because they are the most popular, and then I'll cover personal property Exchanges.

Section 1031 does not cover the sale of securities and shares in corporations, partnerships, limited liability companies, etc. It also does not cover the sale or purchase of shares in real estate investment trusts (REITS) and the like.

Chapter 2:
Held for Investment

In order to qualify for Section 1031, property has to be held as an investment or used in a trade or business. "Held for investment" means you intend to hold the property for future appreciation. For this reason, raw land is always investment property. You can also hold the property for the production of income. A classic example of this is rental property.

"Used in a trade or business" means ownership of the building your business occupies. If Fred owned a bicycle shop and also owned the building it occupied, the building is used in his trade or business. Fred could sell the building and do a 1031 Exchange.

If you get audited, the burden of proof is on you to prove that the property was held for investment. The IRS does not have the responsibility to prove that you held the property for investment or used it in a trade or business. It is your obligation to prove that it was.

Your personal residence does not qualify for a 1031 Exchange. For one thing, there is another Code section that covers the taxability of the gain on the sale of your house. But the real reason is that you don't own your house for the purpose of making a profit (at least not in the eyes of the IRS – in their opinion you purchased your house entirely for your personal enjoyment).

You can change the reason that you hold property. You can change a property from residence to rental property, which changes it from your residence to property that qualifies for a 1031.

In the classes I teach, I use the example of a mythical couple: Fred and Sue. Fred and Sue are both single. They meet somewhere, get married, and Sue moves into Fred's house. Sue then rents out her house. Her house is now 1031 property, and the house that Fred and Sue live in is their personal residence and is not available for a 1031 Exchange as long as they live in it.

One fact that I should point out right here is that it is very common for two or more IRS Code sections to apply to a given transaction at the same time. If Fred and Sue move out of Fred's house, rent it and move into another house, then Fred's house might be eligible for a 1031 Exchange and might also be eligible for a different Code section that makes the sale of personal residences partially or completely tax-free. I'll discuss this in greater detail later.

Property Held for Resale Does Not Qualify

After Section 1031 says that the gain from the sale of your Old Investment Property rolls over to your New Property, it then goes on to say that property "held primarily for resale" does not qualify for an Exchange. There are two classic examples of "held for resale." 1) The developer who buys, say 40 acres, re-plats it into 80 half-acre lots, puts in streets, sewers and gutters, and then puts a "for sale" sign in each lot. The IRS considers these people to be "dealers." You can do things that enhance the value of your property, like re-platting the land from 40 acres into 80 lots, but the thing that is fatal to your dreams of a 1031 Exchange is moving dirt. Once you start doing things like putting in streets and gutters, your Exchange is toast. 2) A "fix and flip" transaction – where you buy a property, fix it up and then resale it a couple of months later. This is probably the most classic example of a property that is held for resale.

Does this mean that you cannot buy a property, fix it up and then sell it and do a 1031 Exchange? The answer is no – you can buy a property and fix it up, but you have to hold it for investment. So how long do you have to hold it before it turns the magical corner from "held for resale" into "held for investment?" The answer that is accepted by most real estate professionals is a year and a day.

The reason that these two examples don't qualify for a 1031 Exchange is that it was your immediate intent to resell the property rather than hold it for investment. If you are in a business where some of your activities are development activities and some are investment type activities, you want to make sure that you keep the different activities in separate entities. There are court cases where Exchanges were disallowed because the developer activities "tainted" the investment activities that were in the same entity. And watch how you record property on the books. There is a case where the court disallowed an

Exchange where a piece of bare land was carried on the books as "work in progress" (which is a development activity term).

Both the Old Property and the New Property Should Be Held as an Investment for at least a Year and a Day

Where does the "year and a day" come from? It is not part of the law; it comes from a very old IRS ruling and a series of court cases that say that to hold a property for investment, you have to hold it for "two tax years." What is two tax years? If you buy a property in January and sell it in January of the following year, that is two tax years. Likewise, if you buy a property in July and sell it in January, that is also two tax years. It is the same if you buy a property in December and sell in January. This is because, as a calendar year taxpayer, when you pass December 31st, you pass into another tax year.

But that's not fair to the unfortunate person who bought his property in January. So, in order to level the playing field, the IRS has said in meetings that I've attended that the acceptable holding period is one year and one day. When Congress rewrote Section 1031, there was a proposal to adopt a one-year holding period as one of the requirements. This proposal was withdrawn at the last minute in favor of the intent test, but the benchmark of a year is still out there.

Another reason that the IRS has adopted the year-and-a-day holding period is that it keeps people from turning short-term capital gains into long-term capital gains by doing an Exchange.

Any asset you sell that you've owned for less than a year is subject to short-term capital gains. Short-term capital gains are currently taxed at your regular tax rates (which at the time I'm writing this tops out at 35 percent federal, plus whatever your state tax rate is). On the other hand, long-term capital gains is how assets you've owned for more than a year are taxed. The tax rate of long-term capital gains can be as low as 5 percent, although the maximum rate of 15 percent is more typical. State income tax is in addition to this, of course.

The IRS does not want taxpayers turning short-term transactions into long-term capital gains by doing an exchange. Again, the year and a day holding period rule helps prevent this. In other words, you couldn't buy a property, fix it up, sell it a couple of months later, do a 1031 Exchange and buy another property and fix it up, etc., doing this for, say six properties, over a two-year period before you decide to cash out and pay the tax. They don't want taxpayers treating the gain as a long-term capital gain just because the first transaction was more than a year before the last sale.

Is it possible to do an Exchange on property you've held for less than a year and a day? Yes, but. Yes, the word "intent" is a big part of this law, and, no, the magic year and a day rule is not mentioned, but if your intent was to hold the property for a long time and something happens that is beyond your control (like someone makes you an offer you can't refuse), the law and the courts allow you to change your intent, sell the property and do an Exchange. But be careful here. If you get audited you can count on the IRS second-guessing the importance of the event that made you change your mind. If you do this, be prepared to fight for it.

We had a client who bought a single-family home as the replacement property for his Exchange. He tried to rent this house for about six months without success. He lost his job and was carrying mortgages on both properties with very little income. He received an unsolicited offer on the house he lived in, so he sold his home and moved into his 1031 Exchange rental house. While he lived in the "rental house" (for almost two years) he made some improvements to the house, like painting it, etc.

When he was audited by the IRS, the IRS noticed that his mailing address on his tax return was the same address as the New Property in his 1031 Exchange and ultimately disallowed the Exchange. The thing that hurt him the most turned out to be the fact that he had tried to rent the house himself with signs in the windows, etc., so they had no proof that he had tried to rent the house. I'll talk about dealing with the IRS later in the book, but be prepared to prove everything.

There have been court cases that allowed taxpayers to do 1031 Exchanges where the holding period was less than a year, but don't lose sight of the fact that the IRS took these people to court. They had to fight with the IRS, which takes a lot of energy, not to mention CPA and legal fees, in order to win this result.

One last thing before I move on. You want to have at least a year and a day between the time that you take title to the New Property and the time that you list the property for sale. If you buy a property, put it on the market to sell it a month later, but then it doesn't sell for a year, that won't cure your year and a day problem because you tried to sell the property before the year and a day holding period was up. In other words, you held it "primarily" for resale.

You Can Sell Any Type of Investment Property and Buy Any Other Type of Investment Property

When the Code section governing 1031 Exchanges was added to the Internal Revenue Code in 1921, trading cattle and horses was pretty standard, and so it became a common understanding of Exchange law that you had to find someone that had property similar to yours, and then you swapped. Not so after the Starker court cases. Now you can sell any type of investment real estate and buy any other type of investment real estate – the two properties do not have to be "like-kind."

If Sue wants to sell her purple duplex, she does not have to go out and find someone else with a purple duplex who wants hers. If you meet the "held for investment" or the "used in a trade or business" requirement, you can sell any type of real estate and buy any other type. You can sell an office building and buy a warehouse. Or you can sell an apartment building and buy bare land. Any type of investment property can be sold and replaced by any other type of investment property.

The properties have to be real estate. You cannot sell real estate (like a rental house) and buy personal property (like a motor home or a boat). In the classes I teach, I tell the students that real estate is dirt and anything that is screwed into it. Obviously this means buildings, but it also means that timber rights, water rights, mineral rights and oil and gas interests qualify for 1031 Exchanges. So, yes, you can sell a royalty interest in an oil or gas well and buy an apartment building. Or you can sell an office building and buy water rights or timber rights.

A common question we get is: "Can I sell my Old Property and buy REIT shares as my New Property?" (A REIT or "real estate investment trust" is like a mutual fund that owns real estate.) The logic behind the question is that since the questioner sold real estate and is buying real estate through this "real estate mutual fund" that person should be able to do an Exchange. Wrong – this questioner is not buying real estate; but rather buying a stock. In other words, this person is not buying a piece of property that has the person's name on it.

It does not matter what the property was used for by the person you bought the property from – it only matters what you are going to use the property for. As an example, if you buy a house that you are going to use as a rental property, it does not matter that you bought it from someone who lived in it as his or her residence.

Types of Investment Property

Besides the obvious types of investment property, like office buildings and apartment buildings, the following items also qualify as investment real estate:

Timber Rights: The rights to remove standing timber from real property. As long as there are no time restrictions against the removal of the timber, you can sell timber rights and buy an office building, an apartment building, etc., (and vice versa). If the right is only for a limited time, it is not Exchangeable.

Water Rights: The rights to remove a certain amount of water per year from a body of water (like a stream or a lake). If the right is perpetual, you can use it to do an Exchange into or out of another piece of investment property. If the right is limited, however, you may not be able to do an Exchange.

Unharvested Crops: Under a different IRS Code section, unharvested crops sold with land are considered real estate and, therefore, can be Exchanged into or out of other investment real estate. When we think of unharvested crops we tend to think of crops like wheat and corn, but trees and shrubs in a nursery are also considered crops. If you are selling land with growing crops, you will want to carefully time the closing of the sale based upon whether you want the crops to be ordinary income or deferred as part of your Exchange.

For example, if Fred is selling farm land with a wheat crop worth $100,000 and that wheat crop is almost ready for harvest, Fred could sell the land before the harvest and roll the $100,000 from the wheat, tax free, into the purchase of the New Property. If Fred needs or wants the income from the wheat crop, he should wait until after the harvest and then sell the bare land.

Cooperative Apartments: In a few parts of the country (mostly New York City), cooperative apartments are popular. An owner in a cooperative apartment building, instead of owning a certain unit, owns a share in the cooperative corporation, with a certain share being associated with a certain unit within the building. If the cooperative shares are considered real estate under state law (which they are in California and New York), you can Exchange an investment co-op for any other type of investment property.

Oil, Gas and Mineral Interests: In general, there are two types of these oil, gas and mineral interests: 1) production payments; and 2) royalty and working interests. Production payments are payments received for efforts to extract the oil, gas or mineral from the ground. They are payments for services and, therefore, are not Exchangeable. Royalty and working interests, on the other hand, do qualify for Exchanges, so you can buy them or sell them as part of an Exchange.

For example, Fred could sell his farm land from the previous example, and buy oil and/or gas royalty interests as the replacement property in his 1031 Exchange. Or, he could sell his royalty interest and buy some other type of investment property such as an apartment building.

Gravel or Quarry Rights: The rights to extract rock from the ground, and in the case of gravel rights, crush that rock into gravel. These rights are Exchangeable into or out of other property.

We did an Exchange several years ago for a client who went through the legal process to get some land that he owned re-zoned as a quarry, which would allow him to remove the rocks from below the surface of the land and crush them into gravel. He sold the re-zoned land for several million dollars, did a 1031 Exchange, and bought an office building.

Leasehold Interests: These qualify for 1031 Exchanges if the lease has at least 30 years left to run, including extensions. In one case the court ruled that a lease with five years left to run, with ten optional renewal periods of five years each (a total potential rental term of 55 years), was 1031 property. If you meet the 30-year requirement, you can sell a lease and do a 1031 Exchange, or buy a lease as the replacement property in a 1031 Exchange.

We don't see a lot of these types of Exchanges, but we do occasionally see commercial tenants who are having their leases bought out by redevelopers. The tenants can take the money they receive on the lease buy outs and use it to purchase investment properties.

What happens if the lease has less than 30 possible years left to run? No one knows for sure. There is one case where a 27.5-year lease was traded into a 27.5-year lease in a similar property. And there is an IRS ruling that allowed an Exchange of a 23-year lease on a motel into a lease of an "unspecified term of less than 30 years" in a golf course.

Vacation Homes: A source of confusion in the 1031 industry. Most Exchange professionals believe that if you are careful with your personal usage the year before you sell your vacation home, it is 1031 property. However, there is a hard-core group of conservatives out there who believe 1031 Exchanges into or out of vacation homes are not possible.

The IRS has issued a ruling that says that you can do a 1031 Exchange with "vacation property," even if you've never rented it, provided you can show "some" investment intent. There has been speculation in our office between the CPAs and attorneys for the last couple of years as to the definition of "some." How much is "some," and how best do you prove it.

Since there is so much confusion and uncertainty in this area, let me spend a few moments and examine this topic in detail. First, the ruling and court case apply to "vacation property." Vacation properties are properties that are in vacation areas – places where people want to go to relax. A property in Vail, Colorado is a vacation property. The exact same property in Bridgeport, Nebraska is not. I'm not picking on Bridgeport, I'm just stating a fact: people don't go to Bridgeport to relax (you're probably asking yourself, "Where in the world is Bridgeport?" See what I mean?) So you only have to worry if your property is in a vacation area.

Second, you have to "show" some investment intent. How do you show intent? Well, the burden of proof is on you to show that you intended to hold the property for investment. A great way to show investment intent is to actually rent the property out during the year-and-a-day period before you sell it. Of course you would declare such rental on your tax return, and this is the best proof of investment intent.

The second best proof is to try to rent the property. Make sure that you keep written proof. If you offer it for rent in the newspaper, for example, keep copies of the entire page the ad is on. You need written proof for your file in case you are audited.

Vacation areas typically have what they call "rental pools," where people who own properties they want to rent make them available for weekend or weekly rental. When you contact a realtor in a vacation area, and you want to rent a unit in a certain area, the realtor or leasing agent will tell you what he or she has available. When you put your property in the pool, you sign a "pool agreement" that specifies the terms of the agreement you have with the pool manager.

You have to ask fair market value rental, but you can put other terms in your pool agreement that protect your property. For example, you can prohibit smoking, drinking or pets in your unit. If you have valuable furniture and art work in your property, you can require a large deposit in order to protect them. But it is critical that your rental rate be fair market value.

While we don't believe that you are prohibited from using your vacation property in the year before you sell it, common sense says that you should minimize your usage in that year if you can (and when I say "you," I also include anyone that is related to you).

Just as I was finishing a draft of this book, the U.S. Tax Court decided a case where one of the issues was whether or not the vacation home qualified as "investment property." Obviously, if it is investment property, it qualifies for a 1031 Exchange. In this particular case the taxpayers had effectively no rental income in the last couple of years – the property was substantially all personal use. Based solely on testimony of the wife that the couple expected that the vacation home would appreciate in value (which it did) the Court ruled that the vacation home was investment property. The great thing about this court case is that it gives us assurance that the courts can be friendly to taxpayers in this area.

How does this affect our future advice to clients about being able to show some investment intent? We will continue to recommend that they build a file proving investment intent, because I don't want any of our clients to have to go to court to win this argument. But having a Tax Court opinion saying that vacation homes can be investment property should help head off an attack by the IRS at the field level.

Timeshares: There are two kinds of timeshares: the first is the kind typically in Mexico where you buy usage not ownership. For example, you pay $25,000 for the right to use a unit in a particular complex for 25 weeks. It doesn't matter if you use the unit one week a year, or four weeks the first year, once you have used your 25 weeks, you're done. While these are common in Mexico, we occasionally see them in the U.S. as well. This type of timeshare does not qualify for a 1031 Exchange because you don't actually own an interest in the property.

The more common type of timeshare that we see in the U.S. is the kind where you own an undivided 1/52nd interest in a certain unit. You may not actually occupy that particular unit during your vacation, but you actually have a deed to the property. These types of timeshares do qualify for 1031 Exchanges, but be careful – there is a U.S. Tax Court case that says that if you use the timeshare the week you sell the Old Timeshare or the week you buy the New Timeshare, the timeshare is not 1031 property.

Both the Old Property and the New Property Have to Be Inside the United States or Both Outside It

Though this seems like a strange statement, it means that if the Old Property is in the United States then the New Property has to be in the U.S. as well. You cannot cross the border. On the other hand, if the Old property is outside the U.S., then the New Property has to be outside the U.S. as well.

If your Old Property is in Seattle, your New Property can be in Miami or Honolulu, but not in Vancouver, B.C., even though it is only 60 miles away, because it is outside the United States. However, if the Old Property is in Vancouver, then the New Property can be in Mexico City, or Paris or Hong Kong, but it cannot be in Seattle because you can't cross the border.

Why does it matter, and who cares if the Old Property is outside the United States? Some people care because if you are a U.S. citizen you are subject to U.S. income taxes on your worldwide income. If you are a U.S. citizen, and you sell a piece of property in Paris, France, you would have to pay tax on the gain to both France and the United States. You can defer the U.S. tax by doing a 1031 Exchange, even though the property is in Paris, since Section 1031 is a U.S. tax law. Of course Section 1031 will not apply to the taxes you pay to France.

Section 1031 also applies to nonresidents who own property in the United States. It is relatively common for Canadian and Mexican citizens to own property in this country, because we are neighbors. When they sell their U.S. property they are subject to tax in the U.S. unless they do a 1031 Exchange.

How Many Properties Can Be Involved in an Exchange?

As long as both the Old Property you sell and the New Property you buy are held for investment, it does not matter how many properties you sell, how many properties you buy or what state they are in. You can sell three and buy one. Or sell one and buy three. Sell the Old Property in New York and buy the New Property in Hawaii. But remember, you have to follow the 1031 rules for each property.

When Does the Exchange Take Place?

A question that frequently comes up is, "When does the Exchange take place?" For example, you sell your Old Property in year one on a contract with a little down and the balance over the next few years with a balloon payment in year five. In different parts of the country this might be called a "Contract for Deed" or "Owner Financing" or "Owner Carry" or "Purchase Money Mortgage," etc.

So, does the Exchange take place in year one when you sell the property and the buyer takes possession? Or does it take place in year five when the bulk of the payment is made? The answer is that the Exchange takes place when risk of loss passes from the seller to the buyer - not when the money is paid.

The concept of the passing of risk of loss is often confusing to clients, so when we get one of these calls we'll usually end up asking them this simple question: "If the property burned down tomorrow, who would be out of luck, the buyer or the seller?" The answer to that question will determine if risk of loss has transferred. If it has, the sale has already taken place and you cannot do an Exchange. This question is a good way to gauge when risk of loss does transfer; at the moment the answer changes from seller to buyer, risk of loss has passed.

In some parts of the country, Contracts for Deed are popular. When the buyer buys the property using a Contract for Deed, it means that that individual is buying the property on contract. The buyer makes a down payment and then promises to pay the balance over time. Title to the property remains in the name of the seller until the final payment is made on the contract, at which time title then passes to the buyer.

When must the seller do an Exchange? In the very beginning, at the time of the sale, because that is when risk of loss passes (if the building burned down in the middle of the contract, the buyer's insurance would pay).

While we typically see Contract for Deed transactions in the northern middle part of the United States, we occasionally see them in other areas as well.

What Happens if a Property Is Both Personal Residence and 1031 Property

If Fred or Sue is a real estate agent and operates a real estate business out of the house, the office portion of the house could be subject to Section 1031. The rest of the house is the primary residence and is subject to a different Code section – Section 121. (Section 121 says that if you have lived in your house for at least 24 months of the last 5 years, when you sell it the first $250,000 of gain is tax-free if you are single, and the tax-free gain is $500,000 if you are married).

Let me give you a couple of examples of how these two Code sections interplay. Let's say that you've lived in your house, your personal residence, for the last five years when a job relocation moves you to a different part of the country, and you rent your residence for a year or two and then decide to sell it. You have a dilemma because your house now qualifies for both Section 121 (the rules governing the sale of your personal residence because you lived in it for at least two of the last five years) and Section 1031 (the rules governing the sale of investment property because it was rental property for the year and a day before you sold it).

Which Code section governs your transaction? The answer is both, which means that you may choose the one that gives you the best tax result. In this case, you should pick Section 121, because this will let you take your money tax-free without having to reinvest it (if you do a 1031 Exchange in this situation you could end up paying tax on the gain somewhere down the road).

To give you a different example of how these two Code sections interact, let me tell you about a transaction we handled for a real estate agent client a few years ago. The agent was selling a rental property for $100,000 at the same time he was buying a personal residence (to be his home) for $400,000. The rental property had no debt against it.

It so happened that the portion that was to be his office was in the walkout basement of the new house and would take up about 25 percent of the new house. So, we did a 1031 Exchange from the sale of his rental property into the office portion of the new residence using the cash from the Exchange as the down payment on the purchase. The client then got a loan for $300,000 for the purchase of the other 75 percent of the dwelling. In effect, what he did was use the cash from the sale of his rental property as the down payment for the purchase of his new residence because of the office in the home.

Chapter 3:
45-Day Identification Requirement

From the day you close the sale of the Old Property, you have 45 days to come up with a list of property you want to buy. This list is called your "45-Day List." The list is not necessarily property that you intend to buy, but merely property that you are interested in. However, as you will see in the next chapter, whatever you purchase to complete your Exchange has to be on this list, so you should take it seriously.

The 45 Days Are Calendar Days

The days start on the day of closing of your Old Property (the day risk of loss passes from you to the buyer). In most cases there is no question of when the closing happens. In some parts of the country (California, for example), a property closes when the deed is recorded. In other parts of the country, there is a "table close" where both the buyer and the seller sit at the same table with the closer, sign documents and pass money back and forth.

Sometimes the closing date is not so black and white. It is more and more common for closings to take place by mail. For example, you send your documents or your money in and the closer tells you when she thinks the closing took place (which is open to second-guessing by the IRS). Let's say you (the seller) sign your documents and send them to the closer on Monday for a Wednesday closing. The buyer does likewise, and her documents are also at the closing on Wednesday. The buyer's lender has a problem getting the loan proceeds to the closing on Wednesday, and they don't actually arrive at the closer's until Thursday afternoon. The closer is on vacation on Friday and doesn't record the sale until the following Monday. The buyer, meanwhile, has keys to the property and spends the weekend moving in. When did the actual closing take place? See my point?

You need to be careful using options and certain types of leases, because there are cases where the courts have ruled that actual ownership starts when the parties enter into the option or lease, because that is when the "risk of ownership" passes from the seller to the buyer, even though title to the property still rests with the seller. If your Exchange has unusual twists, you need to make sure that you are working with a very knowledgeable Intermediary.

You count calendar days, so Saturdays, Sundays and holidays count. If you close the sale of your Old Property on Friday, then Friday is day one, Saturday is day two, Sunday three and so on. Likewise, if the 45th day falls on a Saturday, Sunday or holiday, that is the day your list must be completed – you don't get until the next business day.

The Internal Revenue Code and the IRS Regulations appear to be in conflict about how you count 45 days. The Internal Revenue Code is the actual law, and the regulations are the IRS's interpretation of the law. The regulations explain, through interpretation and example, what the law means.

The Code says that you have 45 days after the date of closing to identify your potential replacement properties. Let's assume that Sue sold her Old Property on November 16, 1992. Counting 45 days starting on November 17th (the day after closing) means that she has until midnight January 1st, 1993 to identify her replacement property.

The Regulations (IRS interpretation of the law) gives an example where the taxpayer closes the sale on November 16, 1992, then says that the identification period ends at midnight on December 31, 1992. In other words, the IRS example counts the day of closing as day one. So we count the day of closing as day one. Occasionally we get an astute client who wants to argue the calculation of the dates. But when in doubt, be conservative. Start your count the day of closing.

You prepare a list of properties, and you have to submit this list to someone involved with your Exchange. This could be your title company or escrow agent, but it typically is your Qualified Intermediary. No, you cannot give your list to your spouse, as one taxpayer tried, unless you want to be convicted of fraud, as they were.

You can put properties on your list during the 45 days and take properties off the list, but at midnight on the 45th day an implicit gate slams shut, and you are stuck with the list that you have at that point.

For example, on the morning of the 45th day you fax a list of three properties (Property A, Property B and Property C) to your Intermediary. That afternoon Property D comes on the market. You could fax your Intermediary a letter that afternoon stating that you are "amending" your list to add Property D and removing Property C. As a result, at midnight your list of properties A, B and D are locked, and that is the list you must work with.

The List Has to Be Clear

The list must be clear enough that an IRS agent can take your list and go directly to that property on the list. You cannot say "a 2-bedroom, 2-bath house on Main Street." Your identification has to be specific: "123 Main Street, Denver, CO." This means that if you want to identify a unit in a condominium complex, you must be as specific as: "Mountain View Condominiums, 123 Main Street, Unit 203, Denver, CO." If the property is bare land and does not have an address, use the legal description.

Sometimes the property does not have a legal description. If that's the case, be creative – just be clear enough that an IRS agent can determine exactly what you identified. We had a client who identified a lot in a development that had not received its final plat approvals (meaning that the lot did not have a legal description yet). The way we had the client identify his lot was to attach a copy of the entire plat plan and shade in the lot that he was identifying. On the formal identification list he would then write, "See attached map."

What if you want to buy two pieces of land: Lots A and B? Does this represent one identification or two? If the two lots are contiguous (meaning that they touch), and you are buying them from one seller in a transaction where you must buy either both of them or neither of them, then that represents one identification. But if the two lots don't touch, or you are buying them from two different sellers, or you have the choice of buying one or the other or both, then you have two identifications.

Submitting Your List

Your list of properties has to be an actual physical list. You submit it to the Qualified Intermediary handling your Exchange. I'll talk about Intermediaries in a couple of chapters, but the typical list used by most Intermediaries has room to identify three properties and asks for the address and purchase price of each property. You do not have to use the Intermediary's form – you can make your own form, but your list has to clearly show the properties you are identifying and their purchase prices.

You can hand deliver your list, mail it, fax it or send it by courier. If you deliver it in person, fax it or send it by courier, it has to be in your Intermediary's hands by midnight on the 45th day. If you mail it, it has to be postmarked no later than the 45th day. We encourage our clients to fax or mail their lists so that we have proof of the delivery date (we keep the envelopes). When clients drop the form off in person, it is harder to prove the receipt date.

Your Intermediary does not submit the list to the IRS. Instead, the Intermediary holds it in your file pending potential audit by the IRS. In other words, if you get audited one of the first things the IRS will do is ask to see the 45-Day list. Usually, as the taxpayer, you will show the agent your copy. It is not unusual for the agent to also go directly to the Intermediary to see the Intermediary's copy, especially where the agent thinks that the two may not agree. The Intermediary's copy is the official one.

Don't Play Games With the List

By this point you've probably asked yourself, "If the 45-Day list is not submitted to the IRS, but I have to buy something off the list, who will ever know if I don't, or if I change the list?" We get this question a lot. The answer is that the 45-Day list is one of the hot topics with the IRS when they audit Exchanges. Let me give you some advice – the last thing you want to do is mess with this form.

In order for a case to get to court and become part of the record, taxpayers have to fight with the IRS. Probably only one or two out of a thousand will actually fight. The vast majority pays the tax and move on, so there no doubt are lots of these types of stories that we'll never hear or read about.

But, from the cases that did make their way to court, here is what we know: If you get caught reporting a replacement property on your tax return that was not on your 45-Day list, you will be hit with a negligence penalty. If you backdate your 45-Day list to meet the deadline you will get hit with a fraud penalty. If you give a copy of your backdated 45-Day List to the IRS agent, you are guilty of criminal charges for delivering false documents to the IRS (as one poor taxpayer found out).

The IRS is aware that there are "wink and a nod" Intermediaries out there who let it be known that they will work with you on the reception date of your 45-Day list, and the IRS is after them. I've heard that if the IRS thinks that the Intermediary is playing games, it will audit every Exchange that the Intermediary has ever handled. There is no statute of limitations here, so if you deal with a shady Intermediary you can pretty much count on being audited at some point in the future. I'll talk more about Intermediaries in a few chapters.

Acquiring What You Identified

It is not necessary that you acquire 100 percent of a property. If you intend to purchase a portion of a property, you need to identify the portion you are considering (25 percent for example) and the amount you expect to pay for your portion. For example, if want to buy 25 percent of a $1 million property, your identification might read something like "An undivided 25 percent share of the property at 123 Main Street, Denver, Colorado, for a price of $250,000."

The IRS has an unstated policy of allowing about a 5 percent variation between what you identify and what you buy, but beyond that the IRS could argue that you did not acquire what you identified. So, continuing my example from above, if you identified 25 percent of the Main Street property on your list, and you actually acquire between 20 percent and 30 percent (i.e., 5 percent either way) you are OK. Outside of that framework the IRS could argue that you have purchased something other than what you identified.

One last comment about identification problems: It occasionally happens that mistakes are made in your identification. For example, you identified 123 Main Street as replacement property on your 45-Day List, when in fact you sincerely meant to identify 321 Main Street as the replacement property. In a perfect world, there is no such property as 123 Main Street, so the error is easy to deal with. But, as so often happens, there may be a 123 Main Street and it also may be for sale. You could try to hide this from the IRS agent if you get audited, but the course of action that has always worked best for me is to document the error as soon as it is found, and if you do get audited, to point out the error right up front. IRS agents understand that mistakes happen, but they don't like to be jacked around. Just be honest.

There Are No Limits if You Identify Three Properties or Fewer

You typically want to put three properties or fewer on your identification list. The IRS does not want you to identify everything in the local MLS book as a potential acquisition, so they restrict your ability to identify a large number of properties. Three properties, on the other hand, is a reasonable identification, and because of that there are no restrictions on the property you identify if you keep your list to three properties or fewer.

For example, if Sue sold her Old Property for $100,000, she could identify three potential replacement properties for $10 million each (a total of thirty million) and she would meet the IRS identification guidelines.

200% Rule

If you identify more than three properties, a different set of rules, called the "200% Rule," kicks in. If you choose to identify more than three properties the IRS limits the combined purchase price of your list – whether your list has four, or ten or 50 properties – to twice the selling price of your Old Property.

For example, Sue sells her purple duplex for $100,000, but chooses to identify four (or more) replacement properties. The combined purchase price of everything on her list cannot exceed $200,000 ($100,000 x 2). If she identifies four properties, for $75,000 each, she'll blow the 200% rule because 4 x $75,000 = $300,000, which exceeds her $200,000 limit for this transaction. The end result of Sue's error is that her entire Exchange will fail. My advice is to keep it simple and stick to three properties or fewer on your list.

What if Sue abides by the rule and lists four little condos for $50,000 each? Her total comes to $200,000 so she meets the 200% Rule. But what happens if she buys one of the condos for $50,100? Because she exceeded the 200% limit, her whole Exchange is toast - even if that is the only replacement property she purchased.

Technically there is an exception to the 200% Rule that states that if you identify more than three properties and the prices exceed the 200% limit, you can salvage your Exchange by acquiring 95 percent of the properties on the list. Truthfully, despite having been involved in more than 30,000 transactions, I've never heard of anyone who has met this exception. Among all my friends in the Exchange community, as of the last time we talked about it, none of them had ever heard of anyone who has met this exception either. Think about it - if you identify 10 properties, and they exceed the 200% limit, you would have to acquire every one to salvage your Exchange!

Occasionally we get a client who truly wants to buy a large number of properties, with an aggregate purchase price in excess of the 200% limitation. Is this possible? The answer is yes, but that client probably needs to get all the purchases completed before the 45th day. The reason for this is that the 45-day identification requirement applies only to those people who have not completed their Exchange by the 45th day. In other words, people who still have an uncompleted Exchange.

If your Exchange is closed by the 45th day, the identification rules don't apply.

Let's say that Sue has sold her purple duplex for $100,000 and her Intermediary is holding $60,000 of Exchange proceeds for her. Sue wants to acquire six properties, each for $100,000, and she has a lender who will loan her $90,000 on each New Property when she puts down $10,000. In other words, she wants to buy $600,000 of replacement property.

Clearly this would blow her Exchange. But there is a way to legally do this, and that is for Sue to close the purchase of all six properties and spend the entire $60,000 before the 45th day. She needs to have her ducks in a row, but Sue could do this.

What if Sue is only able to close the purchase of one of the properties before the 45th day? Is her Exchange toast? Not necessarily. What I would suggest she do is acquire one of the properties by putting down the entire $60,000 before the 45th day. This technically completes her Exchange. She could then borrow against the substantial equity in the first property to get her down payment money for the other five properties. And the other five properties would be outside of her Exchange (she really doesn't need them to successfully complete her Exchange).

One last word of caution: When you do an Exchange, most Intermediaries will tell you what the 45-day "drop-dead" date is, but only a few of them actually monitor your Exchange to remind you and make sure you get your list in on time. Some actually refuse to tell you what the drop-date is and require that you have your accountant compute it for you. Be careful. Make sure you are working with a good Intermediary. This is another one of those areas where saving a couple of hundred dollars may end up costing you your entire Exchange.

Be careful – some Intermediaries are not real sharp. We hear horror stories of taxpayers that have been told by their Intermediaries that because the 45th day fell on the weekend, that their list was not due until Monday. Of course this is wrong and will cost the taxpayers their Exchanges if audited.

What if You Are Selling Multiple Properties?

If you sell multiple properties in the same Exchange, the 45 and 180 drop-dead dates start with the first closing, and the three-property or 200% rules apply to the entire Exchange. To illustrate how this could happen, let's assume that you are selling 300 acres of land to a buyer who wants to close on the purchase of the first parcel of 100 acres in year one, the second parcel of 100 acres in year two and the third parcel of the final 100 acres in year three. All of this is spelled out in the contract between you and the buyer.

An IRS agent, auditing your Exchange, could argue that this is one Exchange. As one Exchange, you only get one set of three identifications, and your 45-day and 180-day drop-dead dates for the entire transaction start in year one. If the agent wins (the IRS has won this one in the past), the net effect is that two-thirds of your Exchange is toast because you will not have met the 45-day and 180-day requirements for parcels two and three.

The solution to this problem is to have three separate contracts for this sale, with the contract for parcel one closing in year one, the contract for parcel two closing in year two, etc. Make sure that each of the three contracts does not reference the other two; otherwise the agent could use that wording to hook them all back together. Each needs to stand alone.

You can also use this to your great advantage. Let's assume that you are selling a property, comprised of three parcels (A, B and C), for $30 million. Acquiring a single $30 million dollar replacement property can be problematic. What you might do is break the sale down into three separate contracts – one for each parcel, and yes, you want three separate contracts. Again, you don't want the IRS to hook all of these parcels together and call them one Exchange. So we would advise you to have three separate contracts, three different closing dates, and, if possible, three different buyers (perhaps subsidiaries or affiliates of the buyer). The end result is that you now have nine identifications – three for each property.

The Days Are Cast In Concrete

The 45-day requirement is "statutory" (meaning that it is part of the law, not something that appears only in the IRS interpretation of the law) – there are no possible extensions to this requirement. The fact that your daughter is getting married, or your son is graduating from college will not buy you extra time. Neither will your vacation to Europe. The term "45 days" means "45 days." So if you close the sale of your Old Property on Friday, then Friday is day one, Saturday is day two, and Sunday is day three, etc. Likewise, if the 45th day falls on a Saturday, or a Sunday or a Holiday, then that is the day. You do NOT get until Monday to file your identification.

Occasionally the IRS will grant extensions for emergency reasons. They did this with the terrorist attacks on New York City on September 11th, and most recently with Hurricane Charlie in the Fort Meyers area of Florida. We had many clients that were caught up in both situations. With the hurricane, for example, people in that area had no power and certainly no mail service. Getting an identification to us was just not possible. And we had other clients who lived elsewhere, who wanted to identify replacement property in that area but who had no way of knowing if the property was still in existence.

I use the term "grant extension," which really isn't accurate. The 45-day and 180-day drop-dead dates are statutory, as I said above. The IRS does not have the authority to change the law, so when it says that it is granting an extension, what it means is that it will be lenient with those who cannot meet the rules because of the special circumstances.

Think of it like this: The speed limit in front of your house is 25 miles per hour. A policeman is sitting in his car at the corner. Because of an emergency down the block, people are now fleeing the neighborhood and are in a hurry to get away. They are not observing the speed limit. The speed limit does not change; it is still 25 miles per hour. The policeman in his car cannot change the law, but because of the circumstances he chooses to ignore the violations and not ticket people.

The IRS announces that there is an emergency situation and that they will not "ticket" violators of the 45-day and 180-day "speed limits." There is a formal announcement that includes revised drop-dead dates, a definition of who is covered by the revised dates, along with special wording that has to be included, usually in red, on the front page of your tax return. If you are working with a good Intermediary they will hold your hand through this process. If not, you are going to have to figure this stuff out on your own.

You can add property to your list and subtract property from it as much as you wish, but once the 45-day identification period has closed, you cannot change your 45-Day list. We hear talk all the time about Intermediaries who will allow clients to change their lists after the 45th day. We know they are out there, but so does the IRS. If the IRS can prove that you changed your 45-Day list, you will go to jail! It's true.

What Happens if You Blow Your 45-Day Limit?

What happens if you don't get your 45-day identification list to the Intermediary on time? Your Exchange is toast, and your Intermediary will return the Exchange proceeds to you on the 46th day.

As sometimes happens, we occasionally get clients who have completed, and forwarded to us, their 45-day identification form, and then decide not to complete the Exchange. If the 45th day is past, as a general rule the proceeds must stay locked up until the 180th day (although there are exceptions to this, as you will see).

However, if you have identified your property, but the 45-day period has not expired and you want your money back, all you need do is "revoke" your identification. For example, Sue has sold her purple duplex and is in the middle of her 45-day identification period. She has located a couple of properties she is interested in and has identified them to her Intermediary already. She then suffers an emergency and needs the balance of her funds from the Intermediary. Sue needs to send a letter to the Intermediary before the 45th day, stating that she is "revoking her identification." Because she revoked her identification, the 45th day will pass without Sue making an identification, and the Intermediary will return her funds to her on the 46th day.

Identifying Construction That Will Take Place on New Property

Later in this book I talk about a "Construction Exchange." A Construction Exchange happens when you use part of the proceeds from the sale of your Old Property to buy a piece of bare land and the balance of the proceeds to construct a building on it. So for example you sell your Old Property for $100,000 and then buy a bare lot for $75,000 and use the remaining $25,000 as part of the funds to construct a structure on the property. This is called a Construction Exchange.

Construction Exchanges have their own set of requirements, as you shall see, but you are allowed to identify property that is either not in existence at the time of the identification, or is in the process of being built. How do you identify construction on your 45-Day list? Well, the best way to do this is to identify the purchase of the bare land AND the construction you intend to do. This means that your identification would read something like this: "The purchase of the bare lot at 123 Main Street, Denver, CO and the construction of a 5,000 square-foot maintenance shop thereon, for a total price of $650,000." If the construction will be a complicated process, as so often happens with our clients, you might attach blueprints or construction drawings to your 45-day identification form.

One thing that you have to be careful of here is that the regulations require that what you receive has to be substantially the same as what you identified. While the IRS doesn't give us much guidance in this area, you want to resist a total change of what you intend to build. In other words, if you identified a 5,000 square-foot building above, and if you end up building a 2,500 square-foot building, or a 7,500 square-foot building, you run the risk that the IRS could argue that what you got was not what you identified.

In meetings that we've attended with the head of the IRS division responsible for Section 1031, he stated that a 5 percent variation between what you identify and what you actually acquire is considered to be substantially the same as what you identified. In other words, if you acquire somewhere between 1.9 acres and 2.1 acres, you've acquired what you identified.

The IRS regulations covering these rules give us no guidance. One example the regulations provide is that if you identify two acres but only acquire 1.5 acres, that is OK. But if you identify two acres with a barn, and then acquire about 1.5 acres and the barn, that is not OK. The examples make no sense, and the IRS officials I've talked to really can't explain them. We feel most comfortable with the 5 percent rule.

Frequently, our clients buy buildings that are in the process of being completed by builders who own the property. If you were acquiring the completed building, you would not identify it as a Construction Exchange. You would wait until the property was completed to close the purchase and complete your Exchange.

If there is question about whether the new building will be completed before the expiration of the 180-day replacement period discussed in the next chapter, you may want to identify it as a Construction Exchange. The key point here is that a partially completed building must be identified as a Construction Exchange on your identification form if that is what you end up acquiring, otherwise the IRS could argue that you did not acquire what you identified.

Identifying Improvements That Will Be Made to Your New Property

An Improvement Exchange is similar to a Construction Exchange, but an Improvement Exchange happens when you sell your Old Property and use a portion of the proceeds to purchase a property that needs work and the balance of the proceeds to fix up the property. I discuss Improvement Exchanges later in this book, but an example of an Improvement Exchange would be the sale of your Old Property for $100,000 and the purchase of the New Property for $75,000 with the balance of $25,000 used to fix up the New Property.

Identifying the improvements in this situation is more difficult. You have to identify each of the improvements you want to make and the amount that each improvement will cost. For example, if you sold your Old Property for $100,000, your identification might look like this: "The purchase of the property at 123 Main Street, Denver, CO for $75,000 along with the following improvements: a new roof – $15,000, exterior painting - $6,000 and new carpeting - $4,000." I'll talk more about additional requirements later in the chapter on Improvement Exchanges.

In an Improvement Exchange you only want to identify what you need to equalize your Exchange or what you know you can complete before the end of the 180th day. In the above example, only those improvements needed to balance the Exchange at $100,000 have been identified. Improvements you plan over and above this or improvements that will be difficult to complete quickly should be left off your form.

Chapter 4:
180-Day Purchase Deadline

From the day you close the sale of your Old Property, you have 180 days to close on the purchase of your New Property and whatever you buy has to be on your 45-Day list. Please note that the deadline is not six months, it is exactly 180 days. Like the 45 days, the 180 days start at the closing of the sale of your Old Property, and the two timeframes run concurrently, which means that when the 45 days are up, you have 135 days left to purchase your New Property.

The 180 Days Could Be Shortened by Due Date of Tax Return

When you file your tax return for the year in which you sold your Old Property, you have to report your 1031 Exchange. Your Exchange is reported on Form 8824, which tells the IRS the details of the Old Property you sold and the New Property you bought. Failure to report the details of the Exchange on your tax return will invalidate your Exchange.

If you sell your Old Property at the end of the year, your 180-day purchase deadline will fall after the due date of your tax return. If you have not purchased your New Property when it is time to file your tax return, you must extend your income tax return. This rule applies to corporations, partnership and trust returns, which all have different due dates for their tax returns, but individuals do most of the Exchanges.

To illustrate this, let's assume that Sue sells her purple duplex on December 1st of year one. That means that her 180-day purchase deadline will fall at the end of May of year two. Sue's individual tax return for year one is due April 15th of year two. If Sue has not purchased her New Property by April 15th, her Exchange will be toast if she files her tax return, because she doesn't have all of the information from her Exchange to report on her return (she doesn't have the details of the purchase of her New Property). What Sue needs to do at this point is file an extension of her tax return. The extension will extend the due date for the return until after her purchase deadline, at which time she will then have the information she needs to file her return.

There are typically two main problems, or issues, involving the 180-day purchase deadline. The first is whether or not you get your New Property closed by the 180th day. The second is whether or not you buy what you said you were going to buy.

When Does the 180 Days Start?

As with the 45-day identification rules, the start of your 180-day purchase deadline is crystal clear in most cases. Sometimes, however, the actual start date is not so clear. Since uncertainty about the actual start date will affect the calculation of your ending date, you want to error on the conservative side just to be safe.

For example, you were supposed to close on Friday, but the buyer's loan didn't close until Monday, at which point the closer recorded the deed. The Settlement Statement says Friday, and the buyer moved their things in over the weekend, but the deed says Monday. Naturally you would like to consider Monday as the start of your 45 and 180 days, because this gives you more time. But be careful – if you use Monday as the starting date and you submit your identification form or close the replacement purchase at the last minute and the IRS argues that the closing actually took place the previous Friday, your Exchange could be disallowed. If you are in doubt, error on the safe side and start your calculations as of Friday.

The 180 Days Are Calendar Days

Like the 45-day requirement, the 180-day requirement refers to calendar days. If you close the sale of your Old Property on Friday, then Friday is day one, Saturday is day two, Sunday is three, etc. If the 180th day falls on a Saturday or Sunday or Holiday, then that is the final replacement day.

Like the 45-day rule, you have until midnight on the final day to close your purchase. I've never experienced a closing in which midnight was a consideration, and I can't imagine a closing taking place at 11:00 at night. Closings take place during normal business hours, Monday through Friday. So if your 180th day falls on Saturday or Sunday, plan on closing on Thursday or Friday.

It is not common, although it sometimes happens, that taxpayers end up closing right at the end of the 180 days. Clients who have control over the closing yet put it off until the last minute make me nervous. You name it and we've seen it: properties that burn down the day before the purchase, sellers who get killed or sued before our clients can close the purchase, even sellers who disappear and can't be found in time for the purchase.

We had a couple of attorney clients a couple of years ago who were buying a piece of bare land from one of their friends. Because they were busy trial attorneys they put off the purchase until we were down to the last week of their 180-day period. We had encouraged them repeatedly to close the deal, but they were too busy, and they weren't too worried. ("It's bare land, and we're friends with the seller, so what can happen? Don't worry about it.")

The weekend before the last-minute closing it started to rain. The rain turned into the biggest flood in over 100 years and flooded their land. The county placed a moratorium on transactions in the flood zone until the cleanup was completed, and the purchase didn't happen. These guys ended up paying tax on their sale.

I can imagine you're creating a lawyer joke out of this right now ("Did you hear the one about the two trial lawyers who met Noah ... ?), but it is a great lesson for everyone: don't put your purchase off. Get it closed as quickly as you can and don't mess around with it. It's not over 'til it's over.

Sometimes there are legitimate reasons why the closing doesn't happen until the very last minute: You're doing a Construction Exchange or the seller is having trouble clearing up a legal cloud on the property. Sometimes taxpayers simply run out of time and the problems cannot be cleaned up until after the 180th day. I have one Exchange right now where the property our client wants to buy is owned by three people, one of whom is serving a life sentence in prison. The purchase requires all three must sign the deed, and they're having trouble getting this prisoner's signature. Meanwhile, the clock is ticking, and there are no extensions.

We occasionally hear of taxpayers who don't have all of the pieces in place to meet the 180-day requirement doing what is commonly called a "dry closing" in which the documents, including the deed, are prepared, dated and signed prior to the 180th day, but are not recorded until some time later when the final problems are worked out. During this time the purchase funds are held in escrow by the closer.

The purpose of a dry closing is to make the paperwork appear as if a closing has taken place, when in fact it has not. The theory is that it would be very difficult for an IRS agent to discover that the actual transfer of risk of loss didn't happen until some period of time after the 180th day. The problem is that if you get caught doing this, because you've tried to hide the actual facts from the IRS, expect that they will throw the kitchen sink at you.

Whatever You Buy Has to Be on Your 45-Day List

If you get audited, you can be assured that the IRS will check to make sure that what you bought was something that you had identified on your 45-Day List. In most cases this is not a problem, but problems occasionally come up. About once or twice a year we get clients who identify a property on a corner as one address and then the legal address turns out to be on the other street. For example, they identify a property on the corner of Main and Long Streets as "123 Main Street." When the final closing takes place it turns out that the correct legal address for the property is "123 Long Street." While we've never had serious problems with this, you can bet that an IRS agent would zero in on it during an audit, and you'll have to prove that the two properties are the same.

As I've said before, mistakes happen and several times a year we have clients who identify a property as "123 Main Street," when they meant to say "321 Main Street." I worry about this a lot, although we've yet to have a problem with it. When we see a discrepancy in the file, we document the mistake very clearly at the time it happens. If the cause of the problem is an incorrect description in the MLS listing or a typographical error by the real estate agent, we add a copy of the MLS listing to the file or get a letter from the agent explaining how the error occurred. Documentation about the problem, at the time the problem occurred, carries a lot of weight with the IRS. Documentation created at the time of the audit is suspicious.

If you get in this position, document the mistake in your file immediately. Explain how the error arose and who was involved at that time. Get letters from everyone right away. Send registered copies (to prove the date) to your CPA and your Intermediary for their files. IRS agents come from a cross-section of our society. Most of them are very nice. My policy is to explain the error up front and provide copies of the supporting documents. Don't wait and hope they won't find it – that makes you look guilty.

You could buy one of the properties on your list, or some of them, or all of them. It doesn't matter as long as they are on your 45-Day List.

Suggestion: Buy Your Replacement Property During the First 45 Days

We don't like it when our clients string out the closing on their New Property until the end of the 180 days. In fact, the advice we give them is to schedule the closing of the purchase of their New Property for about three weeks after the closing is scheduled on the sale of their Old Property. Why three weeks? Because it falls right in the middle of your 45-day identification period. This gives flexibility to the closing of the sale of your Old Property in case of slight delays, and yet still gives you flexibility in the purchase of your New Property in case something happens. If something happens to the New Property, you still have three weeks to find another New Property.

The worst possible scenario would be one in which you have identified only one property on your 45-Day List. If you are past the 45th day and something happens to the property you wish to acquire, your Exchange is toast. What can happen? Anything can happen - we've had clients where their sole target property burns down the night before the purchase, or floats away in a flood, or the seller gets killed, or gets sued, or disappears.

We had one client that was buying a property where the seller left home for the closing. Kissed his wife, hugged the kids, petted the dog, and then never showed up at the closing. They discovered his car several weeks later, but they still have not found him. Needless to say, our client was unable to buy the property within the 180-day limit.

Why Are the Timeframes So Restrictive?

A common question I get in my seminars is why the IRS has requirements as restrictive as the 45-day and 180-day rules. The government loses a boatload of tax due to 1031 Exchanges, so the IRS helped Congress write the law in such a way that it is difficult to comply with, but not impossible. For example, if they only gave you a week to identify your New Property, and you could only identify one potential replacement property, the Supreme Court would probably throw out the law as too restrictive. Three properties and 45 days to identify are just barely acceptable.

Same story with the 180 days. Only having a month or two to close your purchase would be too restrictive. A year was considered too long. Six months (180 days) is about right.

Chapter 5:
Qualified Intermediary Requirement

You cannot touch the money in between the sale of your Old Property and the purchase of your New Property. By law you are required to use the services of an independent third party called a "Qualified Intermediary." Intermediaries wear several hats in an Exchange. First, they prepare the Exchange documents that the IRS requires when people sell their Old Properties and the Exchange documents the IRS requires when those same people buy their New Properties. Second, they hold the proceeds from the sale of the Old Property until the purchases of the New Property. Third, they act as advisors for the Exchange requirements during the Exchanges. And last, they act as something like Exchange cops since they monitor compliance with certain requirements of the Exchanges – like the 45-day identification requirement and the 180-day replacement deadline.

Preparation of Exchange Documents

Section 1031 is a form-driven Code section. The only difference between a 1031 Exchange and a taxable transaction is the form that each step in the transaction takes. Therefore, it should come as no surprise that this is a critical function for the Intermediary.

The Intermediary is the one responsible for preparing the Exchange documents required at the time you sell your Old Property and the Exchange documents when you purchase your New Property. These documents must be perfect, or the IRS can disallow your Exchange. The IRS can disallow them because they don't follow the format required by the IRS, and they can disallow them for not containing all the required information.

While you wouldn't think that a small foot fault would matter, remember that the IRS loses a lot of tax revenue from 1031 Exchanges and if it audits you, its agents will make sure that the documents do, in fact, comply with the law. A couple of years ago the IRS disallowed all of the Exchanges of an Intermediary who had one paragraph of his documents wrong.

It's relatively common in the Exchange industry for Intermediaries to use pre-printed, fill-in-the-blank-type forms for their Exchange documents. We recommend against this because Exchange laws change from time to time as new rulings and court cases come out. In addition, special conditions in your Exchange may require specific modifications to your Exchange documents. Our observation of Exchangers that use pre-printed documents is that required modifications are seldom made, creating a fatal flaw if the IRS closely audits your Exchange. The Intermediary should be professional and prepare the documents for each Exchange from scratch.

We handled an Exchange several years ago where the buyer of our client's property was a famous Hollywood celebrity who was buying the property as the replacement property for his Exchange. Our client was the seller and also doing an Exchange, which we were handling. For some reason we were given a copy of the celebrity's Exchange documents to review. I was appalled. This was a multi-million dollar Exchange, and despite the high-profile client and the dollars involved, the Exchange documents were pre-printed, fill-in-the-blank types and had huge technical holes in them. If the IRS ever audited this person, there were probably three or four reasons an IRS agent could use to disallow the entire Exchange.

Don't Sign a Hold-Harmless Clause

That brings me to the topic of "hold-harmless" clauses. These clauses say that clients can't sue their Intermediaries no matter what they do or how bad they screw up their clients' Exchanges. Most Intermediaries will try to require that you sign this type of clause. Oftentimes this clause is buried in the body of the documents and you may not even be aware, when you sign the documents, you are agreeing to release the Intermediary.

I would caution you against signing away your right to hold someone of unknown background and experience responsible for his or her actions. I've seen some Intermediaries do some pretty grievous things and then hide behind the hold-harmless clause.

I've seen some Exchange documents that give Intermediaries the right to invest Exchange funds in any manner they please. If the Intermediaries are able to make a profit on the investments, the documents say that the profits belong to the Intermediaries. These same documents provide that if the Intermediaries lose money on the investments, the losses are charged to the clients – and the clients agree that they will not sue the Intermediaries for the loss. I think this kind of stuff is blatantly immoral, yet people agree to provisions like this every day. Read your Exchange documents and ask questions about the parts you don't understand. If you don't like a clause, cross it out and initial the deletion on both the original and your copy.

Having said that, there are legitimate items in the Exchange that the Intermediary should not be responsible for, and the Exchange documents may limit liability for those items. Our documents have a clause that limits our liability in matters that you haven't disclosed to us. There are some things that we will never know. For example, if you were selling your Old Property at a loss you probably would not want to do an Exchange. We just would never know that unless you told us.

Holding Your Money

You are not allowed to touch the money in between the sale of your Old Property and the purchase of your New. The money must be held by your Intermediary, so this is the most critical thing they do. And naturally it has the biggest risk.

Intermediaries can hold client Exchange money in one of two ways: one way is in a "commingled account" where the combined proceeds of all of their clients' Exchanges are held in one single account. For example, if the Intermediary has 200 clients, all of their money would be pooled into one bank account. The FDIC guarantee would merely be $100,000 on the combined balance, because there is only one account. Probably 90 percent to 95 percent of the Intermediaries hold their clients' money in commingled accounts.

The alternative way is to hold the money in a separate account for each client. So, continuing my example from above, the Intermediary would have 200 separate accounts – one for each client. And they would have 200 FDIC guarantees.

Commingled Accounts. Commingling all of the money into one account is bad news for a couple of reasons. First, in a recent court case, clients of an Intermediary who commingled accounts were required to return Exchange money they had already received after the Intermediary went bankrupt. Seems the Intermediary was day trading with the Exchange funds and ended up losing most of the money in the commingled account. The Intermediary filed bankruptcy, and the court appointed a trustee to oversee the liquidation of the company. The trustee determined that the Exchange funds, because they were in a commingled account, were available to all creditors, not just Exchange creditors. So the trustee took the money that was left in the commingled account and used it to pay other creditors.

In addition, because the commingled Exchange account was considered a bankruptcy asset, all of the Exchange clients who had received Exchange funds during the 90 days prior to the bankruptcy had to return their funds to the trustee. Most of these clients had used the money to purchase their replacement properties. The trustee's directive meant, therefore, that they probably had to mortgage their New Property in order to comply with the trustee's order.

Think about how they must have felt – they sold their Old Property, the money went to their Intermediary, and a couple of months later the Intermediary transfers their proceeds to the closing where they purchased their New Property. Several months after that they get a letter from a stranger telling them that they have to return the proceeds to the Intermediary company so that the proceeds can be used to pay other creditors (like the Intermediary's landlord). How would you feel? I know how I'd feel!

So it should come as no surprise that a court battle ensued. In the end, the court agreed with the trustee. The judge, in his opinion explaining why the money was to be returned, made it clear that it was because the Exchange accounts were commingled, and he stated that the result would have been dramatically different had the Intermediary put the money in a separate account for each Exchange. It seems to me that the day-trading wouldn't have happened had the money been in separate accounts either – any time you put a large amount of money under the control of someone who is not regulated or audited, you are asking for trouble. Just since I've started writing this book there have been two additional Intermediaries who did similar things with the Exchange account. In each case they were able to mess with their clients' Exchange money because the monies were all commingled.

Probably the biggest problem I see with the above court case is that it has opened the door for future attacks on commingled accounts. It's not hard to imagine a situation where the Intermediary goes bankrupt and current clients who have lost their money sue to force those clients with successfully closed Exchanges to share in their pain. I can also imagine a situation where a plaintiff who is suing an Intermediary could use this case to go after funds in the commingled account. Let's assume, for example, that an Intermediary gets sued by one of his clients, and the client wins a million-dollar judgment. How is that client going to collect on the judgment? Correct - by tapping the commingled account.

Let's go one step further: Anticipating the length of time that it takes for a case to go to trial and the ease at which the Intermediary could switch to separate accounts, what would you do if you were the attorney for the plaintiff in the above case? Correct - try to freeze the commingled account. Could the attorney do that? I don't know, but I can imagine a plaintiff's attorney talking a judge into granting the motion. In the meantime, what if you are one of the poor souls with their funds in the commingled account when the judge freezes it? What are the chances that the account will be unfrozen by the time you need your funds to close the purchase of your New Property?

Another problem with commingled accounts is the ease with which embezzlement is possible. In our modern high tech world, money is handled by banks and large money holders over the internet. Paper transactions are becoming rarer each day. Moving money over the internet requires several passwords. Each password should be held by a different person, but in a small Intermediary firm this may not be possible. This makes commingled accounts vulnerable to theft. If one employee has, or is able to get, all of the passwords, a few mouse clicks on a Friday night can send millions of dollars to Timbuktu. On Monday morning the Intermediary owner can find that the employee and all the money are long gone.

Segregated Accounts. Segregated accounts, on the other hand, keep each client's money separate from the funds of other clients. They protect your money from being messed with by the Intermediary. And they give your account its own FDIC insurance fund. If the Intermediary is holding client funds in 400 separate bank accounts, the Intermediary has has 400 separate FDIC guarantees. The Intermediary's FDIC insurance could be as much as $40 million. If the Intermediary only has one (commingled) account, the FDIC insurance is only $100,000. In other words, if the bank that the funds are in goes down, the Intermediary with 400 separate accounts has essentially protected his or her clients. The Intermediary with the commingled account has only protected $100,000.

Don't go to sleep on your segregated account, however. Remember, the Intermediary controls the account, so check on it periodically. Make sure that your money is still in a separate account. We've made it possible for our clients to view their accounts online at the bank using a process we developed called "**1031Access**™." We give each client a secret portal, if you will, through the backdoor of our Web page, along with a password, that takes them directly to their account at the bank. They can see what's come into their account, what's gone out, how much interest the account has earned, what interest rate the bank is paying that day, etc. They can see all of this in real time, 24/7.

Obviously most Intermediaries are not going to want you to know that the funds are commingled, and some will go to considerable lengths to disguise this fact. There are some who will try to pacify you, and/or distract you, by pointing out that they have an advanced degree, such as a law degree or CPA certificate, or that they have passed some test showing basic Exchange competency. Don't be misled by this. Initials behind an Intermediary's name might show that the Intermediary has some level of knowledge, but it won't protect you against dishonesty. And it won't protect the Intermediary from getting sued.

One last word of caution: Some Intermediaries are not truly honest with clients when they answer questions. One of our clients told us about one he had interviewed, when asked if the accounts were separate or commingled, the Intermediary answered that they were separate (when they were not). When this person persisted in his questioning about how and where the funds were held, the Intermediary finally admitted that the accounts were, in fact, commingled. He tried to cover his lie by claiming that what he thought he was being asked was if the operating funds were "separate" from the Exchange funds (which were commingled). The truth is that he knew what he was being asked from the beginning, but he didn't want to admit that the funds were commingled, so he "spun" the truth. But a lie is a lie. If an Intermediary isn't honest about the little things, can you really trust them with the big things?

Bonding

Based upon the number of people who attend one of several conferences held annually for Exchange Intermediaries, there are some 2,000 Intermediaries in the United States. Some of these people aren't Intermediaries; they are investors or attorneys or CPAs attending for more information. But, at the same time, there are many Intermediaries (some full-time, some part-time) who never attend these meetings. So 2,000 is a rough estimate.

Nonetheless, of all the Intermediaries in the U.S., only 39 are bonded as I write this. How do I know that? Easy – there is only one insurance company that bonds Intermediaries, and it only has 39 clients. If I'm right about the total Intermediary population, this means that only about 2 percent are bonded (and 98 percent are not). Bonding helps weed out convicted felons. And the bonding company plays some role in how the funds are held. While the company currently allows commingled accounts (hopefully that will change as a result of the bankruptcy court case), it does make some suggestions on money-handling procedures. I know when we first got our bond many years ago, the company suggested that we move our operating accounts to a different bank, which we promptly did, even though our accounts were separate from our clients' accounts.

I know there are CPAs and attorneys who act as Intermediaries, and they tell me they consider the bonds for their accounting or legal practices to also apply to their Intermediary practices. They don't (or at least I've never seen one that does). Their bonds are for the "practice of law," for example, and their Intermediary businesses are completely different businesses. This means that if you were to make a claim against an attorney's 1031 practice, that attorney's legal practice bond would not cover it.

So what do you do to protect yourself? If you do nothing else, I suggest that you 1) Make sure your Intermediary has a separate bond for Intermediary work. This at least will ensure that you are dealing with one of the good guys. Feel free to ask for a copy of the bond. The Intermediary should share this with you freely. Ours, for example, is posted on our Web site. 2) Make sure that your money is put in its own segregated account. Don't accept the Intermediary's word for it. And once it is in a separate account, check on it periodically to make sure that it stays that way.

Consulting With You About Your Exchange

The Intermediary is supposed to be the expert in your Exchange. You are paying the Intemediary a fee to handle it, and along with your realtor and perhaps your CPA and attorney, the Intermediary should be part of your team. There are a lot of Intermediaries who refuse to answer even simple questions, like what your 45-day and 180-day drop-dead dates are. What if you hired an attorney to draw up your will and then that attorney refused to explain what the provisions in the will meant and refused to give you any advice about estate planning? How would an attorney like that stay in business very long?

It is your money and your Exchange, and you can pick the Intermediary you want, but for the same fee you can get one who will answer your questions and give you advice about the things that impact your Exchange. Either make them earn their fee or find an Intermediary who will work for you and help you. You deserve the best.

The Intermediary Does Not Take Title to the Property

A common misconception about Intermediaries is that the Intermediary takes title to the property as part of the Exchange. It used to be that this was common practice, and it wasn't all that long ago that this was almost required in some parts of the country.

In the old days, when Sue sold her purple duplex to Bob, title to the duplex went from Sue to the Intermediary and then from the Intermediary to Bob. And when it was time to purchase Frank's red office building, the Intermediary acquired title from Frank and then transferred it to Sue. We called this "double deeding."

Around 1993 the IRS approved "direct deeding" where the deed from Sue's purple duplex would go directly from Sue to Bob. Likewise, when Sue buys the red office building the deed will go directly from Frank to Sue.

It's been a couple of years since I've seen double-deeding by another Intermediary or have seen it required by a closer. Occasionally I get asked about direct-deeding, usually by someone who hasn't done an Exchange in ten or 15 years, but you can be assured that if your Intermediary directly deeds the properties in your transaction, he or she has the blessing of the IRS.

Who Can Be an Intermediary?

The IRS does not define who may be an Intermediary – instead it defines who may not be one (the IRS calls it "disqualified"). The Intermediary has to be someone who is totally independent. Obviously a family member, a family member's corporation, partnership, trust, etc. may not be your Intermediary. Nor can anyone who works for you or has a business relationship with you be your Intermediary.

Your attorney or your CPA may not be your Intermediary. In some parts of the country, real estate closings are handled by attorneys. Often these attorneys or someone in their firms, have a close relationship with clients. The regulations are very clear that these attorneys may not be the Intermediary. Our experience is that many attorneys either don't know this or choose to ignore it.

In some parts of the country (especially most parts of the East Coast), the contracts and closings for real estate are handled by an attorney rather than a title company. It seems common for the same attorney or firm to also handle the Exchange for the seller. While this seems to be common, there is nothing in the regulations that allows this, which means that an aggressive IRS agent could disallow the Exchange as a result. Just be very careful – using your attorney to handle your Exchange could toast your Exchange.

Anyone who has had a professional relationship with you during the previous two years may not be your Intermediary. Your financial advisor, for example, may not be your Intermediary.

I heard a horror story several years ago about an attorney in a large law firm who had acted as the Intermediary for a couple – call them Fred and Sue Jones. After the second Old Property had closed, but before the New Property had been purchased, the attorney discovered that Sue Jones had been married to a different man, and that one of the attorneys in the same law firm had represented her in the divorce. She married Fred, had a new last name and no one in the firm connected the dots until she bumped into the divorce attorney in the hall of the law firm one day. Both Exchanges were therefore invalid, and the last I heard the attorney/Intermediary was sweating bullets worrying about the IRS auditing the transaction.

One additional suggestion about your Intermediary: I see some Intermediaries operating as individuals. This is a bad idea for you as an Exchanger. The reason is that the regulations do not provide for a substitution of Intermediaries. If your Intermediary is an individual rather than part of a company, and that Intermediary dies in the middle of your Exchange, there is no provision in the law for someone to complete your Exchange on that Intermediary's behalf. The IRS could disallow your Exchange because your Intermediary died! Would the IRS do this? I don't know – it probably depends on the agent. But to be safe, your Intermediary should be an entity.

One related comment about this is that no, there is no provision to fire or replace your Intermediary. We frequently get calls from clients of other Intermediaries who want to change Intermediaries because they don't like their Intermediaries, or because they want to do something complicated that the Intermediaries do not have the experience to handle. For example, a client sold her Old Property, and her Exchange funds were with an Intermediary affiliated with her title company. She wants to buy a piece of land with part of her proceeds and use the balance to do construction on the land. Since this will make it a complicated transaction (way beyond the expertise and comfort level of the Intermediary), the client wants to transfer to an Intermediary with more experience. But the regulations don't provide for this, and the only way we can accommodate her is if her Intermediary agrees to hire us to handle the complicated part. Sometimes Intermediaries will agree to this, sometimes they won't.

Intermediaries Can Be Disqualified by the IRS

Intermediaries who are otherwise qualified can be disqualified by the IRS if they are caught doing acts that violate the 1031 rules. Typically these are Intermediaries who allow clients to fudge their 45-day identification forms. Ironically (or perhaps not) all of the Intermediaries that I know who have been disqualified by the IRS are attorneys (or, more properly, former attorneys – because they were typically disbarred for their actions).

The IRS has announced that weeding out unethical Intermediaries is one of its goals, so I expect we'll see more disqualifications in the future. At the same time, there are some clients that really push their Intermediaries to bend the laws. I can't tell you the number of times clients have suggested that I go to the bathroom, leaving their files in the middle of my desk, so that they can change their 45-day forms while I'm out of the room. (Of course I say no.)

Several years ago I was approached by a gentleman who was in the middle of a multi-million dollar Exchange. He was beyond his 45-day identification limit and had just found his dream property. His Intermediary would not allow him to change his identification, so his proposal was that he would switch his Exchange to us. To effectuate the Exchange, he would personally pick up his file from his former Intermediary and hand deliver it to us (during which the 45-day identification would magically change). Because his tax on the transaction was several million dollars, my fee for accommodating him was to be $250,000. I never even considered it and wasn't sure whether I should be flattered he wanted us to handle such a large Exchange or ashamed that he would think I would even consider such an offer.

Intermediaries Are Unregulated

Because of the tremendous amounts of money they hold, and the critical part they play in any Exchange, you would think that Intermediaries would have to have a minimal amount of education, pass a test, and be subjected to rigorous regulatory scrutiny. Wrong. None of the 50 states or the Federal government regulates Intermediaries. There are simply no regulations. The only place that even comes close is Nevada, which requires each Intermediary firm operating there to provide fingerprints of the owner and post a small bond. Our bond for Nevada costs us $250 a year. Not what you would call protection for the public.

The effect of this lack of scrutiny is that anyone who wishes to hold themselves out as an Intermediary may do so – even a convicted felon. As an investor you really need to know who you are dealing with. Despite all of the many tens of millions of dollars that our company holds for clients, I've never had anyone from any state banking or real estate commission even ask to see our books, and our firm is pretty high profile.

Up until recently, the head of the Colorado Real Estate Commission was a gentleman named Gormly. Because my name is Gorman, we occasionally sat next to each other in various meetings. Our headquarters is in Denver, and that is where the people in our firm that handle client money are located. Several times I've invited him to send one of his people to audit our Exchange accounts or at least examine our accounting system. I've made it perfectly clear that he is welcome to inspect us any time he wishes. He never has. The truth is that the states just cannot comprehend the vast amounts of money Intermediaries like us hold.

A couple of years ago I was a speaker on a panel in a seminar in Florida that discussed various investment alternatives for wealthy individuals. The person sitting next to me was the fund manager of a fund that was part of a famous mutual fund from New York. His particular fund was far from the largest in the group but was one of a respected group of mutual funds. He was talking about all of the regulators who audit his fund: the SEC, the States of New York, New Jersey and Florida, etc. A person from the audience asked him how much money the fund held. I was sitting right next to him, and the sum of the funds that we were holding for clients at that moment was far greater than the balance in his fund, and we aren't subject to any regulation – federal, state or otherwise.

How Intermediaries Charge

Intermediaries get compensated in one, or sometimes two ways. First, they charge a fee for handling Exchanges. For most Exchanges this fee runs somewhere between $500 and $1,000. You can expect to pay more if your Exchange is big and/or complicated. But for most Exchanges around the country that is the going rate.

But be careful here. Make sure you know exactly what your total cost will be. Most calls to the Intermediary start out something like this: "Hi! My name is Sue Jones, and I have a rental house I'm selling for $100,000, and I want to do an Exchange. What do you charge?" It is not uncommon for the reply to be something like "$500," when in fact the Intermediary charges $500 for the sale of Sue's Old Property (which is what she asked about) plus $500 for the purchase of her New

Property (which she didn't ask about) and perhaps an additional set-up fee and maybe even a monthly holding fee. I assume that the Intermediary believes they are truthfully answering Sue's question since she didn't ask about back-end fees or set-up fees or holding costs. The total cost could run her as much as $1,750, when she thought she was only going to pay $500.

If you are one of those who are focused on the cost, make sure you pin the Intermediary down as to the total cost you'll pay. Have them confirm this in writing by fax or e-mail so you have proof.

Most Intermediaries also keep all or part of the interest from your money, which is why they hold your money in a commingled account. You read the Sunday papers. Ever notice how the banks pay a higher interest rate for million-dollar certificates of deposit than they do for thousand-dollar certificates of deposit. Imagine what a commingled account earns if you pile millions on top of millions. Few people bother to ask who gets the interest. It's your money, so ask!

If the Intermediary agrees to give you the interest, make sure that completely different sets of Exchange fees don't apply depending on who gets the interest. Make sure that the fees quoted for the Exchange don't go up because you will now be earning the interest. (Intermediaries have dual fee structures depending upon who gets the interest.)

By the way, if the Intermediary puts your money in a separate account, you must be getting the interest (I've never heard of an Intermediary who put his or her client's money in separate accounts and then kept the interest).

Exception to Intermediate Requirement: Simultaneous Closings

Since the Starker court cases were resolved more than 20 years ago, the concept of a "Deferred Exchange" where you sell your Old Property and then go find and acquire your New Property has become the standard type of Exchange. Deferred Exchanges require that you use a Qualified Intermediary.

But if you do a "Simultaneous Exchange," your Exchange is not "deferred," and therefore you do not need the services of an Intermediary. In a pure sense, a Simultaneous Exchange takes place when you find another investor who owns a property that you would like to have, and that person happens to also want your property. For example, Sue is selling her purple duplex and she goes out and finds Frank, who has a red office building. Sue wants Frank's red building and Frank wants Sues purple duplex, so they swap deeds. A Qualified Intermediary is not required for this transaction.

In another scenario, Sue wants Frank's red office building; Frank is not interested in Sue's property. Bob, on the other hand, would love to own Sue's purple duplex. Sue then structures the closings of these transactions so that she, Frank and Bob sit down, along with Carl the closer, in a room together. In one transaction Sue sells her purple duplex to Bob and uses his money to buy Frank's red office building. Carl prepares the deeds for everyone and coordinates the money. Again, Sue does not need an Intermediary for this transaction, but then this type of cooperation among the parties is not very common either. How much flexibility is there in this type of transaction? Not much, although we hear all types of horror stories. The accepted rule in the industry is that if you close the sale of your Old Property and the purchase of the New Property with the same closer on the same day you do not need an Intermediary.

To use my example from above, if Sue sells her purple duplex to Bob in Carl's office in the morning and then purchases Frank's red office building in Carl's office that afternoon, this is considered a Simultaneous Exchange in the Exchange community and does not require the services of an Intermediary.

Does Sue have a Simultaneous Exchange if she closes the purchase from Frank the next day? No. Does Sue have a Simultaneous Exchange if she closes the purchase from Frank the same day but uses a closer other than Carl? No. In some states, like Colorado, title companies handle the vast majority of property closings, and some of these title companies are very large with 25 or 30 offices. Can you close your sale in one office of the title company in the morning and close the purchase in a different office of the same title company in the afternoon? No.

There are lots of horror stories about intended Simultaneous Exchanges that blow up. We received a phone call once from a taxpayer whose Exchange was under attack by the IRS, and she wanted our help. Seems she wanted to do a Simultaneous Exchange, sold her Old Property on Friday, and because of a traffic accident, wasn't able to close the purchase of her New Property until Monday morning. There was no way we could help her.

We had another call about a taxpayer who sold his Old Property in Denver in the morning, had the money wired to Phoenix to an affiliate office of the same title company for the purchase of a Phoenix property in the afternoon and was surprised when the IRS auditor disagreed that this was a Simultaneous Exchange.

It is common in our office for our clients to hire us to handle an intended Simultaneous Exchange as a Deferred Exchange just in case something goes wrong. My favorite example of the wisdom of this was our client who sold a rental property in the morning and was closing the purchase of her replacement property after lunch. Same closer and same title company. The New Property she was buying was a rental property in the mountains outside of Denver, with gorgeous views. The sale in the morning had gone off without a hitch, but at the purchase in the afternoon the wife of the seller broke down in tears and couldn't complete the closing. It seems that this house had been her residence for many years. She and her husband had to sell it because the husband had been transferred by his company to the East Coast. The wife's mother loved the place, with its wildlife and its views, and had moved in and lived with them for the last few years of her life. After her death she had been cremated and her ashes scattered on the property. At the closing, it hit the wife that she wasn't just selling the home she loved; she was also selling her mom.

The couple really had no choice – they had to move to the East Coast, so the next day they completed the closing. The moral of the story is that it is very hard to control all of the pieces in a transaction, and trying to put together a Simultaneous Exchange is very difficult. Had our client not had us involved as insurance to protect the Exchange, they would have ended up with a taxable transaction instead of an Exchange.

Chapter 6:
You Cannot Touch the Money

You cannot touch the money from the sale of your Old Property between the closing of the sale of your Old Property and the purchase of your New Property. Once your sale closes, the proceeds have to go directly from the closer to your Intermediary where they are held pending the completion of your Exchange. You need to commit to doing the Exchange far enough ahead of the closing to allow for the Intermediary to arrange for the Exchange and the transfer of the money.

In the words of the IRS, you can't have control or "constructive receipt" of the money. If you do, your Exchange is toast. We get calls all the time from people who closed the sale of their Old Property two or three (sometimes even more than that) days prior. They haven't cashed the check they got from the closing and seem surprised when we tell them that they can't do an Exchange. The reason is that they could have deposited the check any time they wanted to. They had control of the money.

We got a call from a gentleman a couple of years ago who had just sold a building. The closer, who was an attorney, wired over $7 million into this person's account and then told him to call us because we could show him how to defer the tax on it. Too late – not only did he have control over the money, it was in his account.

You also need a good closer, whether an attorney or a title or escrow company, who is experienced enough with Exchanges to know what to do. We handled an Exchange several years ago where, despite our instructions, at the conclusion of the sale, the closer handed our client a check for a couple of hundred thousand dollars, made payable to our client. Luckily our client had the presence of mind to hand it right back and call us immediately. Had they gone home with the check they would have had control, which would have toasted their Exchange.

Get the Intermediary Involved Early

You need to get the Intermediary involved before you close the sale – in other words before you sign the deed transferring ownership from you to the buyer. You can decide to do an Exchange or not do an Exchange up until you sign the deed. This is typically the moment at which the risk of loss on the property passes from you, the seller, to the buyer.

And don't assume that your Intermediary knows the rules. It seems that the vast majority of Intermediaries only do a handful of Exchanges a year. Someone told me once that the average Intermediary handles only about ten Exchanges a year. You simply can't know the rules when you do so few. Ten Exchanges a year is less than one a month. Look for an Intermediary that is doing at least 50 or 60 Exchanges a month – about two a day. That seems to be the point where the volume requires that the Intermediary know the rules and stay on top of the changes in the law.

We hear the strangest stories of things that Intermediaries allow their clients to do. I got a call from a lady recently who called us to get help reporting her Exchange on her tax return. She had done an Exchange but still owed a ton of tax. She was convinced that her CPA had made an error on her tax return and wanted someone who could show him how to report it properly. Someone had given her my phone number and told her that I could talk to her CPA and straighten out the problem.

When I got into the facts of her case it turned out that she was remodeling her kitchen and her Intermediary had paid her remodel costs out of her Exchange account (no – I'm not kidding!). And then when she was ready to purchase her New Property her Intermediary simply sent her a check, made payable to her, for the balance in her Exchange account. These are major mistakes.

This woman's CPA had rightfully treated her transaction as a failed Exchange, which was why she owed so much tax. She was a really nice lady, and I felt sorry for her. She did everything right, she just got involved with an Intermediary who didn't know what he was doing. Moral of the story – deal only with Intermediaries who have substantial experience.

What About Earnest Money That You Receive From the Buyer?

You have until you sign the deed transferring ownership of the property from you to the buyer to decide that you want to do an Exchange. What happens if you've received earnest money that is not held by your Intermediary? Is your Exchange toast? Some people think so because you "touched the money," but the answer is no – you have until you sign the deed to commit to the Exchange, and the fact that you've received Exchange funds does not toast your Exchange. It doesn't matter if you are holding the earnest money in an account in your name or it's held by your realtor, attorney or title or escrow company.

Now, let's be clear here. While receiving the earnest money doesn't have any consequences immediately, it can have consequences down the line. At the time of the closing of the sale to your buyer, the earnest money must be brought to the closing. If it isn't, it will be taxable to you. You may be just fine with that, but in most cases people aren't, so make sure the earnest money gets added back to the closing.

Assume that Sue is selling her purple duplex, and her next-door neighbor offers to buy it from her for $100,000 and gives Sue a check, made out to her, for $5,000 as earnest money. Sue can deposit this check into her savings or money market account pending the closing of the sale. Sue then gets a title company involved to handle the closing and retains a Qualified Intermediary to handle the Exchange.

On the day of the sale, her neighbor brings the balance of $95,000 to the closing. When Sue signs the Exchange documents she must decide what to do with the $5,000 earnest money. If she brings a check in that amount to the closing, the entire proceeds of $100,000, minus closing costs, will be forwarded to the Intermediary by the title company, and Sue will have no tax liability.

If Sue decides to keep the $5,000, then the $95,000 minus closing costs will be forwarded to her Intermediary, and Sue will pay tax on at least $5,000. I say "at least," because how much Sue pays tax on depends on her Intermediary. If Sue signs a standard set of fill-in-the-blank-type Exchange documents, the entire Exchange will be taxable because Sue "touched" some of the money (she got $5,000). The reason for this is that even if Sue only touched a small portion of the money, the IRS believed that showed that she had control of the money, so they could disallow her entire Exchange.

For the $5,000 earnest money to not toast Sue's whole Exchange, the Intermediary must prepare special Exchange documents saying, in effect, that Sue is doing an Exchange only on 95 percent of the property (or $95,000), and the balance (the $5,000) is outside the Exchange and not part of it. If the Intermediary knows enough to do this, Sue will not have touched any of the money on her $95,000 Exchange.

Only Two Places You Can Get Cash Out of an Exchange

The first of the two places you can get cash out of an Exchange is at the closing table, as Sue has done above. And it is not necessary that the money you take is earnest money. It could be any amount. For example, if Sue wanted $10,000 to buy a car, she could walk away from the closing with $10,000 provided she communicated that desire in advance to the Intermediary so that her Intermediary could prepare Exchange documents showing that Sue did an Exchange on 90 percent of the property, with the balance being outside of the Exchange and going directly to her.

One critically important point here is that once the money is sent to the Intermediary by the closer, you cannot touch the proceeds for the remainder of the Exchange. So Sue needs to communicate her desire for a new car to the Intermediary well before the closing so that the Intermediary can restructure the Exchange to accommodate her. If she doesn't communicate this to the Intermediary, her money is tied up until the end of the Exchange.

The second place that you can get money out of an Exchange is at the end of the 180 days. At that point, any cash left over from the Exchange goes back to you and is taxable. Sometimes clients do this intentionally because they want a few extra dollars to buy a car or pay off a credit card. Other times the amount is inadvertently left over, as frequently happens if the client is estimating the amount of proceeds that will be available from the sale of the Old Property (where it hasn't closed yet) so that an estimate can be made as to the amount of the loan needed on the New Property. As is human nature, clients will estimate high on the amount of loan they need. Again, this amount is entirely taxable.

One very important fact about this money: Any cash you touch in an Exchange is taxable. So in my examples above, the cash that Sue gets is taxable, whether it is $5,000 of earnest money that she keeps or $10,000 of proceeds that come out of the Exchange. And the whole amount that she keeps is taxable. It does not matter that Sue put $10,000 down when she bought the duplex and that she paid $5,000 a couple of years ago to paint it such a pretty purple color, the whole amount of the check she receives is taxable, that is up to the amount of her total gain (you never have more taxable gain in an Exchange than you would have if you didn't do the Exchange).

Can You Get the Balance of the Proceeds Before Your 180 Days Are Up?

This is a tough one. In theory you cannot touch the proceeds before the 180 days are up. The IRS issued a ruling a couple of years ago that on its face said that the Intermediary must hold the proceeds until the 180 days expire before proceeds can be returned to the Exchanger. The ruling covers those people who don't purchase any New Properties as well as those who have small balances left after purchasing their New Properties.

The rumor is that this ruling was forced by an Intermediary company whose Intermediaries kept the interest from the Exchange funds they hold. They constructed their Exchange documents in such a way that the IRS had to rule that, because of the way the documents were constructed, the money must be held until the end of the 180 days. But that is the ruling only if an Intermediary's Exchange documents are written like theirs.

Most people don't find this fair in cases where they can't, or decide not to, buy New Property. Let's say Sue has sold her purple duplex. The proceeds are with her Intermediary, and Sue identifies only one replacement property. After the 45-day identification period, Sue decides that she does not want to purchase that property and wants her money back. Or maybe she has a family emergency and suddenly finds she needs her funds. She knows that she will pay tax on the sale of her Old Property. Why must she wait until the 180 days elapse? What difference does it make?

The reason is that Intermediaries are not allowed to let their clients touch the money. If they do so, they could be "disqualified" as Intermediaries. That makes sense if Sue buys one property and has money left over, but not if Sue has not purchased any property at all.

Most Intermediaries are somewhat accommodating with clients in such a situation. Some of them have a procedure where the client "revokes" his or her identifications. Some have the client write a letter stating that the reason the client cannot purchase the property is for reasons beyond the control of the client (an excuse allowed by the IRS), and some Intermediaries will return the money upon receipt of a letter from the client or the client's attorney threatening litigation.

In the real world I think that this is primarily an issue for Intermediaries who want to hold on to the funds. In reality, if Sue sells her purple duplex, starts an Exchange and then decides not to complete it, there is no trace of the Exchange when she files her tax return and reports the sale as a taxable transaction. If Sue wants to collapse her Exchange and pay tax, few Intermediaries will stand in her way.

On the other hand, if Sue identified two or three properties, bought one of them, has Exchange proceeds left over and wanted the balance of her funds, we would have a different kind of problem. Returning the Exchange proceeds to her could cause her Exchange to be disallowed if her 45-day form was not completed correctly.

Let's say Sue identified three potential replacement properties: properties A, B and C. Sue acquires Property A, which leaves a small balance in her Exchange account. In theory Sue could still acquire one of the other two properties during the remainder of the 180 days, and returning the balance of the money to her could blow her entire Exchange. But at the same time it doesn't make sense for the Intermediary to hold a small balance of funds for the remainder of the 180 days (unless the Intermediary is keeping the interest).

What many Intermediaries do to resolve this problem is have people like Sue indicate on their 45-day forms whether they intend to buy one of the three properties, two of the three or all three. That way if they indicate that they intend to buy only one, and they acquire one, leaving a small amount of Exchange funds remaining, they have acquired what they intended to acquire, and the unspent balance can be returned to them.

In this situation (where Sue has indicated she will buy only one of the three properties she has identified) a smart Intermediary will be reluctant to send one check for the necessary balance to the closer for the purchase of Sue's New Property and a second check to Sue for the amount of unspent proceeds. The Intermediary will instead send the entire balance of Exchange funds to the closer, and the closer will deliver the unspent proceeds to Sue at the time of the purchase.

What Can Be Paid From Your Exchange Account?

If we are talking about your Old Property, the Intermediary can disburse amounts for any items arising in connection with the Old Property. For example, a week after the closing of the sale of her purple duplex, the buyer informs Sue that the water heater needs to be replaced and that Sue should pay for it. After several discussions Sue agrees to pay half the cost of the new water heater. Her share of the cost can come from the Exchange funds held by her Intermediary. Similarly, the Intermediary can pay the closing lawyer's bill she gets a week after the closing is completed.

The logic here is that had the condition of the water heater been known or the amount of the lawyer's fee been known at the time of the sale, the Intermediary would have gotten less in proceeds as a result.

If we are talking about your New Property, the Intermediary can disburse amounts only for items that will come back into the Exchange account if the purchase is not completed. In essence this means that only earnest money can be disbursed by the Intermediary ahead of the closing. Sue calls us and wants us to disburse a check to the lender for loan application fees. We can't do this because if Sue's purchase fails, for whatever reason, the loan fees will not come back to us, which results in Sue having "touched" the money, which will blow her Exchange.

You Cannot Pledge or Borrow Against the Exchange Funds

A question that periodically comes up is whether or not you can borrow against the Exchange funds. Typically the question is: "Can I pledge the Exchange funds the Intermediary is holding against a loan I'm trying to get on another property?" The answer is no, because if you could you would be touching the money. In other words, you have control over the proceeds.

From time to time, clients will want us to park their Exchange proceeds in their bank. You don't really want to do this because the IRS could argue that you were, in effect, pledging (borrowing against) the Exchange funds and could disallow the Exchange.

Chapter 7:
Ownership Issues

Both Old and New Property Ownership Must Be the Same

Both the Old Property and the New Property ownership must be the same. In general, this means that the tax return of the person who owns the Old Property has to be the same as the one that owns the New Property. For example, if Microsoft Corporation owns the Old Property, then Microsoft Corporation must buy the New, not one of Microsoft's subsidiaries and not Bill Gates. It has to be the same tax return.

When the way that you tell the IRS you hold title differs from the way that you legally hold title, this rule can really get confusing. For example, Sue and a couple of her friends buy a building and take title as tenants-in-common (meaning that there are three separate people legally in title). However, instead of treating the property as owned by three separate owners, their CPA files a partnership tax return for the property.

When the CPA files the return, the immediate result is that he just turned the three owners of the property for legal purposes, into only one owner for 1031 Exchange purposes, since the IRS now thinks that the partnership is the tax return that owns the property. In other words, as far as the IRS is concerned, there is now one owner of the property: the partnership. Since the IRS sees the partnership as the owner of the property, the partnership will have to be the one to sell the Old Property and take title to the New Property. The partnership is the entity that must do the Exchange, rather than Sue and her two friends. If Sue and her friends were each planning to go different directions, this would screw up their plans.

It is common for the clients like Sue to call us to talk about their "partners" in the property. When this happens we typically spend considerable time determining the exact legal and tax relationship of the owners of the property, because obviously the options are different if three people own the property than they are if one entity owns the property.

Joint Tenants

To most people, joint tenants are two people who are married to each other. There is only one tax return – their joint tax return, and that joint return owns the property. While it's true that most joint tenants are married, they do not technically need to be married. But for purposes of this discussion, let's assume that they are. What I want to do is assume that there is one tax return.

If Fred and Sue, husband and wife, own a building that they are selling, only one tax return owns the property – their joint return. This means that if they sell their building for $200,000, Sue cannot take her $100,000 share and buy a replacement property in only her name since she (all by herself) is not under the same tax return as the one under which the property was sold (which was the joint return). She and Fred would both have to take title to the New Property to have a successful 1031 Exchange.

Because Fred and Sue file a joint tax return, and because they own the Old Property as joint tenants, they both have to take title to the New Property in both names as joint tenants. The reason for this is because they file a joint return. In other words, since the joint return owned the Old Property, the joint return has to buy the New Property. This is true even if you file as "married filing separately," because in the eyes of the IRS, married filing separate is the same as joint but with separate tax calculations.

Issues With Spouses

If Sue is married to Fred, and Sue owns the building in her name only, then Sue is the one who does the Exchange, and Sue is the one who must take title to the New Property, even though she and Fred filed a joint return.

Let's say that Sue owned the purple duplex before she met Fred. She and Fred got married, but whether she forgot or thought better of it, Sue did not add Fred to the title. She has a buyer for the purple duplex and a week before the closing she learns from the closer that Fred is not on the title. She wants Fred to be part of the purchase of the New Property. Can she add Fred to the title today and then close the sale next week? The answer is no – if the IRS audits the Exchange it can argue that Fred has only owned his half for a week and therefore held it for resale rather than investment. The IRS can, and has, disallowed a spouse's half of the Exchange in real life situations like this.

How does Sue get Fred into title on the New Property? If Sue sold the duplex for $100,000, and her New Property cost her $150,000 she could simply take title to an undivided two-thirds of the New Property, and Fred could take title to the other one-third. As you will see, because Sue sold her Old Property for $100,000, she has to buy her New Property for at least that much to avoid paying any tax on the Exchange. She does this with her two-thirds share.

What if there is no room for Fred on the New Property (Sue sold the Old Property for $100,000, and she is paying $100,000 for the New Property)? Our advice here is for Sue to take title to the New Property in her name only and then to add Fred to the title later. While it would be best for her to wait a year and a day to do this, there probably is very little exposure if she does this sooner because transferring half the property to her husband is not a taxable event (because of a different IRS Code section).

What if the lender demands that Fred be part of the loan for the New Property? While this doesn't seem fair, it appears to be fairly common. The best answer is to have Sue acquire the New Property in her name only, and then five minutes later add Fred as part of the loan. Sometimes this works, but often the lender has a problem with this. If the lender demands that Fred be part of the title in order for the loan to be approved, we suggest that Sue get a letter from the lender stating this and that she and Fred have a written agreement between them that says that Fred is part of the deal solely as an accommodation to the lender.

Tenants-in-Common

Tenants-in-common means multiple separate owners. As a practical matter we assume that tenants-in-common owners are not married, although you could be married and still be tenants-in-common. Tenants-in-common ownership implies that there is more than one owner to the property; therefore multiple tax returns own the property.

If Sue instead owned the building with her brother Frank, and the two are equal owners of a building, two tax returns own the building: Frank's and Sue's. If they sell the building, both tax returns have the potential to do an Exchange. In other words, if they are selling the building for $200,000, Sue can do an Exchange with her half and buy Property A without Frank. Of course she must meet all of the other requirements of an Exchange, but the IRS looks just to her tax return to determine if she has met them. Frank, on the other hand, could also do an Exchange and buy Property B without Sue, or he could take his share of the proceeds and pay tax on them.

The rule that the same tax return has to take title to the New Property as owned the Old Property applies to Sue's tax return (which is separate from Frank's). Sue could not sell her half of the building individually and take title to the New Property as "Jones Investment Corporation," since as a corporation it files a different tax return.

Does it matter that Sue sold an undivided 50 percent of the Old Property but bought 100 percent of Property A? No – as long as she buys Property A in the same manner (meaning within the same tax return) that she held her share of the Old Property. If she does this she has met the requirements of Section 1031.

Of course Frank and his sister Sue could continue on and buy Property C together. As you will see, they each have to buy equal or up, but they could buy Property C in different shares. For example, if they sell their Old Property for $200,000 and each owned half, they could buy Property C for $300,000 with Frank buying one-third for $100,000 and Sue buying two-thirds for $200,000. Again, the fact that each tax return (Frank's and Sue's) sold a half-interest of the Old Property, but Frank bought one-third of the New Property and Sue bought two-thirds is OK, because the IRS looks to each tax return to determine if it has met the requirements of Section 1031.

And, of course, if two people are married but hold title to the property as tenants-in-common, then, in fact, there is only one entity that owns the Old Property and only one tax return – their joint return. The rules that I described in the section above would apply regardless of the wording on the deed. Don't get caught up by the wording on the deed, look through to the actual tax return(s) of the owners of the property.

Partnerships

Let's say that the Old Property is owned by the FGH Partnership. The partnership is owned equally by Fred, George and Howie. Can the partnership sell the Old Building for $300,000, and can Fred take his one-third share, his $100,000, and buy Property A in his name only? No – because the Old Property was owned by the partnership, according to its tax return, which is a different tax return than Fred's, who purchased Property A.

What if the partners want to go different directions? One word of caution as you read this section: The examples that I use involve partnerships. Your results will be similar if you are using an LLC. However, if your property is owned by a trust or a corporation (either a regular "C" corporation or an "S" corporation) the tax laws are much more restrictive, and you should not attempt restructuring unless you have the close guidance of a CPA or tax attorney. Actually having a good CPA or tax attorney hold your hand is a good idea any time you try to restructure an entity.

So let's assume that the Old Property, which is owned by the FGH Partnership, is under contract to sell for $300,000. Fred, George and Howie, the three partners, each want to do an Exchange, and they want to go different directions, and none of them wants to pay tax on their share of the proceeds. How do we accomplish this? First, let's be clear – the Old Property is owned by one entity – the partnership – with one tax return. This means that under the 1031 rules, the partnership has to be the one that does the Exchange, and the partnership has to be the one to buy the New Property.

One solution would be to dissolve the partnership, which would work in this way: each of the partners would give up their membership shares (think of them like shares of stock) in the partnership. In return for their shares, each of them would get a deed to an undivided, one-third, tenants-in-common interest to the property. At this point the Old Property would now be owned by three tax returns (Fred, George and Howie). Each then could take their interest at the closing of the sale and go a different direction.

The fatal flaw in this method is that when Fred, George and Howie each take title to their separate interests in the property it starts their year-and-a-day holding period over again. This means that if the IRS audits them, it could argue that each of them held their shares for resale rather than investment because they each sold their separate shares shortly after receiving them. Of course they could avoid this problem by dissolving the partnership and waiting out the year and a day and then closing the sale. But in real life, Exchangers seem to address this issue only after they have a willing buyer and are facing a scheduled closing in the near future.

The best solution in a situation like this, where the partners want to go different directions, would be for the partnership to sell the Old Property and buy three replacement properties: Property A for Fred, Property B for George and Property C for Howie. Each of these purchases would be done in the name of the partnership. In other words, the same entity that owned the Old Property (the FGH Partnership) is the one that would do the Exchange and would end up owning three new properties. The partnership would hold these three properties for a year and a day after the purchase and then dissolve and distribute the three properties to the three partners: Fred would get A, George would get B, and Howie would get C. In most cases you would want to modify the partnership agreement to provide for the specific allocation of the profits or losses and positive or negative cash flow arising from each property to the respective partner who owns that property during the year that the partnership owns everything.

What if one of the partners wants to cash out? Let's use the same example from above: the Old Property is owned by the FGH Partnership, and the partnership is equally owned by three partners: Fred, George and Howie. The partnership's building is being sold for $300,000, and Howie doesn't want to continue on in the Exchange (or maybe Fred and George don't want to be partners with him anymore). Howie just wants his cash. He knows he will pay tax, but he doesn't care. Fred and George, on the other hand, want to do an Exchange and buy another property. How do we make this happen in a way that doesn't screw up Fred and George's Exchange?

As we discussed above, if we dissolve the partnership, and Fred, George and Howie each take an undivided interest in the property, it starts the year-and-a-day holding period again for each of them, and so we don't want to do that.

If Fred and George buy Howie out, it will cost them each $50,000. (Howie's share is $100,000, remember?) Fred and George are now the only owners of the partnership, but the partnership entity is still the owner of the property, so we don't have a problem with the year-and-a-day rule. The partnership sells the Old Property, does the Exchange and buys the New Property. Our equal-or-up number (see Chapter 8 for a discussion of this rule) for the New Property is still $300,000.

One caveat here – there is an IRS rule that says if you change 50 percent or more of the ownership of a partnership or LLC during a twelve-month period, it results in a defacto liquidation of the partnership (meaning that a new tax return is created). Be careful you don't run afoul of this rule.

A second alternative would be for the partnership to borrow $100,000 against the property and use the money to buy Howie's partnership share. First, remember that we can't touch the money from the sale of the property in an Exchange. If you refinance the Old Property before you sell it, the IRS could argue that, in effect, you touched the money, and the refinancing will be taxable. How long do you have to wait after you refinance so that you don't have to worry about this? Surprise – a year and a day. Fred and George could wait and refinance the New Property after they purchase (the year-and-a-day rule doesn't apply to refinancing the New Property) and use the funds to buy Howie's shares. The problem with doing this is that their New Property now has a $100,000 debt that the Old Property didn't have, their equal-or-up number is $300,000 and Howie has to wait until the New Property purchase closes before he gets his money.

A third alternative might be to sell the property for $300,000 but only do an Exchange for $200,000 and have the other $100,000 go to the partnership (it has to go to the partnership rather than Howie because the partnership is the owner of the property). The partnership would then use the money to purchase Howie's share. The problem with this is that if the partnership agreement does not include a clause providing for disproportionate sharing of cash and gains, the IRS could tax Fred and George each on $33,333 of gain even though they didn't get the cash, which won't make them happy. Howie would also pay tax on $33,333 but would have the entire $100,000 cash. And there are court cases disallowing the arrangement if they try to change the partnership agreement in the middle of the Exchange.

Probably the best way to make this situation work is to give Howie a quit claim deed for an undivided one-third interest to the property in Exchange for his partnership share. Now the Old Property is owned by two entities with two tax returns: the partnerships for an undivided two-thirds interest and Howie's for an undivided one-third interest. In other words, the partnership goes to Howie and gives him a quit claim deed for an undivided one-third interest in the property, and Howie gives back his membership shares.

At this point, can the partnership do an Exchange for its two-thirds share? Yes, because it has owned that share for more than a year and a day. What is its equal-or-up number? $200,000. Does it have any debt? No. Did Fred or George have to put up their money to buy Howie out? No.

Now, can Howie do an Exchange for his one-third interest? No – because he has not owned his share for at least a year and a day. But Howie doesn't want to do an Exchange – he just wants to get his money and pay his tax. How is Howie's gain taxed? Assuming that he was a partner in the partnership for at least a year, part of his gain will be taxed as depreciation recapture and the balance as long-term capital gains. And he will pay state tax (if any) to his state on the sale.

As you can see, there are a number of ways to get to where you want to in an Exchange, but in most cases these solutions take time. Make sure you are dealing with a very good Intermediary, and then give them plenty of time to formulate the solution to your problem.

Buying a new property and then transferring it to a partnership: This is another of those common questions. Fred is selling his Old Property, which he owns in his name, and he wants to buy a share of a partnership that owns his desired New Property. Obviously he can't do this because the partnership is under a different tax return than is he, but what if he took title to a slice of the New Property in his name, and then transferred this slice of property to a partnership?

As you've probably guessed, Fred should wait at least a year and a day after he takes title to the New Property in his name before he transfers that title to the partnership. If Fred makes the transfer quicker than this, he opens the door for the IRS to argue that he didn't buy property to hold for investment, he bought property held for resale since he transferred it within a year and a day.

Death of a Taxpayer

What if a taxpayer dies in the middle of an Exchange? When this happens, the heirs have a large array of tax choices that could cost or save the estate substantial tax. The problem is the heirs are usually not in an emotional place to make the decisions that need to be made.

If the death takes place before the end of the 45-Day identification period: The heirs have the option of ignoring the Exchange and treating the transaction as a sale when the property closed and the taxpayer was still alive. In this case it will be taxed in the deceased final tax return. Or he or she could treat it as a valid Exchange but fail to identify any New Property by the 45th day. In this case the gain would be taxed to the estate. In either of these alternatives the cash, after taxes, would flow to the heirs. What the heirs have to determine, if their motive is to get the cash, is which of these alternatives will result in less tax and therefore the most cash to them (the deceased or the estate will pay tax on the sale, and the estate might pay tax on the net cash).

Alternatively, they could complete the Exchange after which the New Property would pass to the heirs. Neither the deceased nor the estate would pay tax on the sale. But depending upon the value of the property, the estate might pay tax on it. If the estate completed the Exchange it would need to do so as the representative, or trustee, of the estate.

Under current tax law the property would then pass to the heirs, who would get a "step up in basis" on the property when they received it. That means that if the New Property cost $100,000, that amount becomes its basis in the hands of the heirs. If the heirs were to then sell the property for $105,000 they would only pay tax on the $5,000 gain.

On January 1, 2010 that law changes so that the estate would not pay any tax on the value of the property. The heirs would get the property with the same basis that the deceased had and pay tax on all the gain if they sold it.

If the 45-day identification period has passed: The heirs step into the shoes of the deceased, so to speak, if the identification period passes. They can continue and buy something off the 45-Day List, or they can collapse the Exchange, which means that their funds will be locked in the Exchange until the expiration of the 180 days.

Death of a taxpayer in the middle of the Exchange does not happen often. In all of the tens of thousands of Exchange transactions we've handled, this has happened less than ten times. As I've said, the heirs are typically not mentally prepared to handle the choices that need to be made in the timeframes in which they need to be made.

Two of these transactions stick in my memory. The first was a very large, complicated transaction. I had been working closely with our client's tax attorney because of the complexity of this particular transaction when the client was killed in an accident about a week before the expiration of the identification period. I called the attorney, explained the options, and we determined that the most logical option was to continue with the Exchange and the purchase of the property that the client had under contract. We prepared the documents, and the attorney took them to our client's widow for signature. Despite her grief, she signed them because she understood that we were watching out for her best interest. She didn't truly understand what she had signed or why until several months later.

The second transaction involved a client for whom we had handled several Exchanges and who happened to have cancer. When he died in the middle of his Exchange, his wife and his realtor were very clear what his game plan was and the Exchange proceeded without any hitches.

Exceptions (sort of) to the same ownership rule

There are currently four so-called "exceptions" to the same ownership rule. In fact, as you will see, the ownership is the same; it's just the name that is different. These exceptions fall into the category the IRS calls "disregarded entities." The four exceptions are Revocable Living Trusts, Illinois-Type Land Trusts, Single Member Limited Liability Companies and Delaware Statutory Trusts.

Revocable Living Trusts: These are trusts set up to aid estate planning by helping assets bypass probate when you die. Let's take your car, for example. If you wanted to sell your car to me, you would sign the title over to me, and it would be mine. However, after you've died, you (obviously) aren't around to sign the title. Therefore your estate representative would take the title to a judge who would sign the title on your behalf. This process is called "probate." It used to be a lot more costly than it is today, but it can still be quite costly. And it takes a long time.

Revocable Living Trusts are designed to help your estate avoid probate. You set up a Revocable Living Trusts and transfer your assets to it. The Trust has at least two trustees: you and the person you've appointed to be your successor trustee. Your trust documents generally provide that you can sign transfer documents (like an auto title) while you are still alive. After you're deceased your successor trustee will sign transfer documents on behalf of the trust. In other words, the other successor can sign the title of your car over to me after your death without needing to probate it.

What does this have to do with a 1031 Exchange? Two things: Revocable Living Trusts are quite common, and most lenders will not lend to trusts. As a result, it is not unusual to have a situation where you've sold your Old Property, which was owned by your Revocable Living Trust, but not be allowed to close the purchase of your New Property in the name of the trust. Will this screw up your Exchange?

Those of you who own assets titled in your Revocable Living Trust know that the Trust does not file an income tax return – all of the rents, expenses and dividends and interest, etc., are reported in the tax return of the owner of the trust. Because of this, the owner of the trust is the entity who claims the property.

If Sue owned her purple duplex, which was titled in the name of the Sue Jones Revocable Living Trust, Sue's individual tax return (form 1040) would show her ownership of the property. She can sell it, do an Exchange and buy her New Property in her name only since that is the name on the tax return under which she sold her Old Property. In other words, what tax return claimed the Old Property? Sue's (even if the title was held in the name of Sue's Revocable Living Trust). As long as her tax return shows her ownership of the New Property, her transaction will qualify for an Exchange

Illinois-Type Land Trust: In Illinois, all of the details of your real estate purchase and sales are reported in the local paper. As a result, your neighbors, friends and family know the details of every transaction you make. As you can imagine, this doesn't light the fire of very many people. As a result, the Illinois Land Trust evolved. If Fred, George and Howie want to buy equal pieces of a property without sharing the details with everyone they know, they can buy the property in the name of, for example, the FGH Land Trust. The Land Trust does not file an income tax return. All of the income and expense is reported in the individual tax returns for Fred, George and Howie. If they sell the property for $300,000, can Fred take his $100,000 share and buy Property A in his name only? The answer is yes since Fred's tax return is the one that claims his one-third share of the property and reports his share of the income and expense. Again, because the land trust does not file a tax return it is considered a "disregarded entity." Fred's tax return is the one that claimed the sale of the Old Property and the purchase of the New Property, hence the Exchange will be allowed even if the title to the Old and New properties are different.

One of the negative aspects of Illinois-Type Land Trusts is that they do not protect owners from liability. If someone slipped on the ice and got hurt, they could sue Fred, George and Howie individually.

And one other thing before I leave this discussion: we occasionally see Illinois-Type Land Trusts where taxpayers' accountants for some reason had filed tax returns for the trusts. Guess what? The trust tax return now shows the trust as owner of the property and the trust (not Fred, George and Howie individually) must do the Exchange, because the entity whose tax return shows ownership of the property must do the Exchange. Don't let your accountant screw this up by filing a return for the Land Trust.

Single-member LLCs: Limited Liability Companies (LLCs) are entities that combine the best attributes of both corporations and partnerships. As such, they are the preferred investment vehicle for most investors today. LLCs file partnership tax returns (Form 1065). The IRS does not recognize one-partner partnerships. Therefore, if you try to file a partnership return for a single-member LLC showing only one partner, the IRS will send it back and tell you to report the income and expenses from the LLC on the sole partner's (called a "member" for an LLC) income tax return.

In other words, if you are the sole member of an LLC, and you have to report the income and expenses of the LLC on your own return, what tax return owns the property? Correct, yours. Therefore if Fred sells his Old Property, which he holds title to as "Fred Jones," can he buy the New Property as "Jones Investments, LLC," if Fred is the only member of the LLC? Again the answer is yes since the same tax return claims both the Old Property and the New Property. Like the Revocable Living Trust and the Illinois-Type Land Trust, the Single-Member LLC is considered a disregarded entity since it does not file a tax return.

The benefit of a Single-Member LLC is that if someone slips on the ice of a property owned by the LLC, that person can only sue the LLC. The person who slipped could not sue the individual member. In other words, the person could sue Jones Investments, LLC, but not Fred.

Delaware Statutory Trust: A Delaware Statutory Trust (DST), sometime called a Delaware Business Trust, is an entity that combines the best Section 1031 treatment attributes of an Illinois-Type Land Trust and a Single–Member LLC.

Like an Illinois-Type Land Trust, the DST takes title to the property, but the owners (called "beneficiaries" by trust law) are treated as the real owners. If Fred, George and Howie own a property held in the name of the "FGH Trust, a Delaware Statutory Trust," it is the three of them who are considered the owners, and the trust does not file a tax return.

But DSTs are also like Single-Member LLCs in that a person can only sue the DST and not the actual owners of the LLC. So, in effect, a DST provides the legal protection of an LLC with the multi-owner benefit of an Illinois-Type Land Trust.

There is a small problem with DSTs: The trustee who represents the trust must be a person and must be a resident of the State of Delaware.

As I write this, the IRS has just approved DSTs as the fourth disregarded entity for 1031 Exchanges. Although the initial benefits are obvious, I predict that DSTs will become hugely valuable vehicles in the future. Again, if this type of vehicle fits your investment objectives, you'll want to work with a sophisticated Intermediary who can help establish a DST and put you in contact with a Delaware trustee.

Chapter 8:
Equal or Up

In order to not pay any tax, the selling price of your New Property must be equal to or greater than the net selling price of the Old Property. Net selling price is the selling price minus closing costs. Closing costs on the Old Property are typically real estate commissions, title insurance and the fee charged by the title or escrow closer who will prepare the documents transferring ownership of the Old Property to the buyer.

Calculating the Target Price

For example, when Sue sells her purple duplex for $100,000, she'll have real estate commissions of about $6,000, title and closing costs of perhaps $1,500 and an outstanding loan balance of $40,000, which will leave cash of $52,500. And if you are familiar with real estate Settlement Statements, the $1,500 of title and closing costs might be the sum of 15 or 20 small charges. So out of all of this mess, how do you compute Sue's equal-or-up minimum?

In our office we call the equal-or-up number the target price, and a quick and dirty way to arrive at it is to add together two numbers: the debt on the Old Property that was paid off and the amount of cash that goes from the closing to the Intermediary. Add these two numbers together, and the result is the target price on your equal-or-up number. In the above example, Sue could zero in on her target by adding the debt that was paid off (of $40,000) to the amount that goes to the Intermediary ($52,500) to arrive at her target price of $92,500. The purchase price of her New Property must equal or exceed this target number.

One additional thing I want to point out here is that if Sue had decided that she wanted $10,000 from the closing (I've talked about how to do this previously), the amount she takes at the closing would reduce her equal-or-up number to $82,500 (the $40,000 debt that was paid off plus the $42,500 that went to the Intermediary).

What happens if the target number is not achieved? Is your Exchange toast? Must you pay tax on the gain as if you had not sold the property? The answer is no. What happens, as you will see, is that you pay tax on the shortfall, but, no, your Exchange is not toast.

One of the hardest things for people to grasp is that they have to reinvest all of the cash to avoid paying tax. I deal with all of the issues surrounding this in the next chapter. The next question is typically: "What is debt?" Remember, if you touch any cash in the Exchange, at a minimum it will be taxable -- and there is always the possibility that it could toast your Exchange. So can you reimburse your folks for the loan they made you for the down payment? Or the loan you took from your line of credit to make improvements to the property? Read on.

What Is Considered "Debt?"

IRS regulations define debt as that which is "associated with" the property. Why do you care? Because if you can prove that the money from the loan went into the property, then that loan can be paid at closing without being taxable to you and without it toasting your Exchange.

Let's say that Sue, to buy the purple duplex, borrowed $10,000 from her folks. The loan was not recorded as a lien against the property; she merely promised that she will pay back the loan when she sells the property. Now she's selling the duplex, and if she takes a $10,000 check, made payable to her, at the closing she will pay tax on this money. Alternatively, she should direct the closer, as part of the sale, to issue a check to her parents as repayment of the loan. And on the Settlement Statement it should be shown as "repayment of loan from Mr. & Mrs. Smith" (Sue's parents). This way the $10,000 is not taxable as cash to Sue, but is a repayment of debt.

Or let's assume that Fred borrowed $25,000 from his company's line of credit to paint the office building he owns. Now he is selling the office building, and, of course, he wants to use part of the sales proceeds to pay down the line of credit, which, of course, is not recorded as a loan against the office building. Again, the check should show on the Settlement Statement as "repayment of improvement loan from State Bank" and the check for $25,000 from the closing would be to State Bank.

Another common place that this question comes up is in regard to fix-up costs to make the property more saleable. Costs that are paid out of Sue's pocket for paint and supplies, for example, cannot be reimbursed because they are not a "debt," and the money going to her would be taxable. On the other hand, if Sue charged the paint and supplies to her Visa card, a check can be cut to Visa without being taxable to Sue.

All of these amounts are considered "debt associated with" and count toward determining the equal-or-up amount. They have to count toward the equal-or-up target or be a closing cost. If they are not one of these they are taxable.

For example, Sue sells her purple duplex for $100,000, from which she has closing costs of $7,500, a mortgage to the bank of $50,000 and the repayment of the down payment loan to her parents of $10,000, netting $32,500, which goes to Sue's Intermediary. Sue's equal-or-up target is the Exchange account cash of $32,500, plus the debt paid off of $60,000, for a total of $92,500.

Be prepared to prove amounts not backed up by liens against the property. Fred has to be able to show that in fact he did borrow money from his credit line and that he did use the funds for this property. Failure to prove this could end up with the amount being taxable or the Exchange being disallowed.

One final issue to watch for here, although we don't see it often, is the situation where you've used the Old Property as security for another loan, which is not associated with the Old Property. If this loan is paid at the closing, the IRS can make that amount taxable. In this situation you want to make sure the loan is paid off or the security interest shifted to another property prior to closing.

What Happens if You Buy Down?

If your New Property costs less than or equal to your target price, you have bought down. And if you buy down, it does not toast your whole Exchange; you merely pay tax on the amount of the buy-down. For example, in our calculation of Sue's transaction above, her target price was $92,500. What happens if she only pays $85,000 for her New Property? Sue would pay tax on $7,500 -- the difference between the $92,500 net selling price of the Old Property and the $85,000 purchase price of the New Property.

If Sue is buying down by $7,500, should she take cash for this amount, or should she reduce her debt by this amount? While every client's objectives are different, as a general rule if you are going to buy down, take the cash. This way you have cash to pay the tax.

Sue's choice here, for example, is to get a loan on the New Property for $40,000 (the amount of debt paid off on the Old Property) and then use $45,000 of the money the Intermediary is holding, which will leave excess proceeds of $7,500. Alternatively, Sue could use the $52,500 that is being held by the Intermediary and get a loan for $32,500 to balance out the purchase. Either way Sue is going to pay tax on $7,500, but if she takes the first alternative she'll have higher monthly loan payments, but at least she'll have the cash to pay the tax.

How is the $7,500 buy-down taxed? First of all, it is all taxable, meaning that she can't offset any of her cash invested in the Old Property. Sue bought down by $7,500, and even though she invested $15,000 of her own cash into the purchase of the purple duplex, and she invested an additional $5,000 a few years ago to remodel it (for a total cash investment of $20,000), she will still pay tax on the $7,500 buy-down.

The reason for this is that your basis of the Old Property rolls over to the new. If Sue's basis on her Old Property, discussed above, was $25,000, and she sold it for $100,000 and did an Exchange, her potential deferred gain is $75,000. When she buys the New Property for $85,000, her basis in that property is still $25,000 since the basis rolls over from the Old to the New Property. She will pay tax on the $15,000 buy-down, which reduces her deferred gain to $60,000. Her buy-down comes out of the deferred gain, and her basis stays the same.

Computing Net Sales Price

So what about the handling of the closing costs when you sell your Old Property? Some things, like real estate commissions and title insurance add to the basis of your New Property. Some, however, have tax ramifications. For example, if, as part of the closing, you pay your share of the property tax applicable to that portion of the year, you get a deduction for the amount of property tax paid, but you also have taxable income in the same amount because that portion was carved out to pay the tax. The taxable part is taxed at capital gains rates, whereas the property taxes paid at the sale are a straight deduction. In most cases you will get a small tax benefit from this treatment.

If Sue's share of the property tax for the year through the date of sale is $1,500, she will get a deduction for that amount on her tax return and will also report capital gain income of the same amount. The income and expense offset each other.

If you want the deduction for those items paid as part of the sale, but don't want to include a corresponding amount of capital gain income in your return, you have to pay for those items outside of closing. Sue would have to pay the property tax of $1,500 separately at the time of the sale in order to have a deduction for that amount without having to report any income. This will increase the amount of cash that will go to Sue's Intermediary by that amount, which will increase the amount of cash going from the Intermediary to the purchase of the New Property (which will likely reduce the amount of additional cash Sue needs to bring to the closing by the same amount).

What Items in the Purchase of the New Property are Part of the Exchange?

In a typical purchase, you have the cost of the property plus the cost of obtaining the new loan and sundry other costs (such as surveys, inspections, etc.), as well as an adjustment for taxes. What items are considered acquisition costs of the New Property? A good rule of thumb is that if the item adds to the cost of the property, it is part of the acquisition costs of the Exchange. In other words, if it isn't deductible it is a cost of buying the property.

In most cases the costs of the property, plus the acquisition costs, either substantially exceed or are substantially less than the net selling price. It is rare that the price of the New Property is so close to the net selling price of the Old Property that this becomes a problem. In those rare cases where the amounts are so similar, how big a problem is this? Not very – if the net selling price and the net purchase price are the same, the items that are deductible by you offset the taxable gain, and, except for the effect of the tax differences, cancel each other out.

Must New Debt Equal or Exceed Debt That Was Paid Off?

This is one of the most misunderstood areas of 1031 tax law. Most people, especially tax attorneys and CPAs, believe that you must have debt on your New Property equal or greater in amount than the debt that was paid off on the sale of your Old Property. Unfortunately, most qualified Intermediaries also believe this. In fact, this is not a requirement, and it says so right in the IRS regulations. Because this is such a sacred cow to so many people, if you are one of the majority of people in the country that want to argue with me about this, I direct you to Regulation 1.1031(d)-2 and also to Revenue Ruling 79-44. Read the regulation carefully and work through the example, and you'll see I'm right.

Chapter 9:
Reinvest All the Cash

In addition to buying equal or up, you must reinvest all of the cash. Any cash you touch is going to be taxable to you. If, when Sue bought her purple duplex, she put $15,000 down, and several years ago she invested an additional $5,000 to remodel it, she cannot get this money back when she sells the duplex without paying tax. The entire amount of the net proceeds, after paying off the loan(s) and paying closing costs must go to the Intermediary if Sue wants to avoid paying any tax.

This is a hard concept for most people to understand because they have invested their own after-tax cash in the Old Property and feel that they should be able to get this money back without tax. Wrong. In the view of the IRS, what happens when you do an Exchange is that you've merely changed the legal description from that of the Old Property to that of the New Property. If you take cash, you've sold something, which makes it taxable. I don't know a better way to explain it than that. Just know that, no matter how much cash you've invested in the Old Property, if you touch any cash, you pay tax.

Where we see this most often is in situations where people miscalculate the amount of loan they need for the purchase of the New Property. Let's say Sue sold her duplex for $100,000. The unpaid mortgage and closing costs take $47,500 of this amount, and the balance of $52,500 goes to the Intermediary. Now Sue finds the perfect New Property costing $150,000. She's exceeded her equal-or-up amount, so that is not a problem. Because Sue didn't know the exact amount of funds that she would net from the closing of the duplex, she estimated high on her loan application and has been approved for a mortgage of $100,000 on the purchase of the New Property. This means that she will only need $50,000 from her Intermediary to complete the purchase. This will leave $2,500 unspent in her account with the Intermediary. If she doesn't use this in the purchase of her

New Property, this amount will end up being taxable to Sue.

How does she solve this problem? She could always buy a second property and use the cash for that. Of course, if you are beyond the 45-day limit, this second property would have to be listed on your 45-Day List. Alternatively, you could have the lender revise the loan to be $97,500 rather than the original $100,000. The problem with this is that it is usually at the last moment, right before the closing, when you realize that you will have excess funds. Having the lender redo the loan documents at this point will probably delay the closing.

A solution to this would be to have the title or escrow closer use Sue's extra funds to pay down the loan at the closing. In other words, the purchase Settlement Statement would show the full $52,500 coming from the Intermediary with an immediate pay-down of $2,500 against the original loan of $100,000. The end result is that all of the Exchange funds are used in the purchase. and the loan ends up being $97,500 without having to redo all of the loan documents.

The bottom line is that if the purchase closes with the Intermediary left holding the $2,500, Sue will pay tax on it.

What if You Buy More Than One Property?

If you have cash left over from the purchase of one of the properties on your 45-Day List, the best answer might be to use that cash to purchase another property. In the above example, even though Sue bought way up (she sold for $100,000 and bought for $150,000) she still has taxable gain in the amount of the unspent proceeds of $2,500. If Sue bought another property (one that was on her 45-Day List, of course) she could avoid paying tax on the excess funds.

If you are buying two or more properties, there is no requirement that you spread the cash among them equally or even pro rata.

Let's assume that Sue sold her purple duplex for $100,000, and the Intermediary is holding $50,000 cash in her Exchange account. Sue now wants to buy two properties: one for $50,000 and one for $100,000. There is no requirement that she spread the Exchange cash either equally or proportionately based on the purchase price of the properties. It is perfectly acceptable if she buys the first property for cash and gets a loan to buy the second.

What if You Don't Use All the Cash?

If Sue doesn't use all the cash, what happens then? Is her whole Exchange toast, or does she just pay tax on the amount she doesn't use? The answer is that only the amount she doesn't use is taxable.

Using our example from above, if Sue chooses not to reinvest the excess $2,500, then this does not toast her Exchange, she merely pays tax on the $2,500. Although, as I've said previously, she can't touch the money until the Exchange is closed, and then the entire $2,500 is taxable.

What if You Want Some Cash From the Closing?

Let's say that Sue decides that she wants some cash from the sale of her purple duplex to pay off a credit card, and she decides she needs $10,000. When can she get this money? There are two points in the Exchange where she can get this cash. The second place is at the end of the 180 days, after she's purchased her New Property and there is $10,000 of cash left. If you've identified more than one property on your 45-Day List, the IRS assumes that you might buy one of the other properties and, as a result, makes you wait until the 180 days are up. If you take the unspent balance before then, it could toast your whole Exchange.

That's the second place. The first place is at the beginning of the Exchange – at the closing table. To make this work, you are technically doing an Exchange on only a portion of the property. For example, Sue is selling her purple duplex for $100,000 and wants the $10,000 at the time of the sale. Her Intermediary can set up her Exchange so that she is only doing an Exchange for 90 percent of the property ($90,000) with the balance of 10 percent ($10,000) outside the Exchange.

At the closing table, $90,000 (minus loan payments and closing costs, of course) would go to the Intermediary, and the other $10,000 would go to Sue. Of course her $10,000 will be taxable, and as I've said, the entire $10,000 is taxable gain. The most important consideration here is that Sue's Intermediary must prepare the Exchange documents to reflect the fact that she is only doing an Exchange on 90 percent of the property. If the documents aren't changed, the whole Exchange will likely be disallowed if Sue gets audited. This is another one of those places where an Intermediary using preprinted forms can really get you in trouble. The difference between good and bad Intermediaries is usually only a few hundred dollars and is well worth it. Consider it insurance.

Refinancing the Property

Once they learn that they cannot touch the proceeds from the Exchange, most people who want cash but don't want to pay tax on that cash start to wonder if they can refinance the property. If the closing on the sale of Sue's purple duplex is a week from today, could Sue refinance the purple duplex today, have the loan paid off at the closing next week with the lesser balance (because of today's refinance) going to the Intermediary? The answer is no. Guess how long you have to wait after the refinance before you can do an Exchange? Correct – a year and a day. If you refinance it within this time, especially if the refinance is after you've listed it for sale, you risk having the IRS say that you touched the money – especially if it ends up in your pocket.

On the other hand, if you want to refinance the New Property, how long do you have to wait after the purchase before you can do so? The answer in this case is, "one nanosecond." It's true, and nanosecond is the IRS term for it. What you need here is to be able to show that you bought the property and completed your Exchange at least one nanosecond before you financed it. A good Intermediary can show you how to do this so that you can walk away from the closing of the purchase of the New Property with a check without worrying about it being taxable. Make sure you have a good Intermediary, because if structured wrong you'll pay tax on your check.

You're probably wondering why you can't refinance the Old Property while there seems to be very little obstacle to financing the New Property. Their logic apparently is that when you refinance the Old Property, you are very soon released from the obligation, whereas when you refinance the New Property you are obligated to repay that loan forever. Doesn't seem logical, but that is apparently the way they see it.

What Is Boot?

The IRS, tax attorneys, CPAs and real estate professionals call the amount that is taxable in an Exchange "boot." While I generally try to avoid technical and/or slang terms in my writings, boot is one of those terms that is inescapable if you are talking about real estate. When someone says, "you have boot of $10,000" what they are telling you is that you will pay tax on $10,000.

How did the term boot come about? No one really knows for sure. An explanation I heard a few years ago is that back in the very beginning of Exchanges, when people traded horses, for example, if one horse was worth more than the other, the person with the more valuable horse received something extra, a gun, a bag of tobacco, etc. that equalized the Exchange. Whatever was received, because there was no other place to put it, went into the buyer or seller's boot. Over the years the extra became known as "boot," which in today's language means that it is taxable.

When Is the Cash (Boot) Taxable?

As a general rule, when you receive the cash it is taxable to you. Let's say that in December of year one, Sue sold her purple duplex and did a 1031 Exchange. In April of year two she bought the New Property and had $10,000 cash left, which she received at the end of the 180 days in May or June. When is the $10,000 taxable – in year one when she sold the purple duplex or in year two when she got the cash? The answer is year two because that part of the Exchange is subject to the IRS Installment Sale Rules, which provide that the money is taxable when you get the cash.

Do you get the same answer if you buy down? Not necessarily - if you used all of the cash in the buy down purchase of the New Property, the answer is no because of an IRS concept called "debt relief" (meaning that you got the cash and used it to pay off the debt at the time of the sale of your Old Property). In other words, you received the benefit of paying off the loan in year one – so that is the year when the gain from the debt relief is taxable.

Let's say, for example, that Sue sells the purple duplex for $100,000 in December of year one. She has closing costs of $7,500, a loan payoff of $40,000 and has the balance of $52,500 with her Intermediary. In March of year two she buys her New Property for $85,000 and pays the entire $52,500 held by the Intermediary and gets a new loan of $32,500 for the balance.

Sue didn't touch any cash, so therefore the transaction is taxable in year one. The reason is that in year one she received "debt relief" of $40,000 on the loan that was paid off. Her new loan in year two was only for $32,500. Think of it as if she got $40,000 in year one, but only paid $32,500 in year two. The buy-down is taxable in year one.

Had Sue gotten a loan for the purchase of the New Property in the same amount as the one that was paid off ($40,000) she would have used only $45,000 of the $52,500 held by the Intermediary, which would have been paid to her at the end of the Exchange in year two. Receiving the money in year two would make it taxable in year two.

Those of you who are into sophisticated tax planning please note that the taxability of the cash left over in an Exchange straddling tax years provides great opportunities. Let's go back to my example above where $7,500 was left over and paid to Sue by the Intermediary in year two. Remember I stated that it was subject to the Installment Sale Rules and taxed in year two. The Installment Sale Rules provide that that is the required handling unless you specifically elect out of installment sale treatment in a timely filed return which includes extensions.

Sue's tax return from year one (the year of the sale) is due April 15th of year two, but can be extended until October 15th (of year two). If she extends her year one return until October 15th, she will be almost to the end of year two and in an excellent position to determine if the gain would be better if it were taxed in year one or year two. If the answer is year one, she would merely elect out of installment sale treatment when she filed her year-one return and the gain would be reported on that return instead.

Offsetting Boot Against Capital Losses

If you have capital losses in your tax return, you might consider taking boot (taxable gain) in an amount equal to your capital losses. There are a couple of reasons why this might make sense. First, capital losses have a limited carryover period, meaning that they might expire without you using them. Second, this is a great opportunity to get cash out of your Exchange tax-free; the gain that results when you receive cash from your Exchange will be offset by your other losses.

In one of my examples above, Sue wanted $10,000 to pay off a credit card. Her receiving this cash makes it taxable to her. But if Sue has a $10,000 capital loss from another transaction, say the sale of her Enron stock, she could offset the $10,000 gain and the $10,000 loss and pay no tax.

My advice is to carefully plan this if this is what you want to do. Seek advice from your tax advisor. If this is what you want to do, consider taking the cash at the time of the sale. If you're going to pay tax on it anyway, get your cash as quickly as possible. On the other hand, waiting and getting your cash at the end of the deal will give you the opportunity to change your mind.

Passive Activity Losses

While we are on the subject of offsetting losses, let's talk about Passive Activity Losses. Taxpayers who have earned income in excess of a certain level each year, and who also have losses associated with that real estate (called Passive Activity Losses) can only deduct those losses against passive income such as dividends, interest or net rental income. Losses during that year in excess of that year's passive income carry forward to future years when those taxpayers do have passive income or when they sell the properties. In other words, Taxpayers have to have passive income in future years, or they have to sell their properties in order to deduct the losses carried over (on their returns, of course).

If you sell the property and do a 1031 Exchange, does that let you deduct your passive loss carryovers from that property? No, because in the eyes of the IRS all you've done is swap the legal description of the Old Property for the legal description of the New Property.

What we suggest is that you take boot in an amount that at least equals your passive loss carryover. This gives you gain from the sale of the property that you can offset your loss carryovers against. And besides, it gives you tax-free cash equal to the carryover, and it lets you "freshen up" your depreciation on the property in an amount equal to the loss.

For example, Sue sells her purple duplex for $100,000 and will net $92,500 at the closing after paying closing costs. If Sue has a passive loss carryover on this property of $10,000 she could take $10,000 at the closing. This amount will be taxable, but the taxable gain of $10,000 will be offset by the deduction of the passive loss carryover of $10,000, which will result in Sue having tax-free cash of $10,000.

A question that frequently comes up is whether or not you could recognize a small amount of gain on the sale, say $1 or maybe $100 and then deduct thousands of dollars of loss carryover against it. In the above example, could Sue take $100 at the closing, which would be taxable, and then deduct her $10,000 passive loss carryover? The answer is no – you can't contrive a small gain merely to say you've "sold the property" so that you can deduct a much larger loss. Recognize an amount of gain equal to the loss, or else deduct losses equal to the gain recognized, and you'll be OK.

Chapter 10:
Related Party Transactions

Section 1031 specifically prohibits the sale of an Old Property to, or the purchase of a New Property from, a related party. This prohibition is statutory, meaning that it is part of the law, not something that appears only in the IRS interpretation of the law. That means that if you get caught ignoring this prohibition, the penalties are severe.

Who Is Related?

Let's start with the definition of "related." For IRS purposes, only close relatives are considered related: a spouse, parents and grandparents, brothers and sisters, kids and grandkids. Aunts, uncles, cousins, nieces, nephews and the like are not considered related.

Typical questions we get in this area involve in-laws: is your stepfather related to you? Is your son-in-law related to you? There is not a standard answer to questions like these because typically the answer depends upon where you live (such as in a community property state).

What if your daughter is on the title, can she quit-claim her interest to her husband and then you buy from him? No, even though the chances of getting caught are slim, if the IRS catches you doing this, it will throw the book at you because it is obvious the only reason for the transfer is to avoid the related party rules.

What Entities Are Related?

Entities, such as corporations, partnerships and LLCs, are related to you if more than 50 percent of the entity is owned by one, or a combination, of people who are related to you. The words "more than" are critical here. A corporation that is owned half by your dad and half by his college roommate is not related to you because your father does not own more than 50 percent. However, a partnership that is owned equally by your father, your mother and your uncle is related to you because you are related to two-thirds of the owners (your father and your mother). Your uncle is not related to you for these purposes.

Trusts and estates are related to you if you are related to the executor and/or the beneficiaries. A common question we get is whether you can buy a property from your deceased parent's estate. No, because you are a beneficiary. Besides, you are related to your brothers and sisters.

There are two types of transactions with related parties: transactions where you swap deeds (which might qualify for a 1031 Exchange if certain parameters are followed) and transactions where one of you buys the others property for cash (which doesn't qualify for a 1031 Exchange). Section 1031 treats these as different types of transactions subject to different rules.

Deed Swapping

Let's take deed swapping first. You have Property A, which your sister wants, and she has Property B, which you want. The two of you swap deeds and you now own Property B and she owns Property A. This constitutes a 1031 Exchange and IRS rules require that both you and your sister have to hold on to your new properties for at least two years from the time you do the swap. If either of you sells your property before the two years have expired, it toasts the Exchange for both of you. That means that if your sister sells Property A before the two years are up, you are toast and will pay tax on your gain – even though you still own Property B.

The two-year period begins on the date you swap deeds. And two years means 24 months. Don't play games here – the penalties for being cute can be severe. For example, the two-year period is terminated (meaning both transactions are taxable) if you give someone a right to acquire the property. A lease-option, for example, would trigger your two-year period. A contract to sell the property would probably be viewed the same way, so I wouldn't enter into a contract to sell it until your 24 months have expired.

If you own an entity that is considered a related party, and the entity owns the property, disposing of your interest in the entity is the same as selling the property and will trigger the two-year holding period.

Let's say that you own Property A in a corporation in which you own all the stock, and your sister owns Property B, and your corporation and your sister swap properties as above. If you sell the stock of your corporation before the two-year period has expired, both of your Exchanges are toast.

As a point of clarification, you report the tax liability as of the point when you violated the two-year rule, not as of the date that you and your sister swapped properties. So if the swap between the corporation and your sister took place on January 31st of year one, your two-year holding period would run until January 31st of year three. If you sell the stock in the corporation on December 31st of year two, the corporation and you sister would both report taxable gain in their year-two tax returns.

There are a few exceptions to the two-year holding rule. For example, if you or your sister dies during the two-year period, or if either of you is forced to sell under threat of imminent domain, the two-year period ends and you are released.

If Property A and Property B have different values in excess of the debt on the property, the one with the lesser value will owe cash to the one with the greater value. This cash will be considered boot and taxable to the one who receives it unless the receiver does a 1031 Exchange and buys a second property.

Going back to your swap with your sister: Let's say that your property was worth $100,000, and her property was worth $90,000. Assuming that both properties are free of debt, your sister will pay you $10,000 to balance the trade. This $10,000 will be taxable to you. Alternatively, you could put this amount with a Qualified Intermediary, buy a second property and avoid all tax.

Sales for Cash

The second type of transaction happens when one of the related parties pays cash for the property of the related person. The rule here is that you cannot sell your Old Property to, or buy your New Property from, a related party in a transaction where one of you ends up with the property and the other ends up with the cash, and have it be an Exchange. This is so even if the other party would not have had a tax liability.

Let's say that you sell your Old Property to a stranger and you want to buy your brother's residence as your New Property. Your brother and his wife have lived in their house for several years and, since their gain is less than $500,000, they can sell it and not pay tax on the gain under a different Code section. Under 1031 law, however, you cannot buy it as your replacement property even though your brother would not have a tax liability anyway. And it does not matter if your brother and his wife pay tax – for example if they've lived in the house for less than two years (the requirement to receive $500,000 tax free in the sale of your residence). The logic is that the IRS doesn't want you using Section 1031 to construct a transaction where the cash and the property both stay within the family.

The Related Party Rules Are a Hot Topic Right Now

The related party rules are one of the really hot topics with the IRS right now. The IRS is cracking down on abuses in this area, so don't play games. To report your Exchange you must complete IRS Form 8824 for your Exchange. One of the questions this form asks is whether or not you sold your Old Property to, or bought your New Property from, a related party. Checking the box "yes" is to invite scrutiny, so taxpayers who do so have tried to get around this by checking the box "no" under the theory that they "didn't sell the property to their sister, they really sold it to their Intermediary. And they aren't sure who the Intermediary sold it to . . . although come to think of it, they have seen their sister coming and going from the property." No – don't play this game. Be straight here.

If you have questions about whether or not the other person or entity is related to you, call your Intermediary and get their advice.

Chapter 11:
Seller Financing

In today's economic environment, an increasingly common question we get is how to structure a 1031 Exchange for the seller of a property when the buyer wants the seller to carry back a contract in connection with the sale. Seller financing is called different things in different parts of the country. Sometimes it is called an "owner carry note" or a "purchase money mortgage" or "Contract for Deed."

Let's say Sue is selling her purple duplex, which she owns free and clear, for $200,000. The buyer offers to pay $50,000 at closing and wants Sue to carry a contract for the balance of $150,000. Sue has a $75,000 gain on the duplex and would prefer to do a 1031 Exchange and wants to know the procedures so she does not have to pay tax on the sale.

Section 1031 says boot is taxable up to the lesser of the amount of the boot taken or the gain on the transaction. If the contract note, in our example reads "Bob Buyer promises to pay $150,000 to Sue Jones" the note is considered boot, and $75,000 of it is taxable (because the taxable amount of $75,000 is less than the boot of $150,000).

Typically the tax on the boot arises when you receive the cash, although certain taxpayers may owe cash when they get the note itself, before they even get the cash. Typically taxpayers who are taxed on the "accrued gain" instead of the cash know it, but if you are confused, call your CPA before you agree to carry the note from the buyer. If Sue agrees to carry the note from Bob there is no reason for her to do the Exchange because all of the gain in her transaction is attached to the note.

How to Make the Note Tax-Free

In order to defer the gain on your sale you need to have the note paid into the Exchange. This means that the note will be directly between your buyer and your Qualified Intermediary. So if Sue decides to make the note tax-free as part of the Exchange, she needs to have the note structured to read: "Bob Buyer promises to pay $150,000 to Qualified Intermediary X" (Sue's Intermediary). At the closing then, Sue's Intermediary will receive the $50,000 cash and the $150,000 note and will hold both of them pending the completion of her Exchange. Very few Intermediaries will agree to accept and hold the note from Bob as part of Sue's Exchange. You don't want to get to the closing and have the Intermediary pull out when they find out about the note. So if you are thinking of carrying back a note from the buyer, make sure that you discuss this with your Intermediary, that your Intermediary understands what you are saying and agrees to receive and hold the note.

Now that Sue's Intermediary has the note Sue must find a way to make it useable in the purchase of her New Property. If she is unable to do this, her Intermediary will deliver the note to her 181 days after the sale. Sue will now be in the same position that she would have been had the note not gone into the Exchange in the first place (i.e., a portion of each payment will be taxable to her as she receives it). In other words, she has wasted the fee she paid to the Intermediary to handle the Exchange.

If Sue wants to keep the transaction tax-free, Sue must use the note as part of the purchase of her New Property. Sue really has two options if she wants to do this: either transfer the note to the seller of her New Property as part of the purchase or convert it to cash and use the cash for the purchase of the New Property.

Transferring the Note to the Seller of the New Property. As a practical matter it is almost impossible to find sellers who will take notes because they will be immediately taxable to them even though they won't receive any cash until Bob Buyer makes his payments. In other words, sellers of New Properties will pay tax on the notes the minute they get themt, but the only cash they will get is the monthly payments from the buyers.

You could hope that the seller of the New Property doesn't understand the tax ramifications of accepting the note and make it part of your offer, but that just does not seem ethical to me. In all my years of handling Exchanges, I've only seen this work once. That was a situation where the seller of the New Property had a loss large enough to offset the gain from the note. He was willing to take it because it paid a much larger interest rate than what he would be able to invest the money at if he had received cash instead.

Sell the Note. The second option for converting the note to cash before you close on the purchase of your New Property is to sell it. Because the note is not "seasoned" the buyer of the note will want a major discount. Typically unseasoned notes are discounted around 50 percent, which means that if she found a buyer for the note, Sue would only receive about $75,000 for it.

You Buy the Note from the Intermediary. The best solution is for you to buy the note from the Intermediary, and this is, in fact, what happens to virtually all of the notes we hold. Going back to where we are in this transaction, in Sue's Exchange account her Intermediary is holding $50,000 cash and a note from Bob Buyer made payable to the Intermediary.

Sue, or a member of her family, takes a check for $150,000 to the Intermediary and buys the note for face value. In the past, our clients, like Sue, were the ones who bought the notes from us. Over the last several years we've seen a trend toward family members, such a Sue's mom, as the note purchaser. The reason for this is that Sue's mom has her money in a CD at her bank earning maybe 2 percent. If the note pays 6 percent interest, Sue's mom can triple her cash flow by cashing in the CD and buying the note. Where Sue gets the money doesn't really matter. She could even borrow it from the bank.

When Sue buys the note from the Intermediary, the Intermediary will prepare an assignment of the note from the Intermediary to Sue. The Intermediary will also correspond with Bob Buyer and notify him that the note has been sold and direct him to send all future payments to Sue (or Sue's mother if she is the one who bought the note). Assuming that Sue has bought the note from the Qualified Intermediary for $150,000, her 1031 Exchange account now holds $200,000 cash, and she can proceed to the closing of her New Property and the completion of her Exchange.

The ramification to Sue, once the note is in her name, is that her tax basis in the note is $150,000 (the amount she paid for it). This means that as she receives future payments on the note from the buyer of her Old Property, the principal part of the payments are tax-free (called a "return of basis" by the IRS) and she will only pay tax on the interest portion of each payment.

Clients frequently ask us if they can buy notes for less than face value. While the answer, technically, is yes, you really don't want to do this because it reduces the cash in your Exchange account. This means you need to bring more money to the closing of your New Property anyway, and it also means that part of each payment you receive from your buyer is taxable.

So, if Sue bought the note from us for $100,000 (rather than the face value of $150,000), her Exchange account would only have $150,000 in it (the original $50,000 plus $100,000 from the note), and she would need to bring an additional $50,000 to the closing of the $200,000 New Property. And then 1/3 of each principal payment she received from Bob Buyer would be taxable.

What happens if you don't have access to the cash necessary to buy the note from the Intermediary? Don't accept the original offer from Bob Buyer. I got a call from a gentleman several months ago who was selling a piece of property for $5 million. The buyer had offered $500,000 down if he would carry back a contract for $4.5 million. I explained to him how contracts worked in a 1031 Exchange and asked him if he, or anyone in his family, had access to that kind of cash. Of course not. That meant he could not do an Exchange and would pay tax on the payments as he got them.

Can You Do an Exchange on a Contract You Received Several Years Ago?

Another question that comes up frequently is the possibility of doing a 1031 Exchange on the balloon payment from a contract that is several years old. The answer is no. In order to avoid tax on any of the contract payments you must have the contract go into the Exchange in the first place, and you must also convert it to cash during the 180-day replacement period and before the purchase of the New Property.

What if You Want a Small Contract on Your Property?

Sometimes our clients sell property and carry back a small contract with the intention of holding that contract for the higher interest it provides or to defer the tax payments into the future.
Back to our example where Sue is selling her purple duplex for $200,000 and wants to do an Exchange to defer tax on the gain of $75,000: Let's modify the example slightly and assume that Bob Buyer can put up $180,000 and wants Sue to carry back a note for $20,000. This works for Sue because the New Property she wants to buy is only $180,000. If Bob pays cash, Sue will have to pay immediate tax on the $20,000 and Sue will only be able to get 2 percent interest on investing this cash in a CD. Bob's contract will pay 6 percent and will push tax on the gain into the future.

Sue's tax basis on her duplex is $125,000 ($200,000 - $75,000 gain). Therefore Sue's basis in the New Property will be $125,000 with deferred gains of $55,000 ($180,000 - $125,000). Sue started out with a gain of $75,000, of which she will pay tax on $20,000 because of the note, and defer tax on $55,000 by buying the New Property.

Chapter 12:

What Documents Are Part of An Exchange

When You Sell Your Old Property

The vast majority of the Exchange documents are created upon the sale of the Old Property. There are three primary documents that must be signed at or before the transfer of title on the Old Property: an Assignment, an Exchange Agreement and a Notice of Assignment.

You have to show intent to do an Exchange. While an argument could be made that having an Intermediary involved at the point that the deed is transferred to the buyer is proof of that, we suggest that you have a paragraph in your sales contract notifying the buyer that you intend to do an Exchange. The wording of this does not have to be complicated, but it should say that "you, as the seller, intend to do an Exchange and the buyer agrees to cooperate with the Exchange." Notice that it says that you "intend" to do an Exchange. This does not obligate you to do an Exchange; it merely puts the buyer on notice that you might.

Some states, such as Colorado, require a separate Exchange clause be attached to the contract. All of the major real estate companies that we've worked with around the country have Exchange clauses ready to insert into their contracts. Discuss this with your real estate agent. If your real estate agent doesn't have an Exchange clause, call your Intermediary.

Not only does this show your intent to do an Exchange, but is of great importance when you sell your Old Property because you are depending upon the buyer coming to the closing with his cash. You don't want to give the buyer a reason to not close. We had a client several years ago who decided to do an Exchange at the last minute on a property he was selling in Vail, Colorado. Our documents were there as part of the closing to treat the sale as an Exchange, but nobody had bothered to inform the buyer that it was an Exchange – or so we thought. The intent, because of the short notice, was to have the buyer sign an amendment to the contract that contained 1031 Exchange wording at the closing. The buyer showed up for the closing with his attorney, and at the end of the closing, after all of the documents had been signed, and right before the buyer was to hand his check to the closer, the buyer's attorney was handed this document amending the contract and stating that the seller was doing an Exchange. (Keep in mind that Intermediaries cannot interfere in the contract between a buyer and seller. If the seller chooses not to tell the buyer, the Intermediary is not allowed to interfere.) When the buyer's attorney was handed the notice, he leapt from his chair, slammed shut his briefcase, said that the seller doing an Exchange was tax fraud, and with great theatric fanfare he and the buyer scuttled out of the room – with the purchase check still in the buyer's pocket! The seller was stunned because she was obligated to close the purchase of her replacement property about a week later. The failure of the buyer to close was a major problem.

The short version of a long story is that the buyer did finally close that day – but for about $50,000 less than the contract price. I'll always be convinced that the buyer knew it was an Exchange and saw an opportunity to squeeze the seller for a large reduction in the sales price. No doubt the buyer and the attorney split the reduction and spent the week skiing. The moral of the story – you need the buyer to perform, so make sure he or she is notified as early in the game as possible.

Hire an Intermediary. You have a contract to sell your Old Property, and you've notified the buyer that you intend to do an Exchange. If you have not done so already, now is the time to pick an Intermediary to handle your Exchange. Prior to the actual closing the Intermediary will forward a package of Exchange documents to the closer handling the transfer to the buyer. Theses Exchange documents will be included in the package sent to you by the closer. Occasionally, the Intermediary may send them directly to you. If you do what's called a "table close" where you actually go to the closer's office to sign documents, the documents will be waiting for you at the closing.

When do you have to get your Intermediary involved? The Intermediary has to be involved before you sign the deed transferring ownership from you to the buyer, so technically you could be at the closing and decide you want to do an Exchange. (We have a special team in our office that handles last-minute Exchanges.) This may delay your closing by an hour or two, but if you go to lunch, the Exchange documents will be there ready to go when you get back (at least with us).

My advice, however, is to get your Intermediary involved as soon as you list the property for sale. The reason is that most Intermediaries charge the same if you get them involved when you list the property or if you wait until the closing table. As your Exchange progresses you'll likely have questions from time to time about your Exchange, and your Intermediary is a free source of answers. Take advantage of this. (I'm assuming, of course, that your Intermediary is one of the good ones who welcomes your questions and is happy to give you free advice. Not all of them are accessible, and not all of them will answer questions.)

When you get your closing package, the first thing you want to do is identify the exchange documents and make sure they are part of the closing documents. For most closings the exchange documents are sent to the closer by the intermediary to be included in the closing package. Occasionally, they may be sent directly to you from the intermediary. Do not sign any of the documents from the closer until you've assured yourself that the Exchange documents are part of the closing package. They should be on the Intermediary's letterhead, even if they were faxed or emailed to the closer to be included in the package. If you sign the closing documents, especially the deed transferring ownership from you to the buyer, without the Exchange documents, your Exchange could very well be toast.

At the closing table or in your closing package will be three Exchange documents: an Exchange Agreement, an Assignment and a Notice of Assignment. If you are experienced with real estate closings, the only documents that the closer prepares for you to sign that will be different than what you are used to seeing are the HUD-1 (or Settlement Statement, depending on the closing) and the Closer's Instructions (or Title Instructions or Escrow Instructions depending on the part of the country the property is located in). The difference in these two documents is that they list the Intermediary as "seller" and you as "Exchanger."

All of the other documents that you would normally find in a closing remain unchanged. The most important document, the deed, will be the same and will show you as the seller of the property (rather than the Intermediary). Preparing the deed this way (direct deeding) has been the standard in the Exchange industry for the last ten years. Prior to that we did double deeding (where the property was deeded from the seller to the Intermediary and then from the Intermediary to the buyer).

One last thing about Exchange documents: The IRS will examine these documents if it audits your Exchange. If the documents are not prepared correctly, the IRS will disallow the Exchange. The IRS requirements for Exchange documents change from time to time, so it is important that the Intermediary be on top of the latest changes. Good Intermediaries custom tailor a set of Exchange documents for every Exchange. Others use a set of "fill-in-the-blank" forms. If you get a set of Exchange documents that are copies of copies of copies of preprinted forms – pray that everything is OK.

The Exchange Agreement. The Exchange Agreement is the basic contract between you and the Intermediary. It typically defines the terms and timeframes required by an Exchange. It typically sets out what the Intermediary's responsibilities are and what yours are.

The Exchange Agreement will say how your money is to be held and who is to receive the interest. Review this section carefully. It is not uncommon for the agreement to allow the Intermediary to invest the money in whatever manner, and in whatever investment instruments the Intermediary chooses. It might also state that if the Intermediary suffers losses in the account, the Intermediary cannot be held responsible. How do you feel about this? Many investors don't seem to mind, but if you do (and you should), make the Intermediary change this. Your money should be in a separate account with only your money in the account. And you should get the interest.

It is not uncommon for the Exchange Agreement to include a clause that says that you can't sue the Intermediary no matter how bad he or she screws up the Exchange. While the Intermediary should not be responsible for everything that you might do to screw up the Exchange, the Intermediary should be responsible for the things that the Intermediary might do to screw up the Exchange. How do you feel about this? If you are using a low-budget Intermediary, expect that a blanket indemnification will be part of the deal. It's the price you pay for a low fee. On the other hand, if you are paying good money to a good Intermediary, a blanket indemnification is unconscionable.

The Exchange Agreement will include a section that sets out how you are to identify the property for your 45-Day List. Does it have to be mailed to the Intermediary or can you fax it? The Exchange Agreement will also include a section that specifies what needs to happen for you to get your money back if your Exchange fails. Typically, if you are unable to acquire the property for reasons beyond your control, the Intermediary can return the funds to you. There are Intermediaries who construct their documents in a way that makes it virtually impossible to get your funds until the end of the 180 days. Make sure on the front end that you know what the rules are if your Exchange fails.

Assignment. Technically what happens in an Exchange is that you assign the sales contract of your Old Property to the Intermediary, who then sells it to the buyer, in accordance with the contract, and receives the net proceeds from the sale. It should come as no surprise then that there is a document that formally assigns the sale contract between you and the buyer to the Intermediary.

This document assigns the rights but not your obligations (duties) to the Intermediary. This means that the Intermediary has the right to receive the proceeds, but you still have all of your original obligations concerning details like representations and warranties. This means that if you tell the buyer that there are no leaks in the basement, when in fact there are, you cannot hide behind your transfer to the Intermediary. The buyer can still sue you.

Notice of Assignment. This is a simple document that notifies the buyer that you, as the seller, are doing an Exchange. The buyer is not required to sign this, although it is not uncommon for some Intermediaries to require the buyer's signature on the form. Other Intermediaries have the closer sign the form indicating that the buyer was given a copy at or before the closing.

What's the purpose of this form? As I've said, the Exchange documents have to be signed and in place before the actual closing takes place. If the IRS thinks that the Exchange documents may have been created after the Exchange, one of the ways they can prove this is to go to the buyer and ask if he or she was notified at or before the closing and then ask to see a copy of the form.

The Notice of Assignment must be a separate document. It is not sufficient to claim that the clause in the contract that provides that the seller is, or may, do an Exchange satisfies this requirement.

After the Sale Closing

Notification of critical dates. Once the closing is completed, you should receive a packet of documents from your Intermediary confirming the Exchange. One of these documents should be a confirmation of your closing date and should set forth your 45 and 180-day drop-dead dates. Mark these dates on your calendar, and let your real estate agent know the dates so that both of you can monitor them. While good Intermediaries will both track these dates and follow up with you about them, most Intermediaries will not, and some won't even tell you what your drop-dead dates are. Don't assume that your

Intermediary will contact you.

Confirmation of funds received. Also included in this package should be a confirmation of the amount of money the Intermediary received and the date that money was received. Check this carefully. Most of the country uses title companies to close real estate transactions, and it is extremely unusual for us to receive an amount from them that differs from what the Settlement Statement or HUD-1 form says that we are to receive.

On the other hand, closings in some parts of the country, especially the east coast, are handled only by attorneys. When we have clients who are selling property in the northeast, it is common that the amount we receive from the sale differs substantially from what the documents say we are to receive (we always get less than they say we are to get). Furthermore, these attorneys will seldom explain the difference. If you are using an attorney to close your sale, stay on top of it and make sure the amount that the attorney says he or she is transferring to the Exchange account is the actual amount that gets transferred.

45-day identification form. Finally, your packet will include an identification form for your 45-Day List for you to complete and forward to your Intermediary. This form will typically have spots for you to identify three properties. If you want to identify more than three properties, call your intermediary for instructions on how they want you to do that.

45-day handbook. We also send our clients a 16-page booklet that explains the identification process in detail and answers the most common questions about this process. Most good Intermediaries have a similar type of product for their clients.

When You Buy Your New Property

Wording in the contract. You want to insert a clause in your contract that says that you, as the buyer, intend to do a 1031 Exchange, and the seller agrees to cooperate. The wording doesn't have to be fancy, and it can be as simple as what I've just said. Your real estate agent should be able to give you good guidance here – if not, call your Intermediary for suggested wording.

Handling earnest money. Typically the first thing that happens when you contract to buy your New Property is that the seller is going to require earnest money as part of the contract. Since you are the buyer, your contract at this point merely constitutes an offer to buy. Since you probably want the earnest money to come from the

Intermediary, you don't want to advance earnest money until you know you have a deal.

There are two primary ways to handle earnest money in an Exchange. The first way is to attach a promissory note to the contract stating that you, the buyer, promise to pay the earnest money within 48 business hours of acceptance by the seller of the contract. As soon as the seller accepts the contract you want to call the Intermediary and arrange for the transfer of the earnest money.

Your Intermediary is going to want to know if you want the money wired or sent by check. If sent by check, do you want the check sent by mail or by Fed-Ex? Where will the check be sent – to the seller, his real estate agent, your real estate agent or the closer? Since the Intermediary operates similar to a bank in holding money for people, expect that all of these instructions are going to have to be in writing and signed by you.

Our company has an "Earnest Money Request Form" that our clients complete so that we can gather all of the necessary information. Receipt of this form by us starts the process of transferring earnest money for a purchase.

A second alternative for earnest money is for you to write a check from your own funds when you sign the original contract. Once you and the seller have negotiated and signed the final contract you can either leave this check in place or call your Intermediary to have it replaced.

Remember, you cannot touch the Exchange funds once they go to the Intermediary. So if you want it replaced out of your Exchange funds, the Intermediary will transfer the amount of the earnest money to whoever is holding your check. That person will then return your check to you. At this point you will have to go through the same information process with the Intermediary that I discussed above. The Intermediary cannot transfer funds directly to you to reimburse you for the earnest money you put up. Doing so will toast your Exchange.

Assignment of the contract. Remember that what is happening in the Exchange is that you assigned the sale of your Old Property to the Intermediary, who (on paper) sold it to the buyer. Since the Intermediary was technically the seller of the Old Property, the Exchange proceeds went to the Intermediary's account. Now the Intermediary is technically the buyer of the New Property (which the Intermediary will buy with the money being held for you). At the time of the purchase, the New Property is immediately transferred to you to complete the Exchange.

This means that at the same time that the Intermediary transfers earnest money for your purchase the two of you need to execute an Assignment of the Contract, which assigns the contract from you to the Intermediary. Most Intermediaries will prepare this document when they process the Earnest Money Request and then fax or e-mail it to you for signature before, or at the same time, that the earnest money is transferred. To prepare this Assignment the Intermediary is going to need a copy of the contract, so it is easiest to fax a copy when you fax your Earnest Money Request.

Instruction letter to the closer. Your Intermediary will correspond with the closer giving he closer specific instructions on how to put the closing documents together for your purchase. Part of this instruction letter will be a request by the Intermediary for wire instructions so that the Intermediary can wire the funds to the closer to complete your purchase. If you have communicated with the Intermediary, and the Intermediary is doing their job correctly, the funds should be transferred to the closer the business day before the closing so that there is no question about the funds being at the closing in time.

We had a client who was selling a property several years ago, and the buyer was also doing an Exchange. At the closing the funds had not yet been received from the Intermediary. There was some concern about this, so the client called the Intermediary from the closing and was told that the money was being held by one of the major brokerage houses in New York. So, from the closing table they called the broker in New York and were told that he had processed the money that morning and that it should show up in the wire system shortly.

The money didn't get there that day, which was the final day of the buyer's contract. Turns out the wire department at the brokerage house just didn't get it processed that day. Our client, the seller, had back-up offers on the property for more money and sold the property to someone else the next morning. The buyer sued the seller, the seller's new buyer and the Intermediary. The Intermediary sued the brokerage house. Last I heard the whole mess was still in litigation. Moral of the story: make sure your Intermediary transfers the purchase funds the day before the closing.

Notice of Assignment. Just as a Notice of Assignment is required at the time you sell your Old Property; you are required to notify the seller of the New Property that you are doing an Exchange. The Intermediary will prepare this Notice and transfer it to the closer for signature at, or prior to, closing.

After the Purchase Closing

Instructions to contact Intermediary in case of audit. You should expect some type of correspondence from your Intermediary once the closing is completed. Included in this correspondence should be an instruction letter to contact the Intermediary immediately if you get audited. Your Intermediary was your guide during your Exchange and will tell you what to say, or not say, about your Exchange. While Intermediaries all deal with this differently, the good Intermediaries will put themselves between you and the IRS and will deal directly with the auditor.

Reconciliation of your Exchange account. If you earned interest on your account during the Exchange your Intermediary will give you a reconciliation of the account, which will also show you the interest that you earned. Keep this form, because you will need it to prepare your taxes (the interest you earned is taxable). At the end of the year the Intermediary will send you a 1099 for the interest if your funds were in a commingled account. If your funds were in a separate account (which they absolutely should be), the bank will send you the 1099.

Copy of 45-Day List. Most Intermediaries send their clients a copy of their 45-day form. If your Intermediary does not, ask for one. This document is a critical piece paper in an IRS audit, and if your Intermediary is no longer in business it will be impossible to obtain. Get a copy now.

Tax preparation information. The good Intermediaries will give you some level of assistance with the preparation of your tax return. For example, we give each of our clients a our "**1031TaxPak**™" that has about 75 pages of workbook, worksheets and step-by-step instructions on how to complete the tax forms necessary to report your Exchange.

Most CPAs and tax preparers are not very knowledgeable about reporting Exchanges on tax returns, and usually charge for them to research filing requirements. Your Intermediary's tax package should eliminate all or most of this cost. So, while you pay a few dollars more for a really good Intermediary, you make it up in so many ways – like reduced tax preparation fees when you file your tax return.

Chapter 13:
Reverse Exchanges

The IRS will not let you hold title to both your Old Property and your New Property at the same time. However, there are times when you want or need to take title to the New Property before you've sold your Old Property. So, to get around the rule prohibiting being in title to both properties, the IRS has developed another set of rules allowing what we call Reverse Exchanges. If it seems more than a little odd to you that the IRS would have a rule allowing you to avoid another rule, you and I think alike. Nonetheless, it's what we deal with.

Why Would You Do a Reverse Exchange?

For most of you, the need to do a Reverse Exchange will arise in one of two general situations. The first situation is where you've just found the perfect New Property. It's exactly what you want. It's so perfect that this beauty won't be on the market long. You have to move quickly to get it, so you make an offer and get it under contract. If your Old Property doesn't sell in time to do a straight (or "normal") Exchange, you are pretty much locked in to doing a Reverse Exchange (unless you decide to go ahead and pay tax on your Old Property when it closes or else buy a different New Property to close out your Exchange).

The other situation in which a Reverse Exchange will come up is in the case where, for some reason, the closing on your Old Property gets delayed, but yet you still need to close the purchase of your New Property.

Let's say that Sue has a buyer for her purple duplex and that closing is set for Monday. The closing on the purchase of her New Property is set for the following Friday, meaning she has four days between the closings for the sale of the Old Property and the purchase of her New

Property. The Sunday night before the closing of the Old Property, the agent for the buyer calls. Everything is ready to go for the purchase except for a small problem: the lender called on Friday and said that before he will fund the loan for the purchase he needs a survey done on the property. The agent has spent the weekend calling around and has found a surveyor who can do the survey in two weeks, so she needs a two-week extension of the closing date.

That doesn't seem like a serious problem. So Sue's real estate agent calls the agent for the seller of the New Property and tells her about the survey on the duplex and how she needs a two-week extension. The agent informs her that, no, she will not extend the closing date on the New Property because she has two back-up offers for more money than Sue is paying. The agent lets it be known that, quite frankly, she hopes that Sue doesn't close on Friday because if she doesn't the agent will sell the property to one of the other parties for more money on Monday morning. Oh, and, by the way, she will keep Sue's $25,000 earnest money deposit.

Either situation means that Sue will need to do a Reverse Exchange since the IRS will not let her be in title to both the Old Property and the New Property at the same time. What happens in a Reverse Exchange, in simple terms, is that the Intermediary takes title to the New Property (usually) and parks it until the sale of the Old Property closes.

Speed Bumps in a Reverse Exchange

There are two speed bumps you need to know about concerning your Reverse Exchange.

Financing. Since the Intermediary is taking title to the New Property, financing can be a problem if you don't have the cash to buy the New Property without debt. The Intermediary will normally set up a separate entity to take title to the property, and typically this entity will be an LLC owned entirely by the Intermediary.

Let's say that the Intermediary sets up Rocky Mountain Investments, LLC for Sue's transaction. The loan from the lender will be made to Rocky Mountain Investments, LLC and will be secured by the New Property. Sue will typically guarantee this loan personally. A loan of this type is not saleable. The lender cannot sell it in the GinnyMae, FannyMae network as most of them do. You need a lender who will hold the loan. Lenders call this a "portfolio" loan.

If you are doing a Reverse Exchange, don't call your lender and ask if he or she will finance a Reverse Exchange. Most lenders hear the word "Exchange," know that they've financed Exchanges in the past, and say yes without really understanding what you are asking. Simply ask if they plan to sell the loan. If the answer is yes then that lender will not be able to make your loan. Move on and find another lender. Typically banks make portfolio loans (and home mortgage lenders do not), so call the bank you do the most business with first - because it knows you and has a history with you.

The best person to direct you to a Reverse Exchange lender is your Intermediary. Not many Intermediaries do Reverse Exchanges, and those that do them tend to do a lot of them. So they can tell you immediately who to call for financing. An additional benefit is that they have relationships with the lenders. They have a history of working together, which means that the lender will be comfortable with the Intermediary's documents.

Will Reverse Exchange lenders take advantage of you because you need to do a Reverse Exchange? Our experience is that they won't gouge you on the loan, but nonetheless, they won't give you a deal either. They price the loan as they would any other loan, and don't necessarily feel the need to be competitive. My experience is that about half my clients tell me that the loan cost was a lot less than they expected it to be. The other half complains that it was more expensive than a Straight Exchange. That tells me that the loans are fairly priced. Remember, it is your credit and the quality of your collateral that drives the cost of the loan.

Cost of the Exchange. The other speed bump in a Reverse Exchange is the increased cost you'll pay to the Qualified Intermediary to handle the Exchange. You can expect that a Reverse Exchange will add about $5,000 to your Exchange. This is a rough average of what I see around the country right now (maybe $4,000 in one area and $6,500 in another, but $5,000 is in the ball park). The problem is that the $5,000 is in addition to the other costs of your Exchange, and applies regardless if your New Property is $100,000 or $100 million.

The reason for this cost is that the Intermediary has to set up an entity to hold title to the property. This involves legal fees. When the Exchange is completed, the title-holding entity is dissolved, which means more legal fees. Tax returns have to be filed for all tax years for the entity, so now you have CPA charges as well. And during the time that the Intermediary holds title to your property, a staff accountant is making the deposits applicable to your property, then paying the bills and rendering an accounting for you. Believe me, by charging $5,000, the Intermediary is not making much money on the transaction.

You may also have other increased transaction costs, such as additional title fees, loan costs and transfer taxes as well. Since you are giving your New Property, as well as your money, to the Intermediary, it is also a good idea to have your attorney review the Intermediary's documents. So you will likely have some legal fees.

What Happens in a Reverse Exchange, Step by Step

You make an offer on the New Property. You negotiate the terms, and you put up whatever earnest money is required to secure the contract. You then contact the Intermediary. The Intermediary will then prepare an Assignment, which will assign the contract for the purchase from you to the Intermediary's title-holding entity.

Arrange for financing next. Make sure that the lender knows that this will be a Reverse Exchange, and that the Intermediary will be taking title to the property. The lender will need to contact the Intermediary so that the loan documents can be prepared in the name of the entity that the Intermediary will use to take title to the property. In Sue's transaction, the lender will prepare the loan documents as if Rocky Mountain Investments, LLC is the borrower.

Make sure that the closer knows that the Intermediary's entity will be the one taking title to the property. You don't want the closer to have to redo all of the closing documents. So, for example, in Sue's transaction the closer has a contract between Sue Jones (as buyer) and the seller of the New Property. Unless Sue communicates to the closer that this will be a Reverse Exchange and the actual purchaser will be Rocky Mountain Investments, the closer will prepare a set of documents to be signed by Sue, and then will have to redo them later.

As the date of closing approaches, you will need to determine the amount of proceeds, in excess of the loan proceeds, that you need to forward to the closing. These funds need to be "good funds," meaning that you need to wire transfer the funds to the closing or have a cashier's check drawn up for that amount and have it to the closer in time for the closing.

For example, if the New Property will cost $200,000, and the bank has agreed to make a loan of $150,000 for the purchase, Sue is going to need an additional $50,000 for the purchase. Sue needs to arrange to have this money to the closer prior to the date of closing. When the closing happens, the closer will use Sue's funds, as well as the bank's, to pay to the seller.

Once the closing has occurred, the Intermediary will own your New

Property in the name of the entity he or she has set up. So, in Sue's case, the property is now owned by the Rocky Mountain Investments, LLC, and Sue's Intermediary owns Rocky Mountain.

The Intermediary will continue to own your New Property until you have a contract for the sale of your Old Property, or you are notified that your Old Property is ready to close. You need to contact your Intermediary to let them know that you have an upcoming closing on your Old Property so that the Intermediary can prepare the Exchange documents for the closing of your Old Property. Every two or three years we get a client that just forgets to call us about the closing on the sale of their Old Property. The sale happens, there are no Exchange documents, and the proceeds from the sale go to them. A couple of weeks later they realize what they've done, but by then it is too late – their Exchange is toast.

As soon as the Old Property closes, the Intermediary can begin the process of transferring the New Property from the Intermediary's LLC to the Exchanger.

IRS Rules for a Reverse Exchange

Remember I said that the IRS will not let you be in title to both the Old Property and the New Property at the same time, but that it had issued a ruling giving guidance for getting around the problem. This ruling was issued in the form of what the IRS calls a "Revenue Procedure." A Revenue Procedure is what I call a "cookbook ruling." It says that if you do certain things, you will get a certain result. The certain result you get is the assurance of the IRS that it will not audit your Exchange. The IRS calls this a "safe harbor reverse." I call it an "audit pass."

What do you have to do to get your audit pass? There are several critical ingredients:

The Intermediary has to take title to either the Old Property or the New Property. Why can't a friend or neighbor take title to the property? Section 1031 gives very broad powers to the Intermediary to act on your behalf in an Exchange. The Intermediary's role in an Exchange is to sell your Old Property and buy your New Property.

Having the Intermediary take title to the New Property puts the purchase part of the transaction under the umbrella of the Exchange. The Intermediary is not your agent; the Intermediary is merely fulfilling the role set out by Section 1031.

If someone other than the Intermediary takes title to the property, the

IRS could, and probably would, argue that this person was your agent and acting under your direction. This person is not protected by Section 1031. If the IRS is successful in its argument that this other person is your agent, then the IRS can assert that you were the effective buyer, not the agent. That would mean that all of the agent's actions would be treated as your actions, which means, in effect, that you were in title to both the Old Property and the New Property at the same time – and this would toast your Exchange. Using a Qualified Intermediary and following the IRS's Reverse Exchange rules blocks this argument.

The Intermediary has to practically hang neon lights on the Exchange documents. By this I mean that the documents have to be prepared in a special way, and with special wording, that makes them immediately clear to an IRS agent (in case you are audited) that you did a Reverse Exchange and that you have an audit pass. Of course the agent would check to make sure that you've done the things you need to do to earn and keep the pass, but once the agent is assured that you followed the rules, the agent the agent is supposed to back off.

The Intermediary has to file a tax return for the entity that is holding title to the property. While this would seem obvious, I understand from talking to a senior IRS agent that the IRS came out with the safe harbor rules because this was rarely done. I know from talking to other Intermediaries that that there are still some that are pretty loosey-goosey about this and don't file tax returns. The problem is, if your Intermediary fails to file the return, you lose your audit protection. The IRS could then audit your Exchange in detail.

45-day deadline. From the day the Intermediary takes title to your New Property, you have 45 days to provide a list of properties you might sell in order to Exchange into the property the Intermediary is holding for you.

The IRS ruling requires that you follow the straight Exchange rules in identifying this property. Although it doesn't specify exactly what this means, we can deduce that you can identify three properties with no limitation. If you identify more than three properties, then presumably the aggregate value of all the properties you identify could not exceed twice the purchase price of the New Property held by the Intermediary.

With the exception of a handful of clients who intend to sell several properties in order to buy a New Property, people will either have no problem with this rule (because they are only selling one property), or they will not be able to meet this rule because they have so many properties for sale that they have no clue what might sell in the next 180 days.

180-day deadline. Just as you have a 180-day deadline to complete a straight Exchange, you also have 180 days in which to complete a Reverse Exchange. In other words, you have 180 days after the Intermediary takes title to the New Property to complete the sale of your Old Property and take title to the New Property from the Intermediary. The difference here is that this 180-day limit is soft. This means that if you blow it, and your transaction runs beyond the 180th day, your Exchange is not toast. It merely means that you've lost your audit pass. You could still complete a valid Exchange (not so in a straight Exchange).

There are some Reverse Exchanges that, by their very nature, cannot be completed within 180 days. A reverse-Construction Exchange, which I'll discuss shortly, is a prime example. Your problem, however, is that you have a set of Exchange documents that have neon lights hanging on them telling the IRS that the Intermediary bought the New Property before you sold the Old Property.

What does this mean to your Exchange? No one knows for sure, and as of the time that I am writing this there have been no cases disallowing a Reverse Exchange for this reason alone. The big fear among Exchange professionals, however, is that the IRS will try to argue that the Intermediary was your agent and that since you have sailed outside of the safe harbor, you are vulnerable to an agency attack.

I have my doubts about the IRS's ability to win an agency argument in this situation. First, remember, Section 1031 gives the Intermediary broad powers to represent the taxpayer in an Exchange, both for the sale of the Old Property and the purchase of the New. Second, while the 180-day rule for a straight Exchange is statutory (meaning that it is part of the law), the 180-day limit in a Reverse Exchange is merely one of the requirements to get an audit pass. It doesn't create finality.

My advice to you is this: if you know, or strongly believe, that you will not meet the 180-day deadline, do a non-safe Reverse Exchange.

What is a "Non-Safe" Reverse?

A non-safe Reverse Exchange is a Reverse Exchange that is constructed knowing that it will not be able to meet the 180-day requirement. This means that you are not following the IRS rules that you need to follow in order to get your audit pass. The biggest difference here is that the Exchange documents are prepared without any mention of the fact that the transaction is a Reverse Exchange. The intent of this is to make the documents transparent, meaning that an IRS agent auditing the Exchange would not pick up on the fact that the transaction was a

Reverse Exchange. For example, you close the sale of your Old Property on Monday and the proceeds go to your Intermediary. On Wednesday the Intermediary forwards the proceeds to your closer, who pays off the debts and passes title of the New Property from the seller to you.

In this situation there are no 45-day or 180-day issues because the Exchange happened so quickly. You used a Qualified Intermediary, and you bought equal or up and used all of your proceeds in the purchase. It would be almost impossible for the IRS to pick up on the fact that your Intermediary owned the entity from which you are buying the New Property. One reason that this is so difficult is that the Intermediary will dissolve the entity and file a final return as soon as the Exchange is completed. Auditing the entity is as difficult for the IRS as auditing a dead person.

At least that is the theory. There are a number of highly respected Exchange professionals who worry about an agency attack in a non-safe Reverse Exchange. I think their biggest worry is that the implication in the safe harbor ruling is that the reason the IRS established the safe harbor provisions was to protect taxpayers from the stormy seas of agency attack.

One proposed solution to an agency attack if the Exchange fails the 180-day requirement is for the Intermediary to put up his or her own money as part of the proceeds needed to purchase the New Property. The reason behind this logic is that the agency attack in non-Exchange court cases has been defeated when the agent put up their own funds as part of the purchase.

If the Intermediary company puts its own funds at risk, the IRS cannot so easily assert that the Intermediary was an agent acting on behalf of the taxpayer. Five percent of the actual cash equity is the amount most commonly proposed.

The problem with this is that the Intermediary is going to want compensation for having its own money in the deal. This can be expensive. Most of the Intermediaries I know who are willing to put their money into a deal will expect an annual return of at least 20 percent (per year) of the money they put into the deal.

So let's say that Sue is fairly certain that her Reverse Exchange is going to exceed 180 days. She is buying a New Property for $500,000 and has arranged Reverse Exchange financing for $400,000, meaning that she needs to put in equity of $100,000. To protect the transaction from an agency attack, the Intermediary will put up $5,000 of its own money, and Sue will loan the entity the balance of $95,000 from her own funds. And, of course, the Intermediary company is going to charge Sue an additional fee, over and above the normal Reverse Exchange fee, of about $1,000 per year because its own money is in the deal.

There are some other things that you can do to further protect your self from an agency attack in a non-safe Reverse Exchange. For example, you want to make sure the Intermediary collects the rent and pays the bills (in safe Reverse Exchanges this function can be master leased to you). And, if possible, you want to avoid providing funds or guaranteeing loans made to the Intermediary's entity to buy the property. While no single element by itself is fatal to the Exchange, it's best to build as much distance between you and the Intermediary as possible.

Is it Possible for the Intermediary to Take Title to the Old Property Instead?

In the examples above, the Intermediary takes title to the New Property. Are there situations where it works better for the Intermediary to take title to the Old Property rather than the New Property? Yes, for example when the Reverse Exchange arises suddenly, and there isn't time to get new financing on the New Property (remember, we need a portfolio lender to make a Reverse Exchange loan), or perhaps the seller objects to the Intermediary taking title to the property instead of you.

Going back to our original example, what if Sue's sale of her purple duplex on Monday got postponed for a couple of weeks, but the seller of the New Property won't let her postpone her Friday purchase? If Sue has really excellent financing ready to go on the New Property, it may make more sense for the Intermediary to take title to the purple duplex, which would then allow Sue to do a straight Exchange into the New Property.

The mechanics of this kind of Exchange are fairly simple. Let's say Sue owes $40,000 on the purple duplex. Since the sale price on the closing that was postponed is $100,000, that will be the amount for which the Intermediary will buy the property from Sue. To make this happen, the Intermediary will need to borrow the balance of $60,000 ($100,000 - $40,000) from Sue.

A normal real estate closing is set up, the Intermediary's entity (Rocky Mountain Investments, LLC) takes title, and the proceeds of $60,000 flow from the closer to the Intermediary, who immediately turns around and sends the $60,000 to the closer handling the purchase of the New Property. What's happened here is that when Rocky Mountain Investments buys the purple duplex, it "wraps," or assumes, the existing loan of $40,000 and borrows from Sue the amount representing the difference between the sales price and the amount of debt and closing costs. The Old Property is now fully encumbered by a $40,000 mortgage to the bank and a $60,000 mortgage to Sue.

When Rocky Mountain Investments finally sells the purple duplex to the real buyer, there will be a closing, and the real buyer will pay $100,000 for the property. The first $40,000 will go to pay off Sue's mortgage on the property, and the balance of $60,000 (minus any closing costs) will go to Sue to pay back the loan she made to Rocky Mountain Investments.

There are not that many Intermediaries who do Reverse Exchanges and the ones who do don't like taking title to the Old Property. There are several reasons for this. For one thing, the Intermediary really does not want to own the property. Taking title to the New Property keeps the Exchanger motivated and keeps him or her working toward selling the Old Property. The fear if the Intermediary takes title to the Old Property is that the Exchanger will give up on it and the transaction will drag on.

The biggest problem, however, is how the transfer price that the Intermediary is paying for your property is determined, and how that impacts the Exchange. For example, let's assume that you don't have a buyer for your Old Property, so you guesstimate what you think the final selling price will be. Based upon this, you determine that the fair market value of the property is $100,000, so this is the amount that the Intermediary pays you for it. The Intermediary will buy it from you by assuming any loans that you have on the property and then borrowing the balance from you.

In a perfect world, a real buyer then comes along and agrees to pay $100,000 for the Old Property. At a closing, the title is passed from the Intermediary's title holding entity to the buyer. The buyer brings $100,000 to the closing (either all his or her own cash, or usually part from a lender). This $100,000 is used to pay off the existing real debt with the balance going to repay the loan. This works great.

But what if you overestimated the property's value, and the best price you can get for it is $95,000? How is the $5,000 shortfall handled? There really is no choice but to reduce the amount owed to you by that amount. You have a $5,000 loss.

How are You Protected in a Reverse Exchange?

In a previous chapter I talked about the risk you take dealing with Intermediaries, especially small local Intermediaries. Intermediaries should scare you. I'm absolutely amazed by the number of people who will risk tens (or even hundreds) of thousands of dollars of Exchange proceeds on an Intermediary with little knowledge or experience because that Intermediary charges a couple of hundred dollars less in Exchange fees.

When you do a Reverse Exchange your risk goes up a hundred-fold because you are, in effect, giving the Intermediary your money and your property. Be very careful.

How do you protect yourself from the Intermediary in a Reverse Exchange? I'm not positive how other Intermediaries do it, but I'll tell you how we protect our clients from us. Yes, from us. You have to make sure you protect yourself from the Intermediary ending up with your cash, your property or both.

The largest Reverse Exchange we've handled was in excess of $100 million and involved attorneys in New York, Dallas and Los Angeles. All of them reviewed our documents in detail in order to make sure their clients were protected from us. I'm happy to report that none of them changed our procedures, so I feel very comfortable that our methods are effective in protecting our clients.

First and second mortgages. The first thing we do is to make sure the lender records a first mortgage (or a "deed of trust" in some parts of the country), payable by the entity, in favor of the bank. Then we record a second mortgage (or deed of trust) from our entity, in favor of the client, for the amount of money the client is putting up. This fills up the equity on the property and prevents Intermediaries from borrowing additional money against property.

Special protection document. At the time that we purchase the New Property, we prepare a special document that is recorded as a blot against the title of the New Property by the closing agent. This document says three things: first, we cannot sell the property to anyone except the client. Second, we have to sell the property to the client at cost (meaning that we cannot jack up the price of the property). We have to transfer it back to the client at the price we paid including any holding costs incurred. We've heard horror stories about other Intermediaries who have taken advantage of this situation and inflated the transfer price of properties before they will transfer them to the clients. Lastly, this document says that we cannot borrow against the property – we can't put further encumbrances on it. While this would seem unnecessary because we filled up the equity when we bought the property, we believe it is important because this would prevent us from going out and finding an appraiser who would appraise the property at an inflated price, allowing us to borrow money against the property to the detriment of the client.

While these safeguards may seem like overkill, I can't stress enough how important it is that you build protection into your transaction. Remember, you're dealing with an Intermediary who is not regulated by any one. No one is out there, on your behalf, protecting you. As one judge put it: "Caveat Exchanger" (Exchanger beware).

Master lease. The last thing we do in safe harbor reverses is to prepare what we call a "master lease" between our entity and the client. Those of you who have some experience with commercial real estate might call it a "triple-net-lease." With a typical triple-net-lease, the tenant is responsible for everything associated with the property, including maintenance, property taxes and insurance. Most leases with large commercial tenants are triple-net-leases.

When we master-lease a property to a client, the lease provides that the client is responsible for collecting the rent on the property and paying all of the bills, including the ones I just mentioned. The client can also negotiate the leases of any tenants and sign the leases in his or her own name. Similarly, the client can negotiate contracts with vendors in the client's name. If the client needs to evict a tenant or cancel a contract with a vendor, the client can do that without involving the Intermediary (us) in the process.

So as you can see, between the document that protects the client and the master lease that provides that the client collects all the money and pays the bills, the client truly does completely control the property even though the property is in our name.

Chapter 14:
Construction Exchanges

A Construction Exchange happens when someone sells an Old Property and uses part of the proceeds to buy a piece of bare land and uses the balance of the proceeds to construct improvements on the property. Typically the improvements are a house or a building, but technically they could be any type of constructed improvement.

The IRS regulations define a Construction Exchange as a transaction where the New Property doesn't exist, or only partially exists, at the time it is identified as Exchange property. However, in the real world, Construction Exchanges also refer to transactions where construction will not be completed at the time the taxpayer takes title.

For example, Sue has sold her purple duplex and has entered into a contract with Bob Builder to buy one of his houses. The house is not completed at this time, but will be finished within the next 90 days (well within Sue's 180-day drop-dead date). Sue will not take title to the house until it is completed and has received a certificate of occupancy. This is not considered a Construction Exchange by 1031 terms.

Let's change the facts slightly. Bob Builder has just broken ground on the house. Completion is schedule for a year from now, but Bob has agreed to transfer title of the partially constructed house to Sue right before the expiration of her 180 days. This is what the industry considers a Construction Exchange because Sue will take title to a partially constructed building.

Rules for Construction Exchanges

Once you take title to the property your Exchange is over. There are specific rules for Construction Exchanges, but the most important, and the best place to start is the rule that once you take title to the property, your Exchange is over for that property. In other words, once title is in your name your exchange is finished, at least for that property. In our example above, if Sue takes title to the bare land, she cannot use any of her Exchange funds for construction. What she wants to do, therefore, is to wait until almost the last minute to take title to the partially built building.

Construction does not need to be completed. The second most important rule is that the construction you do on the New Property does not need to be completed (meaning that you do not need a certificate of occupancy) to satisfy the Exchange. You do have to equalize your Exchange values, and you have to do so within 180 days from the date that you sold your Old Property.

You need to equalize your Exchange. Assuming Sue sold her Old Property for $200,000, that is her equal-or-up target. If she and Bob agreed that the land was worth $150,000, she would have to do $50,000 worth of construction by day 180 in order to equalize her Exchange at $200,000.

Let's change our example a little. Let's keep the assumption that Sue sold her purple duplex for $200,000 and found a piece of land that will cost $150,000. Let's change it and assume that she wants to build a $350,000 house on it, for a total package of $500,000. The house does not need to be completed, but she needs to "equalize" her Exchange at $200,000 by the 180th day.

Costs must be installed costs. In our example, the $50,000 of construction must be installed costs, meaning that Sue cannot buy $50,000 worth of lumber and have it delivered to the site and nothing more. That doesn't count. To count, the lumber must be nailed together. Things that the construction industry typically calls "soft costs" count when they are paid – assuming that the service has been rendered and is not simply being prepaid. For example, your building permits and your sewer hookup fees count when you pay them. So do architect fees where construction plans are required in order to get building permits.

What Happens if You Fall Short of Your Equal-or-Up Target?

What happens if you don't meet your equal-or-up target by the 180th day? Your Exchange is not toast, but you have a taxable gain for the amount of the shortfall. Going back to my example, Sue's target is $200,000, and by the 180th day she has only completed $40,000 of construction, which brings her total to $190,000. She has a valid

Exchange, but she will pay tax on the $10,000 short-fall. Sometimes this is not something a person has any control over, and it is better to pay tax on $10,000 than to pay tax on the entire Exchange.

Be realistic in what you want to do. In Sue's example, Sue has 180 days to do $50,000 worth of construction on a $300,000 building, which shouldn't be too tough. But if the facts are different and you are selling for $200,000, buying the land for $75,000 and building a $130,000 structure for a total cost of $205,000, your structure will need to be essentially completed, within the 180-day timeframe, to meet your equal-or-up target. Start-to-finish completion of a property in 180 days is pretty much an impossibility anywhere in the United States.

We had a client several years ago who identified a house being built in Winter Park, Colorado as his replacement property. At the time of his 45-day identification deadline, the house had been framed, the exterior siding and roof were on, and most of the interior had been sheet-rocked. Since the builder needed only to paint the interior, install fixtures, cabinets and tile, the client felt comfortable that this could be easily completed in the remaining 135 days. Guess what? 135 days later, despite constant prodding by our client, virtually nothing had been done toward completing the property, and the value of the construction that was completed fell far below the client's target price. The builder got involved in another project and just let this house sit. One year later the property was still not completed. The client ended up losing his Exchange, and the transaction ultimately ended up in litigation.

The advice we give our clients is that when they negotiate contracts with builders they should negotiate performance clauses in the contracts. Such a performance clause might say that if the building is not completed to a certain stage by, say, day 170 (to allow time for final documents), the builder will be subject to penalties (usually the tax on the amount of the client's gain). Obviously the builder will exempt items beyond his or her control (such a strikes, acts of God, war, etc.), but if you can get this kind of clause in the contract (even with exemptions) it will help keep the builder focused on your property.

Types of construction contracts. There are two types of contracts involving construction: what I call "turnkey" contracts and the true construction contracts. In a turnkey construction contract, the builder is in title to the land and the building until it is completed. When construction is completed, and the builder has a certificate of occupancy, there is a closing, and you give the builder the money, and he gives you the key. Key fits lock, etc. This is the typical arrangement when you buy a house in a subdivision that a builder is developing. It's very common with the national builders. You have very little say over the building or the timing. When it's finished, it's finished. Typically in these types of transactions your cash investment is minimal until the building is completed.

A true construction contract, on the other hand, is a transaction where you own the land and then hire Bob Builder to construct your building. Bob works for you, and you have lots of control over the project. The flip side of this, however, is that you pay for construction as you go.

Converting turnkey contracts to true construction contracts. It is important if you are buying a property subject to a turnkey contract and the building is not completed by the end of the 180th day that you have to be able to take title to the property before the end of construction. You are changing the contract from a turnkey contract to a true construction contract. Our clients have had both good and bad experiences making this change with large builders. We've worked with some that are truly delightful, that have gone way out of their way to accommodate the client. And we've worked with some who go as far out of their way to be uncooperative, which usually results in the Exchange failing.

We had one client who was buying two tract homes from a large national builder. The salesman who sold the property and the construction supervisor in charge of building the houses had promised the client, and us, on several occasions that the houses would be completed by the 180th day. Toward the end, the salesman got pulled off that project to work on another project for the company, and even though the houses could have been completed in time, they weren't. Despite frantic calls from the client during the last month, the construction company did no work on the homes (each was about a week from completion). The company also refused to let our client take title to the mostly completed houses at that point, which caused his Exchange to fail. This, too, ended up in litigation.

Add a conversion clause to your contract. My advice to you is to add a clause to your turnkey contract that says that the builder agrees to convert the contract to a true construction contract before the 180th day so that you can take title if the property is not completed.

Here is how this would work in our example with Sue: She starts out with a turnkey contract to buy a property for $500,000. Her equal-or-up target is $200,000. She gets close to the 180th day, and the building is not completed, and only $180,000 worth of construction is completed. At this point she would exercise her conversion clause by taking title to the partially completed building for $180,000. This completes her Exchange, and only $20,000 of the gain will be taxable.

She would then immediately enter into a new contract (in effect a true construction contract) with the builder to complete the building to the original specifications for the balance of $320,000. Without an agreement by the builder to convert the turnkey contract to a true construction contract, her transaction could be dead in the water because she wouldn't be able to take title to the property by the 180th day.

Identifying a Construction Exchange on Your 45-Day List

If you are doing a Construction Exchange, you have to identify the construction in an addendum to your 45-Day List. Be careful you don't put yourself in a position where the IRS could argue that what you got was not what you identified.

Typically, a Construction Exchange identification will read something like this:

> *The purchase of the 2-acre parcel at 123 Main Street, Denver, Colorado, and the construction of a 4,500 square foot, cement block, single story warehouse, with 1,000-square-foot office, landscaping and paving for delivery trucks and customer parking.*

I prefer that your program be well-defined when you make the identification. If you are far enough along that you have blueprints, attach them to the identification. If the identification above was your identification, and you ended up only building 3,800-square-feet, would that be a problem? Or if you build 4,500 feet, but you build a two-story warehouse, would that be a problem? Or what if you build it out of lumber rather than cement block? The IRS doesn't provide any guidance about how much variation is allowable. Therefore, you want to be as precise as possible.

If you are doing a transaction that follows my suggestion for turning a turnkey transaction into a true construction contract, you should identify the property as a Construction Exchange. That way, if the turnkey project is not completed, this identification will let you properly take title to a partially completed building. If construction is completed, this identification will be okay also – you just took title to the finished thing rather than a partially completed building.

Doing a "True Construction" Deal

If you've found a piece of property you want to buy, and you intend to hire your own contractor to construct the building, you have a problem. If you take title to the land, your Exchange is over on that property. In this situation you really have two options: either get the builder to take title to the land or else have the Intermediary take title to it.

Having the builder take title to the land. It's usually cheaper to have the builder take title to the property. This creates a couple of problems, however. The first problem is the reputation, integrity and financial stability of the builder. How well do you know the builder? How much do you trust the builder? Is he or she financially stable? The second problem you have is that the builder is going to need to obtain a construction loan for the bulk of the construction, because if you provide the funds you have a huge agency risk (meaning that the IRS could say that the builder is your agent). This would end your Exchange as of the date that the builder took title to the land.

If the Intermediary takes title you don't have an agency problem, and you can use funds from your Exchange account for the purchase of the land and the construction costs. The negative, however, is that the Intermediary is going to charge you at least $5,000 or $6,000 to handle the Exchange.

The procedures that the Intermediary will follow in structuring a Construction Exchange mirror the procedures for a Reverse Exchange.

Reverse Construction Exchanges

If you don't think that you can complete sufficient construction within 180 days to meet your equal-or-up target, there is still a way that you can make the Exchange work. It's called a reverse Construction Exchange. What happens in a reverse Construction Exchange is that you couple together a Reverse Exchange and a Construction Exchange.

This is how it works: As in a Reverse Exchange you have your Qualified Intermediary acquire the New Property (land) while you are still in title to the Old Property. Then you, through the Intermediary, start construction on the land. Construction work commences and progresses until you reach a point where the construction costs, including the cost of the land, are close to the selling price of your Old Property. At that point you can close the sale of your Old Property and the proceeds then roll over to the purchase of the partially constructed building, from the Intermediary, to complete your Exchange.

For example, your Old Property is a manufacturing plant worth $2 million. You want to sell it, buy a piece of land and build a new building on it for a total price of $3.5 million. If you did a straight Construction Exchange, you would have 180 days from the day you closed the sale of your Old Property, to buy the land, get your permits and approvals and do a substantial amount of construction.

By doing a reverse Construction Exchange, you find the land you want and have the Intermediary buy it, as in a Reverse Exchange. Of course you have to provide the funds or the finance, to make this happen. Likewise, you arrange for the funds necessary to pay for construction until you get to a point where the cost of the land and construction approximates the $2 million selling price of the Old Property. At that point you could close the sale of your Old Property.

If your cost on the New Property equals or exceeds the selling price of your Old Property, the Intermediary can transfer title of the New Property to you immediately. If you are a little short of your equal-or-up target, you have 180 days from the closing date of the Old Property to make up the difference. And remember, "construction costs" means installed costs.

Financing of Construction and Reverse Construction Exchanges is relatively easy. Banks are the typical lenders on construction projects, and the fact that you have an Intermediary in the middle of the transaction because you are doing a Reverse Exchange, or Reverse Construction Exchange will typically not prevent the bank from making the loan.

Remember, too, that the Intermediary will set up an entity to take title to the land and to do the construction until the Exchange is completed. That means that money you put up to pay for the land and/or construction will go though this entity and will be treated as a loan from you to the entity. Construction loans from the bank will also be made to the Intermediary's entity and guaranteed by you. And don't be surprised if you have to pledge your equity in the Old Property against this loan.

Chapter 15:
Build-to-Suit Transactions

Before I explain what a Build-to-Suit transaction is, let me give you one really big caution: Before you attempt this, talk to your CPA or your Intermediary (if you are using a really good one). Build-to-Suit transactions are controversial. Although, as I write this, the IRS has blessed them, it is having second thoughts and may revoke this blessing. Check and make sure it will still approve them before you consider Build-to-Suit. Let me say also: I don't like Build-to-Suit transactions. I think the IRS rulings are wrong, and I believe that they will be withdrawn at some point in the future.

My big fear is that when the IRS does withdraw its blessing, we'll have eight or ten clients in the middle of transactions like this. In other words, my clients will be out at the end of the limb, and the IRS will cut the limb off!

What Is a Build-to-Suit Transaction?

A Build-to-Suit Exchange is one where you sell your Old Property, and then you use the proceeds from the Exchange to build on land that you already own. In other words, the difference between a Construction Exchange and a Build-to-Suit Exchange is that you own the land on which you are going to build at the same time you own the Old Property.

Lots of people would like to do this, but up until recently these types of transactions were not allowed. In a landmark 1951 court case, *Bloomington Coca-Cola vs. Commissioner*, the courts disallowed such a scheme. In that court case, the company had sold a piece of property and used the proceeds to build an extension onto their existing production plant. The IRS disallowed the Exchange, and the company sued and lost.

Up until recently this case was one of the pillars of 1031 law: You can't do an Exchange into something you already own because you can't have a tax-free sale and then use the proceeds to enhance something you already own. In other words, you can't have your cake and eat it too.

Now, in two almost back-to-back rulings, the IRS has approved a similar setup. The taxpayers did their construction through a series of leases to avoid having a direct improvement on property owned by the same taxpayer as the one who sold the Old Property. What the IRS is saying is that the lease very slightly alters the transaction, but the small difference is enough to make it different than *Bloomington Coca-Cola*.

Let's say Fred owns a piece of property he is selling for $100,000. He wants to roll this into the construction of a building on a piece of land that he owns across town. And of course, like all of us, he doesn't want to pay tax on the transaction. *Bloomington Coca-Cola* won't allow this, so this is an example of how the IRS rulings could structure this transaction:

First, Fred sets up an LLC. This LLC is owned 99 percent by Fred and 1 percent by Sue, his wife. This LLC leases the land from Fred on a lease of at least 40 years. Why 40 years? In order for a lease to be considered real estate under 1031 law, it has to have an unexpired term of at least 30 years remaining on the lease when the transaction is finalized. As you will see in a moment, by setting the term of the lease to be at least 40 years, it gives Fred and Sue time to properly structure the Exchange and complete the transaction. In our office, we typically structure such transactions to have a term of at least 50 years, and preferably 99 years.

Why did we add Sue to the LLC? *Bloomington Coca-Cola* won't allow a person to build on something that person owns. But an LLC jointly owned by both Fred and Sue is considered by the IRS to be a different taxpayer separate from Fred. According to these new IRS rulings, adding Sue makes the transaction just different enough to avoid a *Bloomington Coca-Cola* problem. Since Sue is Fred's wife, you could say this is a blatant change to avoid a *Bloomington Coca-Cola* problem because now the taxpayer doing the Exchange (Fred) is not the same taxpayer as the owner of the replacement property. But it is all legal; the IRS currently allows such setups.

Fred's Intermediary then sets up a separate entity to do the construction. The Intermediary will use essentially the same procedures as if Fred were doing a Reverse Exchange.

The Intermediary's entity then enters into a sublease of the land with Fred and Sue's LLC. The lease is set up to allow the entity to improve the property by constructing a building on it. The sublease will be of shorter duration than the lease from Fred to the LLC in order to make the sublease appear to stand on its own, so we might structure it to have a 35-year duration (remember, when the transaction is completed we need to have at least 30 years left on the lease).

The IRS has only approved this Exchange structure when done as part of a Reverse Exchange. Therefore it is important that all of the title and leasing arrangements be done prior to closing the sale of the Old Property.

At this point the Intermediary's entity constructs the building on Fred's property. In both of the IRS rulings the taxpayer (Fred in our example) sold the Old Property and immediately constructed the new building using Exchange proceeds from the Intermediary to pay the construction costs. In both of the rulings the building was apparently constructed within the 180-day period following the sale of the Old Property.

I don't know how practical this would be, because it is difficult to build anything, anywhere in this country, in 180 days. Consult your Intermediary about this, but if you can pull it off, this would be great, because you have proceeds from the Exchange that can be used to pay for construction.

If you decide to start construction before you close the sale of your Old Property, or if you won't have enough proceeds from your Exchange to pay for the construction, you're either going to have to make up the difference with your own funds or with a loan from a bank (or perhaps a combination of the two).

If you need construction financing you need to deal with a bank rather than a mortgage company, and you can expect that a banker will have a problem with the goofy lease arrangement necessary to follow the IRS rulings. Expect a bank to want a guarantee from Fred and perhaps subordination of the two leases.

Remember, from the chapter on Construction Exchanges, you don't need to complete the building, but you must equalize your Exchange in order to avoid having a taxable situation, and you must equalize your Exchange before the 180th day following the close of the sale of the Old Property. Build-to-Suit transactions are a little different in that the 180-day period starts with the signing of the sublease by the Intermediary's holding entity.

In my example, because Fred sold his Old Property for $100,000, there must be at least $100,000 of construction to avoid a taxable situation. And, as in a Construction Exchange, this means installed cost. Also, remember that the value of the land itself is not counted – only the cost of the installed construction.

What happens if Fred doesn't get to equalization (in this case $100,000) by the 180th day? The shortfall is taxable. So if he only completes $90,000 of construction by day 180, he will pay tax on the shortfall of $10,000 (and, yes, the whole $10,000 is taxable).

Now, one of the requirements of a 1031 Exchange is that the same taxpayer must take title to the New Property as held title to the Old Property. How do we do this with this goofy lease/sublease structure? We have Fred take title to the entity that owns the construction. The entity was set up by the Intermediary as an LLC, so to complete the Exchange the Intermediary transfers all of the ownership interest in the LLC to Fred. Because Fred owns all of the shares of the construction LLC, the LLC is considered a disregarded entity, and Fred is considered the owner of the building via the construction LLC. If this is confusing to you, I suggest that you read the section on single-member LLCs as disregarded entities in the chapter on Ownership Issues.

The transfer of the Intermediary's construction entity's ownership has to take place before the 180th day. This then completes Fred's Exchange (subject to all of the other 1031 requirements, of course). So as soon as the transfer to Fred happens, ownership of the property looks like this: There is a piece of land owned by Fred, that is leased to an LLC owned 99 percent by Fred and 1 percent by his wife Sue, and then subleased to an LLC owned by 100 percent by Fred. The LLC owns a building that was built tax-free as part of an Exchange from the sale of a different piece of property owned by Fred. With the minor addition of a 1 percent ownership of the first LLC by Sue, Fred owns both the land and the new building. With the exception of the use of the leases and the minor 1 percent ownership by Fred's wife, this transaction looks just like *Bloomington Coca-Cola* to me, and that is why I don't like it.

Since the transaction is pretty much Fred, you may be wondering if Fred couldn't just terminate the leases and dissolve the LLCs. Most clients want to do this fairly quickly to get rid of the hassles of the screwed-up title and the multiple LLCs. We strongly recommend to our clients that they leave the structure untouched until the statute of limitations has closed (in other words until the third anniversary of the filing of the tax return that reported the Exchange).

Chapter 16:
Improvement Exchanges

In its simplest form, an Improvement Exchange happens when you sell your Old Property and use a portion of the funds to buy a building and the balance of the funds to make improvements to the building. The rules for an Improvement Exchange are similar in many ways to those of a Construction Exchange, but are dramatically different in other respects. Let's start with the similarities.

Similarities to Construction Exchange Rules

As in a Construction Exchange, you can use the proceeds from the sale of your Old Property to fund the purchase of the New Property and to pay for the improvements. This means that Sue's Intermediary could use part of the funds that he holds to buy the New Property, and the balance of the funds to pay for the improvements.

Like Construction Exchanges, you have exactly 180 days from the closing of the sale of your Old Property to equalize and complete your Exchange. If you fail to meet your equal-or-up target, the shortfall is taxable. And, as we've discussed before, the whole shortfall is taxable.

If Sue sold her purple duplex for $100,000 but only spent $90,000 on purchasing the New Property and fixing it up, she will pay tax on the $10,000 shortfall. And the entire $10,000 is taxable – she cannot offset any of her investment in the purple duplex against this amount.

Also like a Construction Exchange, once you take title to the property (once title goes into your name) your Exchange is over on that property. This means that your Intermediary will set up a separate entity to take title to your property. Through this separate entity the Intermediary will own your New Property until the improvements are completed. Once the improvements are completed, title will then be transferred from the Intermediary's entity to you.

Let's assume that Sue sold her purple duplex, which was free and clear, for $100,000. After closing costs her Intermediary is holding $92,500. Sue's New Property is a rental house that she can buy for $80,000. The rental house needs $30,000 worth of improvements. If Sue takes title to the house, her Exchange is over. However, her Intermediary can set up an entity to take title to the property, using Sue's Exchange funds. The Intermediary can also pay for the improvements out of the balance of Sue's Exchange funds. Once the Exchange funds are depleted and the improvements are completed, ownership of the property will be transferred from the Intermediary's entity to Sue to complete her Exchange.

You are allowed to play an active roll in the actual improvements to the property. You can pick the contractors, pick the colors, supervise the work, etc. Of course, no moneys can flow to you from the Intermediary while all of this is happening. In other words, Sue could not be compensated from the Exchange proceeds for hours worked by her. Nor can the Intermediary reimburse her directly for monies she spent for supplies and the like. In other words, the Intermediary should not cut checks from the Exchange account directly to Sue for anything. The Intermediary could disburse funds to Visa for supplies Sue charged on her charge card or to Home Depot for materials Sue has ordered, but has to pay for when she picks them up. But it would be bad for any funds to flow from the Exchange account to Sue directly because that could give the IRS an opening to argue that Sue touched the money, which could toast her whole Exchange.

How Improvement Exchanges Differ from Reverse Exchanges

So how is an Improvement Exchange different? In a big way, because you must list the improvements you plan to make on your 45-Day List. And the Intermediary can't transfer the property to you until those improvements you listed are completed. That's right – the improvements need to be completely finished. Of course, you don't have to list every single improvement you plan to make – just the ones necessary to equalize your Exchange.

So to flesh out our example from above, if Sue sold her purple duplex for $100,000 and the Intermediary is holding the net proceeds of $92,500 after closing costs, Sue must spend the $92,500 to avoid paying tax. If she plans to buy the New Property for $80,000 and make improvements costing $30,000 (for a total of $110,000), Sue would only want to list $12,500 of the improvements because that is all she needs to equalize her Exchange. She has to list the $12,500 of improvements on her 45-Day List, and her Intermediary cannot transfer the New Property to her until these improvements are completed.

The secret here is that, of all the improvements Sue plans to make, she will want to list only enough of them to equalize her Exchange. She'll want to pick the biggest, easiest, quickest ones; because once they are completed the Intermediary will deed the property to her. For example, a new roof for $10,000 and repainting the exterior of the building for $2,500 is all it might take to equalize her Exchange. She should avoid listing improvements that are small in dollar amount or take a long time to complete.

You Need a Really Good Intermediary

One thing I need to stress at this point is that in the typical Improvement Exchange, the Intermediary will take title to the New Property and hold that ownership until the improvements are made. Make sure at the beginning that your Intermediary can do an Improvement Exchange, and as in a Reverse Exchange, plan on paying an additional $5,000 or more for the Exchange because of the extra work the Intermediary must perform. These things just cost that much.

If you are planning to do an Improvement Exchange you absolutely have to have a really good Intermediary. Improvement Exchanges are complicated, and the Intermediary should be giving you a lot of guidance about what things you want to put on the list, how you want your list to read, how the contractors will be paid, etc.

A good Intermediary is simply critical here, so if you know at the time of the sale of your Old Property that you are going to do an Improvement Exchange, make sure you get a good Intermediary with a lot of experience. The cost difference between a pro and a rookie Intermediary is pretty insignificant to the whole transaction, so get a good one.

It is human nature to want to save a few bucks, but a fairly common situation that we see where taxpayers hire less experienced Intermediary in order to save a few bucks. Then they find their dream properties and realize they can add a lot of equity by making some basic improvements to the properties from their Exchange accounts. Their offers are accepted, and they are off to the races until they call their Intermediary and discover that the Intermediary cannot handle Improvement Exchanges (very few Intermediaries can). They call us, but we can't help them because the law will not let them switch from their existing Intermediary to us. So they are stuck. They either lose the properties, or they end up paying a lot of tax because they can't wrap the improvements into the Exchange.

How to Handle Small Improvements

What happens if the improvements you want to make are pretty insignificant to the transaction, but without including them in the transaction your Exchange would fail to meet the equal-or-up requirement? Let's say that Sue sold her purple duplex for $100,000 and needs to meet an equal-or-up target of $92,500. She's found a New Property for $90,000 that needs $3,000 of repairs. Once Sue takes title to the New Property her Exchange is over. Sue should do a formal Improvement Exchange, but it does not make sense to pay an Intermediary $5,000 or $6,000 in Exchange fees in order to save paying tax on a $3,000 buy-down.

My advice in this situation is to offer to buy the property from the seller for $93,000 (instead of the $90,000 that the seller is asking for the property) with the seller making the $3,000 of improvements before the closing. Sue should expect to have to put up $3,000 of additional, non-refundable, earnest money so that the seller has the funds to pay for the improvements (if the seller could afford to make the improvements he or she would have already done so because it enhances the salability of the property). We often see sellers agree to this sort of scenario.

What if the seller won't agree? Sue's only other alternative is to have checks cut, as part of the purchase, for payment of the improvements she wants to make. In other words, the closing statement for the purchase of Sue's New Property would show the purchase of the New Property from Sam Seller for $90,000 and the payment of $2,000 to Acme Construction for structural repairs to the porch and a check to Betty's Painting for $1,000 to paint the porch. The total of these three items gets Sue past her equal-or-up target of $92,500.

Since the repairs to the porch are not completed on the day of the purchase (if fact, they have not even been started), Sue will want to take charge of the two checks and hold onto them until the work is completed. This should be within a short time after the closing – say several weeks.

From a technical standpoint, the $3,000 of improvements does not qualify as part of the replacement cost of the New Property. Because the work has not been completed, Sue is not paying for $3,000 of "real estate" on the purchase Settlement Statement, but rather she is paying for a promise to do the work (promises from Acme Construction and

Betty's Painting). If she were audited, the IRS could allow only the $90,000 of the purchase because that is the true cost of the real estate, and Sue would pay tax on $2,500 (the actual amount of the buy-down from her $92,500 equal-or-up target).

Most Intermediaries will look the other way when a client does this, provided the amount of the uncompleted work is insignificant to the whole transaction. We, and most Intermediaries I know, have a 5 percent fudge limit (meaning if the amount of the fudge factor is less than 5 percent of the sales price of the Old Property, the client is OK). Beyond that level, the client either does a formal Improvement Exchange or has to pay tax on the shortfall.

But again (I want to be clear here), technically the 5 percent fudge factor is a violation of the law, so don't be surprised if the uncompleted work is disallowed by the IRS, and don't be surprised if your Intermediary refuses to work with you on this.

Chapter 17:

Tenants-in-Common (TIC) Transactions

These transactions have become the rage in the 1031 world since the IRS issued guidelines for structuring them in 2002. Notice that I did not say that the IRS approved them – they merely issued guidelines for how the Exchanges are to be structured.

What Is a TIC Transaction?

Let's start with an example of tenants-in-common, or TIC (rhymes with "lick") transaction. If you and two of your friends were to buy a building, the three of you would most probably take title as tenants-in-common, which is a legal term meaning that the three of you each own an undivided one-third of the building. In other words, the property is claimed on three different tax returns.

Even though you are tenants-in-common, your transaction is <u>not</u> what the 1031 community calls a TIC because you know each other. When we talk about a TIC we are talking about a property owned by a group of people who don't, and probably never will, know each other. These people are brought together by a "sponsor" – a salesman who is compensated to find investors for the property. The sponsor may also be the same person who found the property and put the deal together.

For example, Sam Sponsor has found a property on the market for $8 million. The seller of the property has agreed to hold the property off the market for nine months while Sam tries to market the property as a TIC. Sam has a lender who will loan $5 million against the property. Sam is looking for 20 investors willing to put up $250,000 each, for a total of $5 million. In other words, Sam is marketing the property to the public for $10 million. Sam's profit on this transaction is $2 million, if he can put it together. Sam advertises the property to local investors as well as national investors via the internet. This is clearly a TIC since it is unlikely that the investors will know each other, and because the transaction was put together by a sponsor (Sam).

As in my example above, a TIC is a transaction comprised of strangers brought together by a salesman, and only TIC transactions are subject to the rules I'm discussing in this chapter. The building you own with your two friends is not affected by these rules. Only if there are strangers involved, and someone is being compensated to bring them together, do you have a TIC. And then it is only a TIC if we are talking about rental real estate. A transaction to buy a piece of bare land or a corporate jet would also not be covered by the TIC rules.

IRS Has Issued TIC Guidelines

The IRS issued their TIC guidelines as a Revenue Procedure. As I've said before, Revenue Procedures are cook book rulings – if you do certain things, you will get a certain result. In Revenue Procedure 2002-22 the IRS provides a checklist of the things you must do before the IRS will issue an opinion on whether or not your TIC qualifies as replacement property for a 1031 Exchange.

Notice that the ruling does not provide a checklist of things you must do for a property to qualify as replacement property; it merely provides a list of things that are necessary before the IRS will even look at whether or not the property qualifies as 1031 replacement property. After examination, the IRS may or may not approve it. The problem is that the review process takes approximately six months – a period of time that most sponsors are not willing to wait.

My recent search for the acronym "TIC" on Google returned approximately 550,000 hits – most of them sites of sponsors seeking investors. However, in the almost three years since the ruling came out, there has only been one ruling application that has been published (which was approved). We have no way of knowing if there have been applications that would have been disapproved had not the sponsor withdrawn the application. But clearly the vast majority of TIC sponsors are not getting their TICs reviewed by the IRS.

Why would the IRS disallow a TIC transaction? Well, one of the primary requirements of a 1031 Exchange is that if you are selling real estate, you have to buy real estate. Partnership interests do not qualify as replacement property for your Exchange, even if the partnership owns only real estate. The risk you run in a TIC exchange is that the IRS could determine that what you are purchasing is, in essence, a partnership share; because the deal is structured more like a partnership than a group of individual owners (the IRS have disallowed Exchanges because of this).

For example, if Sue invested $100,000 in a building costing $100 million, she would own a 1/10 of 1 percent of a share of the property. If the deal were structured in such a way that she had no say in how the building was run, when to sell it (if she could), to whom, for how much, the IRS would very likely decide that she really owned a partnership interest – even though she had a deed to her small slice.

So the IRS's ruling sets out the minimum requirements that the deal must meet before it will tell you if you have a good TIC or merely a partnership. Unfortunately, what we are seeing is many TICs that meet most of the requirements of the ruling. However, they are being marketed as "good" TICs qualifying as 1031 replacement properties because they meet almost all of the requirements. As each new deal comes out it seems to meet fewer of the rules than the deal before it. It seems that the standard is not the minimum requirements that the IRS ruling sets forth (merely to submit a transaction for approval, don't forget), but that the standard is how close it comes to the last deal. The quality seems to be sliding, especially as we see more and more small deals.

IRS Requirements for TICs

So what are the IRS requirements? First, the investors must own their interest in fee simple, meaning that they have a deed for their slices of the property. For liability protection we see a large number of deals that have each member take title as single member LLCs. The problem with single member LLCs is that if a husband and wife owned the Old Property, and they don't live in a community property state, a single-member LLC becomes a problem from a 1031 Exchange title holding standpoint.

With a TIC, the number of co-owners in the property cannot exceed 35, although there are allowances built into the rules that count a husband and wife as one owner. Also, if a co-owner dies and leaves his or her share equally to heirs, the heirs still collectively count as one owner.

The group cannot conduct business under a common name, and it cannot file a common tax return. In other words, you cannot set up a partnership or LLC to take title to a building. If there are 35 investors you have to have 35 separate deeds, and each investor has to report each share of the income and expenses on each tax return.

It is OK to have a Co-ownership Agreement that sets forth in writing the important guidelines for investment in the property. This Agreement will explain how revenues are split among the investors and how each investor pays the expenses for which he or she is responsible. The agreement will also provide for which business actions have to be voted on and how many votes are required for each action.

Under the IRS ruling, some actions require unanimous approval. Selling the building or refinancing the debt must be unanimous. Leasing space in the building also must be unanimous. Each lease has to be approved unanimously by the owners. Requiring unanimous approval is one thing when there is only one or two investors or when the building only has one or two tenants but quite another when there are many investors or the property is a 20-story office building with tenants moving in and out each month.

Hiring of a property manager and approval of the management contract also require unanimous approval of the investors. If the manager is also the sponsor of the deal (which is almost always the case), not only do you need unanimous consent for each investor, but the management contract needs to be approved each year. Not surprisingly this is the area where we see the most compliance issues.

It will be interesting to see how the unanimous approval provisions work in real life. It seems hard to imagine that you can get everyone to agree on everything all the time. What happens if you can't find one of the investors right away? For example, what if one is on active duty in the Navy and is out at sea?

Another problem that is beginning to come to light with the 100 percent approval rule is the fact that one unhappy investor can make life miserable for everyone else. For this reason we are starting to see deals that give the sponsor or the other investors the right to kick someone out. While I understand the reasoning behind this, I think it is probably fatal to the deal.

All the decisions that don't require 100 percent approval require the approval of a simple majority. (By the way, you are not allowed to give power of attorney for your vote to the sponsor or the property manager.)

What to Look for in a TIC

The following advice will hopefully help you when you look at a possible investment:

First, the "playground" rule has to be part of the deal. Remember when you were a kid and didn't like a game anymore, and you wanted to go home? You simply picked up your ball (or your toys) and went home. The same rule has to be part of the TIC transaction. You have to be able to leave anytime you want.

You have to be able to sell your share to anyone you want, whenever you want, for however much you want. Anything that limits your ability to "pick up the ball and go home" should be fatal to the deal. You can be required to notify the other investors first that you intend to sell your interest so that they can be first in line to make you an offer, but there cannot be a right of first refusal that gives them the right to block the sale to any one you might want to sell it to.

While TIC investments fill a certain role in the market, I don't like them as a general rule. Yes, I understand the desire of many investors to move to a property that provides a fairly certain cash flow with good upside potential and no management hassles. But there are a lot of deals out there that are simply not good investments.

Not uncommonly we will see Sam Investor, who sold his Old Property and is now looking for replacement property for his 1031 Exchange. He finds a building that he likes and goes through due diligence on the property: he reviews the leases, analyzes the credit worthiness of the tenants, has every inch of the building inspected, has the property surveyed, scrutinizes the title report so that he understands each easement to the property, etc. But then, for whatever reason, toward the end of his 45 days, he decides against buying the building. Instead, he has a slick TIC brochure with pretty pictures and glowing descriptions and decides that he will buy a slice as his replacement property. No due diligence, no reviews, no analysis. He likes the pictures in the brochure and has made up his mind.

Don't be like Sam. You need to approach the purchase of a TIC share the same way you would the purchase of an entire building. You need to do more due diligence on a TIC then you would do if you were buying all of the building, because not only do you need to do the same due diligence on the building, you also need to do due diligence on the sponsor.

We've seen some pretty bad deals. Perhaps a building is on the market for $14 million. It's really worth maybe $12 million, and sits there unsold until a TIC sponsor comes along and offers the seller $15 million if the seller will delay the closing until the sponsor puts together a TIC offering, which the sponsor. The sponsor then sells interests totaling $18 million. If you're one of the investors, you and the rest of the group now own a property you just paid $18 million for, but which is really worth $12 million. How long will it be before you can even get your original investment back? Will you ever get your investment back? Who will buy your interest? At what price?

Another common device that we see is where the sponsor "master-leases" the building for a predetermined amount (usually yielding the investors around 7 percent a year). Under the master lease the sponsor collects the rents and pays the bills, pays 7 percent of each investor's original investment to them and pockets the rest. This is a great way to get around the rule requiring unanimous approval of each lease. Except for three problems: first, the IRS guidelines require that this type of setup has to be approved by 100 percent of the investors annually. Provisions to do this annually almost never appear in the governing documents to the deal.

Second, what if there is not enough money, after collecting rents and paying the bills for the sponsor to pay the promised 7 percent to the investors? The promotional materials typically provide that the sponsor will make up the difference out of pocket. But is there money set aside for this contingency? Almost never. So in other words, the sponsor has just stripped out all of the upside cash flow, and the investors (although unknowingly) have all of the downside. As part of your due diligence make sure that you are clear on how the sponsor will make up any negative cash flow and where the sponsor will get the funds to do so. Has the sponsor set aside funds to do this? Are the funds really there?

And third, the sponsor has pegged the maximum amount of income. Therefore, if similar buildings have a higher level of income (say 10 percent), the actual value of your building as a whole, as well as the value of your share, goes down accordingly. Again, the investors have a property that could be very difficult, if not impossible, to sell at anything approaching their original investment.

Why do sponsors do this? Greed is probably the best answer. There is so much money chasing these things right now, and they are so new that few problems have yet come to light (which implies little or no risk to current investors). Investors are simply caught up by the pretty pictures and lack any sense of caution. In addition to the markup on the purchase price, sponsors make an additional 3 percent to 5 percent of the selling price of the properties as commissions. Add to that amount the annual management fees they are paid to oversee the properties, and you can see why sponsors are so eager to put together TICs.

You Need a Good Exit Strategy

Which brings us to perhaps the biggest problems with these investments, and that is the exit strategy. How are you going to get out? Who's going to buy your interest? How are you going to connect with investors who might want your share of the property? How are potential buyers going to find you? How do you value a small slice of a large project? Who will prepare the documents transferring ownership from you to the buyer?

What Are the State Laws Regarding TICs

What do the individual states think of TIC transactions? The states are all over the map on this one. Most states "piggy back" federal tax law, so if your state is one of those and the IRS considers your investment to qualify as 1031 property, you should be OK that it qualifies as investment property for your state. But all states seem to have security "blue sky" laws. If you live in Atlanta, the sponsor is in New York, and the property is in Texas, which state has jurisdiction? Has the sponsor met the requirements of each state involved? In other words, is it even legal for the sponsor to sell you, or even offer to sell you, your interest?

I paint a pretty bleak picture of TIC transactions. Are all of them bad? No, there actually are some that are quite good. And the concept of a TIC makes sense - it's a way that a number of investors can band together to buy a large property that none of them would be able to purchase on their own. My rule of thumb is that the larger the minimum entry into the deal, the better the deal probably is. If each investor is putting up $500,000, or $1 million or more of his or her own cash, the sponsor runs a huge risk of getting sued if the deal is not correctly structured. On the other hand, if each investor is only putting up $25,000, there is not enough money to justify hiring an attorney and incurring legal fees to go after the sponsor.

So what should you do if you are interested in buying one of these interests? First, get a good tax attorney to make sure the sponsor's documents are correct. If you are unwilling to pay for legal advice going in, it's probably a good indication that you shouldn't be making this investment. Make sure the deal is properly structured and meets the requirements of the ruling. And then do the same due diligence you would do if you were buying the property yourself: review the leases, analyze the tenants, etc. Have your specialist review the engineer's report about the property. Don't stop there - do a background check on the sponsor. Find out as much as you can about the deal. Ask every single question you can think of about the property, and then go back and ask the questions you can't think of. And make notes of every conversation you have with the sponsor so that there are no questions in the future about what you were told.

I constantly hear clients say that there are no good individual deals out there, and then they act as if every TIC deal is a gift from heaven. It's hard for me to believe that there are more good TIC deals out there than there are individual properties. Please be careful.

Do Your Own Research

Now, one last thing to watch for with these deals: Is your Intermediary getting a kickback, or referral fee, for sending you to the sponsor? While the number of sponsors offering referral fees seems to have decreased dramatically since a recent supreme court case that seems to imply that it is illegal to pay referral fees to someone who is not licensed by the SEC, I know that a number of Intermediaries get referral fees, and some have even set up SEC-licensed subsidiaries or employees to receive these kickbacks. I think this is highly unethical – whether it is illegal is yet to be seen.

Be Careful!

The best advice I can give you about TIC transactions is this: If the deal is really that good, why does the sponsor need your investment to make it fly? Why didn't the property get bought up before it ever hit the market?

Remember these three things: (1) Be careful! (2) Be really careful! And (3) really, really be careful! If you invested in partnership tax shelters during the 1970s you understand what I'm talking about. How many people do you know that actually invested in a good tax shelter back then? If you are too young to remember the 1970s, seek the advice of someone who does before you make this investment.

Chapter 18:
Personal Property Exchanges

When I talk about "personal property" in this section, I'm talking about the IRS definition of personal property, which is "things that can be moved." When many people hear the term "personal property" they automatically assume that we are talking about their residence because that is their personal property. No – to the IRS personal property means something that can be moved. And most of the time when we talk about personal property we're talking about movable property that can be depreciated, although as you will see, not all personal property is depreciable.

Things that can be moved include planes, boats, office equipment, over-the-road trucks and trailers, construction equipment, computer systems, cars and buses, communication satellites and even cattle. There are very large Exchanges done for fleets of automobiles owned, for example, by rental car companies.

Many of the rules governing personal property Exchanges mirror the rules for real estate Exchanges, but some of them are completely different. Let's take the biggest difference first.

"Held For Investment"

Like real estate, both your Old depreciable personal Property and your New depreciable personal Property have to be of like kind and held for investment. But "like-kind" or "like-class" are defined more narrowly for personal property. A depreciable asset or a group of assets is "like-class" to other assets only if they are in the same asset or product class. How do you know if the assets are in the same class?

General Asset Classes

The IRS starts by dividing personal property into thirteen broad General Asset Classes:

1. *Office furniture, fixtures and equipment.* This class includes items that are not a permanent structural component of a building such as desks, files, safes, etc.
2. *Information systems, such as computers and peripheral equipment.* Peripheral equipment is equipment related to computers, such as external disk drives and storage devices, optical scanners, etc.
3. *Data handling equipment other than computers.* This includes typewriters, calculators, adding machines and copiers.
4. *Non-commercial airplanes and helicopters.*
5. *Automobiles and taxis.*
6. *Buses.*
7. *Light general purpose trucks.* This class is typically pickups and delivery trucks – trucks with an unloaded weight of less than 13,000 pounds.
8. *Heavy general purpose trucks.* This class includes trucks heavier than 13,000 pounds, such as concrete ready-mix-trucks and ore trucks used over the road.
9. *Railroad cars and locomotives.* This does not include those owned by railroad transportation companies.
10. *Tractor units for use over the road.*
11. *Trailers and trailer-mounted containers.*
12. *Vessels, barges, tugs and similar water-transportation equipment.*
13. *Industrial steam and electric generation and/or distribution systems.*

In order to do a 1031 Exchange, you have to stay within the same General Asset Class for both the Old Property you are selling and the New Property you are buying. If the two assets are in different General Asset Classes, you cannot do an Exchange. For example, if you sold a pickup (i.e. Class #7 – light general purpose trucks) you could do an Exchange if you bought another pickup truck or a light delivery truck, but you could not do a 1031 Exchange into a cement mixer that fell into Class #8 – heavy general purpose trucks, because those are two different classes. To do an Exchange you have to stay within the same class – if there is one.

Product Classes

Not every type of depreciable personal property is covered by the above list. So, if your type of asset is not one of the 13 types of assets listed above, you next look to Product Classes to see if your asset is listed there. Product Classes are generally classes broken down into four-digit classes by SIC (Standard Industrial Code) set out in a Standard Industrial Classification Manual published by the government in 1987.

The SIC breaks down assets into more detailed classifications than the 13 General Asset Classes set out above. For example, Division G is a subsection of the SIC that covers assets used in the retail trade industry. Division G is further broken down into assets owned by eight major groups:

Major Group 52: Building materials, hardware, garden supply and mobile home dealers
Major Group 53: General merchandise stores
Major Group 54: Food stores
Major Group 55: Automotive dealers and gasoline service stations
Major Group 56: Apparel and accessory stores
Major Group 57: Home furniture, furnishings and equipment stores
Major Group 58: Eating and drinking places
Major Group 59: Miscellaneous retail

Each one of these Major Groups is broken down into subgroups with the four-digit designations. For example, Major Group 58 (of Division G) is then broken down into the following four-digit subgroups:

Industry Group 581: Eating and drinking places
• 5812 Eating places
• 5813 Drinking places (alcoholic beverages)

These two Class codes (5812 and 5813) encompass really broad types of places. Class code 5812, for example, covers everything from the hot dog pushcart stands that you see on street corners in major cities to dinner theaters.

So let me put this into perspective for you:

Fred and Sue are selling their restaurant. They are selling the tables, the chairs, the decorations, the stainless steel tables in the kitchen, the walk-in cooler and all the dishes and silverware. If they buy a lounge, can they do a 1031 Exchange?

To determine if they can do an Exchange, we start with the 13 General Asset Classes at the beginning of this chapter. If there were a General Asset Class that covered both restaurants and liquor establishments, our work would be done, and the answer would be yes. If there were separate Classes for restaurants and for liquor establishments the answer would be no.

Since there is not a General Asset Class that covers either restaurants or liquor establishments, we must go on to Product Classes, and we search the SIC listings for restaurants and liquor establishments, where we find that there is an Industry Group (#581) under Division G that covers both eating and drinking establishments. So far, so good. We then review the detail of Group 581, where we find that there is an SIC (5812) for eating places and one (5813) for drinking places. Since restaurants and lounges fall under different SICs we cannot do a 1031 Exchange. Fred and Sue's choice at this point is to either pay tax on the sale of the restaurant and use the net proceeds to buy the lounge (in other words not do an Exchange) or to buy another restaurant instead. They could sell a steakhouse and buy a pizza place (since they are both covered by the same SIC category), but they could not buy assets for a business that did not fall under Section 5812 – eating places.

One further thing that you have to watch for with SIC is that some Product Class codes end in "9." These are miscellaneous classes that are essentially a dumping ground for items that don't fit in any of the other sections under that Industry Group. If there were a section 5819 (which there is not), it would cover eating and drinking establishments (which is Group 581), and it would cover every type of eating and drinking establishment that was not specifically covered under section 5812 or section 5813.

Section 1031 says that you cannot do an Exchange just because your Old Property and your New Property both fall under the same section if it ends in a 9 (5819 in our example) because these are merely catch-all sections.

What do you do if there is not an SIC category that covers the type of assets you sold? How do you know if you can do an Exchange? In that case, you can move forward with an Exchange provided that both your Old Property and your New Property are essentially the same (in other words – they are like kind). This is a subjective test that is easily second-guessed by the IRS, so any time we have a client that gets to this level in a personal property Exchange we start to get very nervous.

However, at times it is still reasonable to do Exchanges on assets in miscellaneous classes. For example, several years ago we had a client who sold a manufacturing plant full of machines that used an injection molding process to make a certain product. The client did a 1031 Exchange, which we handled, and bought a manufacturing plant full of injection molding equipment that made a different product. The old equipment made a plastic product that was listed in the 3089 section (plastic products, not elsewhere classified) of Industry Group 308 – miscellaneous plastic products manufacturing. The plastic product manufactured by the new equipment was not listed anywhere in the SIC. Since this was a multi-million dollar Exchange, there was considerable concern about whether injection molding equipment that makes product x is "like-kind" to injection molding equipment that makes product y. Although we were clear about the "like-kind" determination, we all breathed a sigh of relief when the statute of limitations closed on that Exchange.

Because so many of the SIC covered such broad categories, the government revised the SIC system and issued the North American Industrial Classification System (NAICS) in 1997. The NAICS breaks the old SIC categories into much greater detail. It expands the four-digit SIC system into a six-digit system. The NAICS reference manual we have in our office looks like the phone book of a major city.

For example, where we only have one SIC section that covers restaurants (Section 5812), there are four NAICS sections covering restaurants:

> 722110: Full service restaurants
> 722211: Limited service restaurants (like fast food restaurants)
> 722212: Cafeterias
> 722213: Snack and nonalcoholic beverage bars

Here's the problem: The IRS has never switched to the NAICS. As I write this, you could sell your Burger King restaurant equipment and do an Exchange into the equipment in a fancy seafood restaurant, because they both fall in the same SIC section. After the switch to the NAICS you won't be able to do the Exchange because the two restaurants fall in different NAICS sections.

Not long ago the IRS announced that it was starting the process of switching from requiring use of the SIC to requiring the use of the NAICS. As I write this, we are still under the SIC without a definite date for the switch.

Shortly after the IRS announced that it was finally going to start using the NAICS, the Office of Management and Budget announced that it was upgrading the NAICS to a different system that has not been released yet. This means that just at the time the IRS switches from an abandoned system to a current system, the current system is being abandoned and will be replaced by an even more current system. Presumably by the time the IRS makes its switch, it will still be using an abandoned system. This means that you need to be very careful which classification system you use. Don't do anything without checking with an Exchange expert to see if the requirements have changed. A really good Intermediary will be on top of which system you must use for your Exchange.

Deminimus Rule for Personal Property Part of Real Estate Exchanges

One point that often comes up is that when you sell real estate, unless you are selling bare land, there is often a certain amount of personal property that is present in the building you are selling. For example, if you are selling a rental house, your sale might include the drapes, stove, refrigerator, dishwasher and perhaps the washer and dryer. Must you have two separate Exchanges – one for the real estate and one for the personal property? The answer is no – Section 1031 has a "deminimus" clause that says that any personal property that is appropriately included with the sale of that particular type of real estate is ignored as long as the personal property constitutes less than 15 percent of the sale price. If you are selling the rental house for $100,000, you can ignore the personal property as long as it is worth less that $15,000 (15 percent).

So how do you determine the value? The value is based on the "fair market value," which generally means garage sale value. In most parts of the country any type of improved real estate is worth at least $100,000, which means that you most probably will be working with $15,000 or more of garage sale value. If you've ever been "garage saling" you can appreciate how much stuff $15,000 can buy. I don't think we've ever had a client that has had to worry about the 15 percent limit.

Intangible Personal Property

Intangible personal property includes items like patents and copyrights, and there is no classification system that covers them. The IRS rules state that whether one type of intangible personal property is like-kind to another depends on their nature or character as well as the nature or character of the underlying property to which the intangible personal property relates.

For example, a copyright on a novel can be Exchanged for the copyright on a different novel, but the copyright on a novel cannot be Exchanged for the copyright on a song. While that makes sense to me, the IRS has ruled that FCC television licenses can be Exchanged for FCC radio licenses, apparently because both are licenses to send signals through the air, just on different frequencies. This logic is harder to understand.

There are Intermediaries who specialize in personal property Exchanges, and if this is what you are contemplating, I strongly urge you to use one that has experience with the type of property you are selling. Interview Intermediaries and ask what their experience is with your type of property. Ask for the names and phone numbers of some of their past clients and attorneys and then verify that they truly do have the experience they claim to have.

Personal Property in the Sale of a Business

When you sell a business, you are selling a whole bunch of things, some of which might be Exchangeable, and some of which are not. If some of the sales price of the sale is allocated to the land and buildings, their Exchangeability is pretty straightforward. Likewise, if part of the sales price is allocated to personal property (such as manufacturing equipment) that property's Exchangeability is explained above. Some of the pieces in a sale are less obvious, however.

Personal property items included in a sale considered like-kind are customer lists, trade names, franchise rights, licenses and permits. Goodwill, at least according to the IRS, is not like-kind, meaning that it cannot be Exchanged. A large number of Exchange professionals disagree with the IRS's position, but as of this writing there has not been a court case that gives us guidance on this issue. Service contracts, employment contracts and covenants-not-to-compete are not Exchangeable because the value received is for services (i.e. your agreement not to compete with the buyer), rather than an actual piece of property.

What this means to you, as you sell your business, is that you want to allocate as much as you can to the land and buildings, because you can Exchange these into any other type of investment or trade-or-business real estate. You want to allocate an amount to inventory equal to the cost assigned to it on your books. The reason for this is that the inventory value will come back to you, in cash, without tax as a sale at cost without any gain being realized.

Then you want to allocate as much of the sales price to the items that are Exchangeable (such as trademarks, franchise rights, licenses and permits), because they are Exchangeable, and you want to allocate as little as you can justify to goodwill, because you will pay tax on the gain associated with it.

Let's talk about allocations for a minute. If you, the seller, and the buyer draw up a list allocating a value to each of the items I've discussed above, as they are appropriate to your situation and if the two of you follow this allocation, it is virtually impossible for the IRS to override the established market price between buyer and seller and to allocate your sale any other way. On the other hand, if you don't have an allocation, or if you don't follow the allocation, the IRS is free to allocate the pieces any way it wants to – and, of course, it won't be in your favor.

The problem with allocations is that sellers and buyers have different, and often opposing, motivations about how they want things allocated. If you're selling your business and you want to minimize your taxes, when you put the business up for sale, before you even have an offer, form a team of your attorney, CPA, real estate agent or business broker and your 1031 Intermediary. Have a meeting so that everyone knows what the objective is at the beginning because there often isn't time to properly strategize once you get an offer. Have a game plan.

Non-depreciable Personal Property

Just as with intangible personal property, non-depreciable personal property is not covered by a classification system. While the regulations are not clear, it seems that to be of like-kind for an Exchange the property must be of the same use. Examples of like-kind non-depreciable personal property are Exchanges of major league sports contracts, non-currency bullion-type gold coins and gold bullion for Canadian maple leaf coins.

Non-depreciable personal property is another one of those areas that has gotten very little guidance from the regulations or the courts. Unless there is absolutely no room for argument, you're better off using an Intermediary who has a lot of experience in this area. There are Intermediaries who are competent to handle a gold bullion transaction, but there are only a couple who handle sports contract Exchanges. Stay away from an Intermediary who has no experience in your area of interest.

Handling Trade-ins in a 1031 Exchange

No doubt most of the personal property transactions that could be treated as Exchanges are not treated that way, and as a result taxpayers end up paying more tax, and paying it more quickly than they would if they treated the transactions as Exchanges.

For example, Fred needs a new delivery truck for his business. He goes to his dealership and picks out a New Truck for which he agrees to pay $35,000. The dealership agrees to give Fred $5,000 trade-in for his Old Truck which Fred has depreciated down to a basis of $0.

In most cases, this transaction is reported as the sale of the Old Truck with Fred paying tax on the $5,000 trade-in. At the same time, Fred records the purchase of the New Truck at its cost of $35,000, which becomes his depreciable basis. If Fred treated the transaction as an Exchange, his result would be much different. Fred would not pay tax on the trade-in, and his depreciable basis in the New Truck would be $30,000 (the basis in the Old Truck of $0 plus the buy-up of $30,000). This would save him a lot of tax dollars in the present, and although he would get less depreciation on the truck in the future, the annual difference would not be great in most cases. Fred's CPA merely would need to treat the transaction as an Exchange on Fred's tax return.

Identifying Personal Property on Your 45-Day List

Real estate is easy to describe – you have an address, a street, a city and a state. There seldom is much question as to what you've identified. Personal property is much harder. The regulations state that personal property must be unambiguously described. The regulations use the example of a truck and say that you meet this requirement of unambiguous if you describe the truck by specific make, model and year. While you have to be pretty clear about what you are identifying there is no requirement to identify a specific asset. Using the truck example, you would have to know what make, model and year of truck you were going to buy, but you wouldn't need the serial number of a specific truck.

If the type of property you want to buy doesn't have a specific make, model and year, meeting the identification becomes more difficult. Make sure that you have a first class Intermediary and then work closely with that person to make sure you meet the identification requirement.

The last thing about identifying personal property is that personal property Exchanges are also subject to the same three property or 200% identification rules as real estate Exchanges. In most personal property Exchanges, the property is part of a group of assets in the same class. As a result the three property rule will be essentially impossible to meet. As a practical matter you'll use the 200% identification rules when you do personal property Exchanges. For example, if you sold 10 pieces of equipment from your restaurant's kitchen for $100,000, you wouldn't identify 30 pieces of restaurant equipment as possible replacements. Instead, you would identify a list of restaurant equipment adding up to $200,000 or less.

180-Day Rule

In real estate you have 180 days after the sale of your Old Property in which to buy your New Property. Likewise, in personal property you also have 180 days in which to buy your New Property, but with New Property the property you buy should be placed into use by the 180th day. That means that if your New Property is a piece of manufacturing equipment, you need to add it to the processing line at the plant so that it is used in your manufacturing process by the end of the 180th day. Merely buying it and having it sit on the loading dock is not enough.

Ownership Issues

There are no differences between real estate and personal property in how you have to take title to your New Property.

Buy Equal or up and Reinvest All of the Proceeds

The rules on buying equal or up and reinvesting all of the cash are the same for personal property as for real estate. However, there is a subtle trap that you have to watch out for, and that is that you have to meet the rule for each SIC section.

Continuing our example from earlier sections, let's assume that in the restaurant that Fred and Sue are selling, there is a bar or lounge separate from the restaurant. They are selling the business for $100,000, but the contract breaks down the sales price as follows: sales price for the restaurant equipment, tables, chairs, decorations, etc. is $60,000 and sales price for the bar tables and chairs, bar fixtures, etc. is $40,000.

Fred and Sue do a 1031 Exchange and subsequently find a lounge for which they agree to pay $100,000. The lounge has a separate dining area, and so the purchase contract breaks down the items as follows: restaurant equipment, tables, chairs, decorations, etc. for $40,000 and sales price for the bar tables and chairs, bar fixtures, etc. for $60,000.

Even though they paid exactly the same price for the new lounge as they sold the old restaurant for, they are going to end up with $20,000 of taxable gain. Here's why: They sold the old SIC section 5812 property (the restaurant) for $60,000, but they are buying the new SIC section 5812 property for $40,000, which results in taxable gain of $20,000 even though the overall purchase price is the same.

Notice that for the SIC section 5813 property (the bar/lounge) they sold the Old Property for $40,000, and they are buying the New Property for $60,000. They bought up by $20,000. The $20,000 buy-down on the restaurant property is not offset by the $20,000 buy-up of the bar/lounge property even though it is all one transaction. The reason for this is that the two are different SIC sections.

Personal property exchanges, as you can see, can get very complex. Just make sure that you are working with a really good Intermediary who specializes in personal property Exchanges.

Chapter 19:
Mixed Use Exchanges

Mixed Use Exchanges are Exchanges that involve multiple components being sold. Sometimes they include both real estate and personal property. In other cases a Mixed Use Exchange can involve both 1031 property and non-1031 property.

Exchanges of Both Real Estate and Personal Property

In our example of Fred and Sue selling their restaurant and buying a lounge we were only talking about the personal property aspect of the transaction – the tables, chairs, equipment, etc. If we throw in the real estate component, the transaction becomes a "Mixed Use Exchange" (meaning it is part real estate and part personal property).

Let's assume that Fred and Sue are selling their restaurant for $200,000, which includes everything – the land and building, the restaurant and the bar/lounge. If they don't allocate a specific sales price for each of the pieces in the sales contract, the IRS could re-determine the allocation if it audits Fred and Sue. Some part of the sale could be allocated a larger price by the IRS and some parts a smaller price. If this happens, Fred and Sue will most certainly end up paying tax because they won't have purchased enough property to cover the Exchange of items allocated a larger sales price.

Let's say that Fred and Sue, outside of the contract, arbitrarily allocate a price of $100,000 to the land and building (which are real estate), $50,000 to the restaurant equipment (which is personal property) and $50,000 to the bar/lounge equipment (which is also personal property). When they purchased their New Property, Fred and Sue bought exactly as much property as they needed to cover their

Exchange ($100,000 of real estate and $50,000 each of restaurant and bar/lounge equipment). As far as Fred and Sue were concerned, and according to their tax return, they had covered their Exchange and had no gain or loss on the transaction.

Let's say that upon audit, the IRS decides that the land and building should have been valued at $80,000 (rather than $100,000) and the restaurant and bar/lounge equipment should have been valued at $60,000 each (rather than $50,000 each). This means that Fred and Sue sold their real estate for $80,000 and replaced it with Property worth $100,000. In other words, they bought up. But for both the restaurant and the bar/lounge equipment they sold for $60,000 and bought down for $50,000 resulting in a $10,000 gain on both the restaurant and bar/lounge equipment. In other words, Fred and Sue have a taxable gain of $20,000, on which they will most certainly pay recapture tax of 25 percent federal, plus state tax. Their tax bite will equal at least $5,000.

What Fred and Sue should do to protect themselves against this is to break the sale down into the separate components and assign a price to the land and building (which is real estate), the restaurant equipment (which is SIC section 5812 property) and the bar/lounge equipment (which is SIC section 5813 property).

It is important that each piece be assigned a price in the contract and that both the buyer and the seller follow the allocations in their tax returns. If Fred and Sue do this, it is almost impossible for the IRS to allocate the sale different than they and the buyer did.

Assigned values should be clearly stated in the body of the contract or in an attachment to the contract. If you already have a signed contract on a transaction with which you are involved, prepare an addendum or an amendment to the contract, signed by both the buyer and seller, before the transaction closes.

Once again, if the buyer and seller both agree, in the contract, about the values of the individual pieces, the IRS really has no power to change these values. The courts almost always agree with the buyers and sellers on the values they determine in arm's length negotiations.

A suggestion that we make to our clients in situations like this is to show the different allocations on the Settlement Statement. The Settlement Statement in a closing is the document with all the numbers. Most places in the country we see Settlement Statements with both the buyer and seller's information on the same statement. We would suggest that the Settlement Statement from the above example show the sale of the real estate for $100,000 and then separately the sale of the restaurant and bar/lounge equipment for $50,000 each so that there is no question that the parties agreed to the allocation. The allocation is also clear to the CPAs of both parties, which minimizes the chance that one of them could screw it up.

If you don't agree as to the allocation of the values or if you have an allocation in the contract, but you don't follow it, the IRS is free to reallocate the sale however it wants. For this reason we really push our clients to get the allocations in writing and agreed to by both the buyer and seller. Frequently, the seller and buyer don't agree about how each item should be allocated. Their tax motives are different.

One last thing before I move on, and that is that my examples in this book have over-simplified the normal transaction in order to teach you the concepts in a way that makes sense. In real life, these types of transactions are much more complicated and often involve subjects like the transfer of licenses, covenants-not-to-compete, inventory, customer lists, etc. They can get tremendously complicated and you need to get your CPA, your real estate agent and a first class Exchange Intermediary involved before you get, or at least accept, an offer on your property.

Get your ducks in a row before you start, and make sure you are crystal clear what the different components are for your Exchange. Make sure you (and each member of your team) understand the tax options and ramifications for each component. Otherwise you could wind up getting burned bad by taxes.

Exchanges of 1031 Property and Non-1031 Property

Sometimes, not all of the property you are selling qualifies for a 1031 Exchange. Typically these types of Exchanges involve property that is part investment real estate, and part personal residence. We generally see three of these types of personal use properties: multi-dwelling units, farms and ranches, and business use of part of the home.

Section 121. Before I begin an explanation of each of these types of mixed use properties, I need to explain a different IRS Code section – Section 121. This IRS Code section provides that if you have occupied your residence for at least two years out of the five years that precede its sale, up to $250,000 of the gain if you are single ($500,000 if you are married) is tax-free.

Multi-Dwelling Units: Involve buildings with more than one dwelling unit, one of which is occupied by the taxpayer as his or her principal residence. The building could be a duplex with one of the units occupied by the seller and the other unit a rental unit. Or it could be a four-plex with one of the units occupied by the seller and the other three units as rental units. In other words, one of the units is Section 121 property, and the other(s) is Section 1031 property.

Your allocation of the purchase price for the sale has to be consistent with the allocation you used when you filed your income tax returns on the property, but if you follow this allocation, part of the sale will be tax-free in Section 121, and the balance could be a 1031 Exchange. For example, on the four-plex, approximately 1/4 of the sale will be the sale of your personal residence under Section 121, and the other 3/4 of the sale a 1031 Exchange. And to avoid any confusion in the Exchange we recommend that you have two seller's Settlement Statement at the close – one for the sale of the residence part and one for the sale of the 1031 property.

Assume that Fred and Sue are selling their four-plex for $400,000. They have lived in one of the units for more than two years, and the other three units have been rented during that time. At the closing of the sale, there would be one Settlement Statement for the sale of the Section 121 property (Fred and Sue's residence) for $100,000. This money is theirs, tax-free, to do with as they wish. The second Settlement Statement would show the sale of the 1031 property for $300,000. This is the equal-or-up number for the Exchange (before closing costs, etc.).

Farms and Ranches. The typical farm or ranch includes a residence surrounded by farm or ranch land. The law generally provides that the sale of a personal residence does not include the surrounding land if the land was used in a business or held for investment. Since a farm or a ranch is a business, you cannot include the farm or ranch land in the $250,000/$500,000 exclusion under Section 121. It does qualify for a 1031 Exchange, however.

Rarely is there an allocation between the value of the residence and the value of the farm and ranch portion of the land, so confusion is common because of the values at the time of the sale. You could have the house appraised separately, or you could do an allocation of the components of the sale similar to the allocation we do in sales involving personal property (as I discussed above).

Your objective if you do a separate allocation is to allocate as much of the sales price to the personal residence as you can, because the gain, up to the maximum limits, is tax-free. You can do what you wish with the cash, and you don't have to buy any replacement property.

Let's say Fred and Sue are selling their ranch for $1.25 million. They and the buyer negotiate an allocation of this amount as follows:

$500,000 for the residence, $350,000 for the ranch equipment, $250,000 for the out-buildings and $150,000 for the land. The value of the residence is probably higher than it is really worth so that Fred and Sue can maximize their Section 121 exclusion.

What I suggest in this situation is to allocate the purchase price in the sales contract. Even better, if the buyer will accommodate Fred and Sue, I would suggest that there be two contracts – one for the sale of the residence for $500,000 and the second for the sale of the ranch for $750,000. Either way, at the closing Fred and Sue want to end up with two Settlement Statements – one for the sale of the residence and one for the sale of the ranch. Handling the sale this way will be a huge firewall between Fred and Sue and the IRS.

Business Use of Part of the Home. The IRS regulations contain a number of examples of 1031 Exchanges where there is a business use of part of the home. The classic example is for an office in the home.

For example, let's say Fred and Sue are selling their home for $200,000. Fred has had his real estate office in the basement of the home for the last several years, and the CPA has allocated 25 percent of the house to his office. Therefore, when Fred and Sue close the sale, 25 percent (or $50,000) of the sale is 1031 property and 75 percent (or $150,000) is tax-free to them under Section 121.

The 1031 portion must be rolled over into the purchase of other investment property. Presumably it will be the portion of Fred and Sue's new residence that they will set aside for Fred's new office, but it could be any other type of investment property. Fred and Sue just need to make sure that the $50,000 Exchange value covers the value of the new office. For example, if the new house costs them $300,000 and Fred's office is 20 percent of this house (or $60,000) the Exchange will be covered. But if the office only comprises 15 percent ($45,000) of the new house, Fred and Sue will pay tax on the $5,000 buy-down.

A variation of this type of Exchange that gets really complicated is an Exchange involving a bed-and-breakfast. In the typical B&B, the owner(s) live in a portion of the house and rent out bedrooms on a nightly basis. Right off the bat we have an allocation issue between the portion of the real estate that is occupied by the owners (which is Section 121 property) and the business portion of the real estate. But the thing that makes most B&B transactions difficult, at least with the ones that we've handled, is that the furnishings of the house are usually antiques. These furnishings are personal property that is being purchased by the buyer also. These furnishings are usually worth a lot of money so the buyer wants to allocate their value to them, if not more, because they can be depreciated much quicker than the real estate can. The problem is that because the furnishings represent personal property, to avoid paying tax on the sale the seller must do a 1031 Exchange into similar furnishings. Sellers seldom want to do this and see the sale instead as their way to get out of the B&B business. As a result, a substantial portion of the sale will be taxable.

Chapter 20:
Exchanges of U.S. Real Estate by Nonresidents

Section 1031 is a U.S. Tax Code that governs the sale of property within the borders of the United States. Some of this real estate is owned by people (and entities) who are not residents of the United States.

Types of Foreign Persons

There are two simple classes of foreign persons: the first class includes those who live here (typically called "resident aliens"). These people typically have green cards and usually work here. They have tax identification numbers (like social security numbers) and file U.S. income tax returns. Then there are those who come to this country periodically for visits then leave. They are called "nonresident aliens." Of course, they don't have U.S. tax numbers and they don't file tax returns. Some of these people own real estate in the U.S. The IRS calls these nonresident alien owners of U.S. property "Foreign Persons," even if the owners are corporations, partnerships, etc.

Many Europeans get a month vacation and like to take that vacation in the United States during the winter. For this reason they may own a home there. In our southern Florida offices we see a lot of property owned by Europeans, especially Germans. We see similar patterns in other parts of the country as well. The Miami area has a large number of properties owned by South Americans. The mountain communities of Vail, Aspen, etc. have a large number of properties owned by Mexican and Canadian citizens. Hawaii, not surprisingly, has a large Asian ownership.

Withholding Is on the Sales Price

When these foreign owners sell their U.S. real estate they are subject to FIRPTA (Foreign Investment in Real Property Tax Act) withholding. FIRPTA is actually a withholding, or advance payment, of the tax. The rate of this withholding is 10 percent of the sales price, regardless of whether the sellers had real gain or not and regardless of the amount of the gain. In many states there is also a similar state withholding that is imposed on out-of-state residents.

For illustration, a nonresident Japanese couple who bought a condo in Hawaii at the top of the market for $1.5 million and then sold it several years later at the bottom of the market for $1 million, would still be subject to FIRPTA withholding of $100,000 (10 percent of the selling price) when they sold it – even though they had a real loss of $500,000.

FIRPTA Can Be Avoided by Doing an Exchange

Nonresidents can avoid paying the FIRPTA tax, as well as most of the taxes imposed by some states on out-of-state sellers, by doing a 1031 Exchange. While you typically would not do a 1031 Exchange if you have a loss, the Japanese couple in the above example very likely would simply to avoid having to pay the $100,000 FIRPTA withholding. It is simpler to do an Exchange than to not do the Exchange, pay the FIRPTA withholding and then file the appropriate U.S. tax forms to get the withholding back.

The rule covering 1031 Exchanges by foreign persons is the same as those for U.S. citizens, with the exception of several special rules:

U.S. Tax Identification Number Requirement

First, since November 2003, the IRS now requires that every foreign person who sells U.S. real estate must have a U.S. Taxpayer Identification Number. This is part of the Homeland Security changes – it's O.K. to own real estate in the U.S., but the government now wants to know who you are.

Individuals apply for this identification number on IRS Form W-7. A business would use IRS Form SS-4. The closing attorney or title company will typically not close the sale until this number is obtained, whether you do a 1031 Exchange or not.

Withholding Exemption Requirement

Once the foreign person has a tax identification number, that person must apply for a withholding certificate for exemption from the FIRPTA withholding. This withholding certificate is applied for on IRS Form 8288-B. This application must include the U.S. tax identification number, so typically that has to be applied for before the withholding certificate can be applied for.

The last thing a foreign person has to be careful of is that in order to avoid the application of the FIRPTA withholding, he or she has to buy New Property at least equal in price to the sales price of the Old Property. If the person fails to do so, the full FIRPTA withholding applies.

For example, our Japanese couple who sold their Hawaii condo for $1 million must buy replacement property at least equal to $1 million to avoid the withholding. If they buy their replacement property for $999,000 (in other words, they bought down by $1,000), the entire FIRPTA withholding of $100,000 will apply.

You Can Be Liable if the Intermediary Doesn't Pay Withholding

If you are a U.S. citizen buying from a foreign person doing a 1031 Exchange, you can be held liable if the Intermediary does not pay the FIRPTA withholding to the government. You have liability, but you probably have no control over the Intermediary the seller has picked. My advice here is to get an Indemnification Letter from the Intermediary that says that if the Intermediary doesn't pay the FIRPT withholding to the IRS, and the IRS comes after you, you have recourse against the Intermediary. If you're lucky, the Intermediary will realize at this point that the deal is over his or her head, and you might be able to steer the seller to a more knowledgeable Intermediary.

Of course, a foreign person who sells U.S. real estate and does a 1031 Exchange must buy the replacement property within the United States.

Chapter 21:
How to Turn Exchange Property into Cash With Little or No Tax

Most people think of 1031 Exchanges as simply a way to defer the tax on the sale of their real estate. If they believe this, they totally miss the vast flexibility of an Exchange – though the deferral all by itself is a pretty big incentive.

To demonstrate the power of the deferral, let's say you're selling your Old Property for $100,000. And let's say this property is free of debts, and that your taxable gain on this property is $60,000. To keep the comparison with an Exchange reasonable, let's assume that you intend to buy another piece of property. If you sell the Old Property and don't do an Exchange, you're tax on the gain will run at least 25 percent of the $60,000 gain ($15,000). I'm assuming some federal depreciation recapture and some state tax, but even if this were bare land, with no depreciation, and you live in a state with no state tax, like Florida, you'll still pay 15 percent. (Think of depreciation recapture as the payback of depreciation deductions you've taken on your rental property. You pay these depreciation deductions back at a different tax rate than the rate on long-term capital gains).

If you use the cash from the sale as the equity on the purchase of your New Property and you decide to borrow $2 for every $1 you put down as equity (in other words a 66 percent loan), losing the $15,000 to taxes will decrease the buying power on your New Property by $45,000 ($15,000 of cash equity and $30,000 of new borrowing). In other words, because you didn't do an Exchange you'll end up buying $45,000 less property than you could have if you had chosen the 1031 route.

If your property appreciates at 5 percent per year, in ten years the additional $45,000 will have appreciated to about $73,000. Of course you'll have to pay back the additional loan of $30,000, which means that your $15,000 will have grown to $43,000. In other words, doing a 1031 Exchange and not paying the tax allows you to almost triple, in ten years, your cash equity dollars. You're making money off the government's money. Now that's a switch!

You can argue with my assumptions all you want, (maybe it will only appreciate at 4 percent a year, and maybe you feel more comfortable with a 50 percent loan) but the fact remains that doing a 1031 Exchange allows you to make money off the tax you would have paid had you not done an Exchange.

Interplay With Section 121 – Sale of Your Personal Residence

Let's get back to ways that you can sell real estate with little or no tax. Savvy real estate investors use two completely different IRS Code sections to avoid all, or almost all of the tax on the sale of their real estate. Code section 1031 (which is the subject of this book) rolls the gain from the sale of your old investment property into your new investment property, and Section 121 provides that all, or a portion of, the gain from the sale of a residence that you have occupied for at least two of the last five years could be tax-free.

Many of you are familiar with Section 121 – this is the law that governs the sale of your home (your personal residence). Section 121, as you recall, requires that your house be your personal residence for two of the last five years. Did you ever wonder what it was the other three years? Exactly – very likely it was Section 1031 investment property. These two Code sections overlap and used together can be a very powerful tool.

Section 121 says that if you meet the two of the last five year requirement of a house as your primary residence and then sell it, the first $250,000 of gain if you're single ($500,000 of gain if you're married) is tax-free. Congress just amended Section 121 to provide that if you buy the residence as rollover property in a 1031 Exchange, you have to own it for five years in order to take the Section 121 exclusion. In effect, this amendment increases your holding period two years because prior to the amendment you had to hold the property for three years (a year and a day to meet the 1031 Exchange requirements and 24 months to meet the Section 121 requirements).

To summarize the new law, the day you take title to the New Property starts the five-year holding period. The first year and a day the property has to be investment property to meet the requirements of Section

1031. Then, during the following four years you have to occupy the property as your primary residence for at least 24 months.

In other words, you sold your Old Property, and you did a 1031 Exchange. For your New Property you buy a house that you wouldn't mind living in. This New Property has to be investment property for at least a year and a day to qualify as your replacement property for the 1031 Exchange. To meet this requirement you lease, or try to lease, the New Property during that period.

Once you have met your 1031 replacement requirement of a year and a day, you have four years left before you sell the residence and take your Section 121 exclusion. Any time during this period you can move into the new house and make it your replacement property. And the day you move in marks the beginning of your two-year residence requirement.

We advise our clients to take a number of steps to document the start of the two-year residence requirement: Change your drivers license to the new residence. Register to vote at that address. Change your credit card, as well as your tax return mailing address. Get a library card, etc. Failure to do these things allows the IRS to question your starting date.

Let's take a real life example: Fred and Sue sell their purple four-plex near their home in Minneapolis for $600,000. They have a gain of $400,000, which they defer by doing a 1031 Exchange into a nice house on a golf course in Scottsdale, Arizona that they buy for $600,000. This completes their Exchange and starts the five-year holding period required under Section 121 (because they bought the residence as rollover 1031 property). Then they rent the golf course property out for the following year and a day, which confirms that the New Property is investment property. After the year and a day holding period, Fred retires. He and Sue sell their Minneapolis home (the one they've been living in for years) and pocket the gain of $500,000 tax free. They then move to Scottsdale and move into their Scottsdale rental house. This then starts their new two-year residence holding period. After two years of living there, they can continue to live there or they can move into another residence – either way they have to wait out the five-year holding period. Once the five years is up, they decide to sell the Scottsdale house, which they do for $700,000. Their gain when they sell the Scottsdale house is $500,000, which is comprised of the $400,000 rollover gain from the sale of their Minneapolis four-plex and $100,000 appreciation in the value of the Scottsdale house.

This $500,000 is tax-free under Section 121, because the Scottsdale house meets the two-year residency requirement and the five-year holding period. And the $500,000 is tax-free even though the majority of the gain is rollover gain from the 1031 Exchange. In fact, the only tax Fred and Sue will pay on this transaction is tax on the recapture of any depreciation they took on either property after May of 1997 when the tax laws changed. Depreciation they took before that is not recaptured.

In a very short period of time, Fred and Sue were able to turn $1 million of real estate gain into tax-free cash. There is no requirement for them to reinvest the gain under Section 121. This gain, and the cash, is tax-free forever.

What if the Gain on the Sale of Your Residence Exceeds $500,000?

Because of the astounding appreciation of property values in some parts of the country, we're getting more calls every day from clients whose gain on their residences exceeds $500,000. And, as we tell them yes, there is a way to turn a gain this large into cash and not pay tax.

First, let's make sure that we are all on the same page. Section 1031 involves rolling the gain from one investment property to another. You have to buy another investment property.

Section 121, as we've discussed, is a different Code section, which allows you to take $500,000 ($250,000 if you are single) of the gain tax-free on the sale of your personal residence. You don't have to buy a replacement residence, but you are limited to $500,000 (assuming that you are married) in gain. What do you do if your gain is greater than that? Is there a way to get all of the gain tax-free? Yes, but it involves several steps, and it's done by combining Section 121 and Section 1031 of the Internal Revenue Code.

The first thing you must do is to turn your residence into investment property. This means that you must move out of the house and try to rent it. Notice that I didn't say you have to rent it. You merely must try to rent it.

After you move out you have a period of a year and a day during which you rent or try to rent your property. After the year and a day is up you can sell it, but you only want to do a 1031 Exchange on the amount of the gain that exceeds $500,000 (assuming that you are married). The balance of the gain is tax-free under Section 121. The important technical consideration here is that you are not required to do a 1031 Exchange on the entire property – you can do it on just a portion if you wish.

So, as an example, let's assume that Fred and Sue are thinking of selling their home in Minneapolis. This is their home that they've lived in for many years. The value of the home is $1 million, of which the gain is $750,000. Obviously this gain is in excess of their exclusion under Section 121. If they don't want to pay tax on any of the gain, the first thing they need to do is to move out of the house and rent it (or try to rent it) for the following year and a day.

Once the year-and-a-day investment period is up, Fred and Sue sell the house for $1 million (with its $750,000 gain). They've lived in the house for four of the last five years, so they meet the requirement of Section 121. And they've rented the house for the last year and a day, so they also meet the requirements of Section 1031.

To get them where they want to be, Fred and Sue first take their Section 121 exclusion of $500,000 on the sale. They want to take this first because this amount is tax-free (you always want to take the tax free money off the table first). This leaves them with a remaining gain of $250,000, and this is the part that we have them do a 1031 Exchange on. Of course they must buy a replacement property for this Exchange, and most likely they will choose to reinvest in a rental house that they could live in someday – as they did in the example above. There is no limit to the number of times you can use Section 121 (the sale of your personal residence) over a lifetime, but you can't use it more than once every two years.

Leaving a Legacy

We, like other good Intermediaries, are frequently called upon to help our clients structure their Exchanges in order to implement some part of their estate plans. A really good Intermediary will meet with you to go over your plan and point out ways that an Exchange can help you accomplish your goals.

I've given you some examples of ways to turn real estate into tax-free cash. Now let's look at an example of how you could leave some property to your heirs as part of your estate plan – a legacy, if you will.

Let's go back to Fred and Sue. They are older now, and they own a large apartment complex, with no debt, worth $3 million. Like many of our clients, they are tired of the management hassles and simply want out. They would like some cash to make the rest of their lives comfortable, and yet their primary concern is that they leave a legacy to ease the lives of their grandchildren.

The first thing they need to do, of course, is sell the apartment complex and do a 1031 Exchange. Their New Property will be what real estate experts call a "triple-net-lease" property. A triple-net-lease property is one where the tenant pays all of the expenses associated with the property: the maintenance, insurance, property taxes, etc. Since the tenant pays all the expenses, the property owner typically has no obligations to the property and merely receives a monthly check for the rent. A good example of a net-lease-property might be a Wal-Mart store, for example.

So Fred and Sue buy a Wal-Mart building for $3 million as their replacement property, and they enter into a lease with Wal-Mart for 30 years. Because they had no debt on their Old Property, Fred and Sue's New Property is also free and clear.

The next step for Fred and Sue is for them to go to the bank and borrow against the Wal-Mart property. Generally the amount they are able to borrow is based upon the interest rate the bank will charge for the loan. What typically happens in these situations is that the bank calculates the amount of loan that creates a monthly loan payment approximately equal to the amount of monthly rental income paid by Wal-Mart on the lease. Typically, Wal-Mart would then send its monthly lease payment directly to the bank, rather than to Fred and Sue.

Let's assume that our plan calculates out to a loan of $2.5 million. There are no tax ramifications to Fred and Sue when they take this loan. So at this point they own a $3 million building and have $2.5 million in tax-free cash. We could stop there, but let's take it one more step and see what happens.

To go to the next level, Fred and Sue take the $2.5 million cash and buy a second triple-net-lease property. Let's say they buy a building with a 30-year lease to Home Depot. Again, they borrow against this lease, and let's assume that they are able to borrow $2 million against it – again tax-free.

At this point Fred and Sue decide that they have achieved their objective: they have $2 million in cash (tax-free) and they have $5.5 million in property that will pass to their heirs after their deaths.

Using Section 1031 to Transfer Property to Your Heirs

There are a number of ways that Section 1031 can be used to transfer property to your heirs. A simple one involves the parents selling their Old Property and buying New Property with the intent to pass the New Property to their heirs after their deaths. The New Property(s) are purchased with the intent that the heirs will ultimately own it/them.

For example, Fred and Sue have three adult children: One is a lawyer in San Francisco; the second is a doctor in Chicago; and the third is a teacher in Boston. Fred and Sue sell their Old Property for $300,000 and do a 1031 Exchange and buy three New Properties for $100,000 each.

The San Francisco daughter is starting her career, can use extra income, but has no extra time to manage property, so the first property they buy as a replacement property is in the San Francisco Bay area, has good rental income but requires minimal management.

The Chicago son is well established in his medical practice with an income that puts him in the highest tax bracket. He doesn't need additional income but would like something destined to grow in value. To accomplish the investment desires of this son, Fred and Sue buy a piece of bare land in an excellent location in the Chicago area.

The Boston daughter and her husband (also a teacher) love home improvement projects. Having summers off makes it natural for them to buy distressed property that they can fix up and add substantial value to. Fred and Sue, therefore, buy a distressed rental house as their third replacement property close to where their daughter and son-in-law live.

The intent of buying these three properties is to buy properties that are tailored for each of the children in type and location. Fred and Sue, of course, are the owners of each property and are responsible for the income and expenses of that property, but upon their death each property will pass to that specific child. The San Francisco daughter would get the Bay Area property, the Chicago doctor the bare land, etc.

Transferring Equity to Your Heirs Tax-Free

Building upon the prior example, you can use Section 1031 to transfer property to your heirs tax-free. The way we do this is to have the heirs (let's assume that the heirs are the owners' offspring) be co-owners in the property. As each property is sold, the parents, and the kids do 1031 Exchanges – but the difference is that the parents do an Exchange into an equal dollar amount of property, while the children also do Exchanges, but buy up.

Assume that Fred and Sue (the parents) sell their Old Property for $500,000 and do a 1031 Exchange into a 50 percent interest in Property A, which costs $1 million. The other 50 percent is bought by their children. Property A, therefore, is owned 50 percent by Fred and Sue and the other 50 percent by their children.

Does it matter that Fred and Sue sold 100 percent of their Old Property and purchased 50 percent of Property A? No, but to not pay any tax they have to buy equal or up, which they did. They also have to take title to Property A in the same name in which they held title to their Old Property, which they did. So Fred and Sue have a good Exchange.

Several years later they sell Property A for $1.5 million and buy Property B for $2 million. Fred and Sue's share of Property A is $750,000. They do a 1031 Exchange and just buy equal in dollars. In other words, they buy a $750,000 interest in Property B, which satisfies their Exchange. Meanwhile, the kids also do a 1031 Exchange, but they buy up from $750,000 to $1.25 million. When the dust settles, Fred and Sue own a 37.5 percent ($750,000) interest in Property B, and the kids own a 62.5 percent ($1,250,000) share.

If they sell Property B for $3 million, Fred and Sue's share (at 37.5 percent) is worth $1,125,000. The replacement property is Property C, which is being purchased for $4 million, so Fred and Sue do a 1031 Exchange and again buy exactly equal, which means that they buy a 28 percent interest in Property C for $1,125,000. The kids' share of the sale of Property B is $1,875,000, and they also do a 1031 Exchange, but they buy up to a 72 percent share of Property C, which they purchase for $2,875,000.

To summarize where we are, Fred and Sue own 28% of Property C at a cost of $1,125,000. The kids own the balance of 72%, and their cost is $2,875,000.

If Fred and Sue were to die at this point, their ownership in Property C is considered a "minority interest." Because it is a minority interest, their share of Property C is valued at a reduced rate in their estate return. The amount of their reduction will be determined by their CPA when he prepares the estate return, but it is likely that the reduction will be at least 30 percent and could exceed 50 percent. This means that it is possible that Fred and Sue's estate would pay little or no estate tax on Property C.

Fred and Sue's share of Property C will then pass to their children, who now own 100 percent of Property C, which is worth at least $4 million. And the end result is that the children own 100 percent with no capital gains, and virtually no estate tax having been paid on the property. Had Fred and Sue owned all of Property C when they died, it is likely that substantial estate tax would have been due.

Chapter 22:
Conclusion

If you've worked your way through this book, you've learned the critical parts of an Exchange: Both the Old Property and the New Property have to be held for investment, and you cannot hold them for resale. And you've learned the difference between "held for investment" and "held for resale."

You've learned that you have 45 days from the closing of the sale of your Old Property to submit a list of properties that you might buy, and you've learned that you want to keep this list to three properties or fewer.

You've learned that you have 180 days from the sale of your Old Property to complete the purchase of your New Property and that whatever you buy has to be on your 45-Day List. And you've learned that both the 45-day and 180-day requirements are calendar days. You've learned that there are no extensions to these requirements.

You've learned that you cannot touch the money in between the sale of your Old Property and the purchase of your New Property and that you must use a Qualified Intermediary to handle your Exchange. You've learned what to look for in an Intermediary, and most importantly, you've learned that they absolutely must hold your money in an account separate from everyone else.

You've learned that how you hold title to the Old Property is how you have to take title to the New Property. You've learned how to structure the ownership of your property to avoid problems with this, and you've learned how to identify and work through the problems if they do arise. And you've learned what disregarded entities are and how to use them to your advantage.

You've learned that in order to have no tax liability in your Exchange you must do two things: You must buy equal or up, and you must reinvest all of the cash. And you've learned what happens if you buy down or if you end up with unspent cash.

If you had stopped there, and hadn't read the rest of the book you still would have known more than 95 percent of the CPAs and attorneys about Exchanges. But you didn't stop there, because you'd only scratched the surface. To really supercharge your investment plan, you learned about Reverse, Construction and Improvement Exchanges, because this is where the big dogs make the really big dollars.

You've also learned that after you build your real estate empire, there are many ways you can legitimately use current tax laws to turn your real estate empire into cash or transfer it to your heirs, with little or no tax.

Don't be afraid of 1031 Exchanges. Thousands of Exchanges are handled every day in the United States. Find yourself a good Intermediary, one who will guide you and keep you from getting into trouble, and you'll be fine.

Good luck!

Appendix A

Complete Copy of IRS Section 1031

Internal Revenue Code
Section 1031

TITLE 26--INTERNAL REVENUE CODE

Subtitle A--Income Taxes

CHAPTER 1--NORMAL TAXES AND SURTAXES

Subchapter O--Gain or Loss on Disposition of Property

PART III--COMMON NONTAXABLE EXCHANGES

Sec. 1031. Exchange of property held for productive use or investment

(a) Nonrecognition of gain or loss from exchanges solely in kind

(1) In general

No gain or loss shall be recognized on the exchange of property held for productive use in a trade or business or for investment if such property is exchanged solely for property of like kind which is to be held either for productive use in a trade or business or for investment.

(2) Exception

This subsection shall not apply to any exchange of--
    (A) stock in trade or other property held primarily for sale,
    (B) stocks, bonds, or notes,
    (C) other securities or evidences of indebtedness or interest,
    (D) interests in a partnership,
    (E) certificates of trust or beneficial interests, or
    (F) choses in action.

For purposes of this section, an interest in a partnership which has in effect a valid election under section 761(a) to be excluded from the application of all of subchapter K shall be treated as an interest in each of the assets of such partnership and not as an interest in a partnership.

(3) Requirement that property be identified and that exchange be completed not more than 180 days after transfer of exchanged property

For purposes of this subsection, any property received by the taxpayer shall be treated as property which is not like-kind property if--

   (A) such property is not identified as property to be received in the exchange on or before the day which is 45 days after the date on which the taxpayer transfers the property relinquished in the exchange, or

   (B) such property is received after the earlier of--

      (i) the day which is 180 days after the date on which the taxpayer transfers the property relinquished in the exchange, or

      (ii) the due date (determined with regard to extension) for the transferor's return of the tax imposed by this chapter for the taxable year in which the transfer of the relinquished property occurs.

(b) Gain from exchanges not solely in kind

If an exchange would be within the provisions of subsection (a), of section 1035(a), of section 1036(a), or of section 1037(a), if it were not for the fact that the property received in exchange consists not only of property permitted by such provisions to be received without the recognition of gain, but also of other property or money, then the gain, if any, to the recipient shall be recognized, but in an amount not in excess of the sum of such money and the fair market value of such other property.

(c) Loss from exchanges not solely in kind

If an exchange would be within the provisions of subsection (a), of section 1035(a), of section 1036(a), or of section 1037(a), if it were not for the fact that the property received in exchange consists not only of property permitted by such provisions to be received without the recognition of gain or loss, but also of other property or money, then no loss from the exchange shall be recognized.

(d) Basis

If property was acquired on an exchange described in this section, section 1035(a), section 1036(a), or section 1037(a), then the basis shall be the same as that of the property exchanged, decreased in the amount of any money received by the taxpayer and increased in the amount of gain or decreased in the amount of loss to the taxpayer that was recognized on such exchange. If the property so acquired consisted in part of the type of property permitted by this section, section 1035(a), section 1036(a), or section 1037(a), to be received without the recognition of gain or loss, and in part of other property, the basis provided in this subsection shall be allocated between the properties (other than money) received, and for the purpose of the allocation there shall be assigned to such other property an amount equivalent to its fair market value at the date of the exchange. For purposes of this section, section 1035(a), and section 1036(a), where as part of the consideration to the taxpayer another party to the exchange assumed (as determined under section 357(d)) a liability of the taxpayer, such assumption shall be considered as money received by the taxpayer on the exchange.

(e) Exchanges of livestock of different sexes

For purposes of this section, livestock of different sexes are not property of a like kind.

(f) Special rules for exchanges between related persons

(1) In general

If--
   (A) a taxpayer exchanges property with a related person,
   (B) there is nonrecognition of gain or loss to the taxpayer under this section with respect to the exchange of such property (determined without regard to this subsection), and
   (C) before the date 2 years after the date of the last transfer which was part of such exchange--
      (i) the related person disposes of such property, or
      (ii) the taxpayer disposes of the property received in the exchange from the related person which was of like kind to the property transferred by the taxpayer,

there shall be no nonrecognition of gain or loss under this section to the taxpayer with respect to such exchange; except that any gain or loss recognized by the taxpayer by reason of this subsection shall be taken into account as of the date on which the disposition referred to in subparagraph (C) occurs.

(2) Certain dispositions not taken into account

For purposes of paragraph (1)(C), there shall not be taken into account any disposition--
   (A) after the earlier of the death of the taxpayer or the death of the related person,
   (B) in a compulsory or involuntary conversion (within the meaning of section 1033) if the exchange occurred before

the threat or imminence of such conversion, or

(C) with respect to which it is established to the satisfaction of the Secretary that neither the exchange nor such disposition had as one of its principal purposes the avoidance of Federal income tax.

(3) Related person

For purposes of this subsection, the term ``related person'' means any person bearing a relationship to the taxpayer described in section 267(b) or 707(b)(1).

(4) Treatment of certain transactions

This section shall not apply to any exchange which is part of a transaction (or series of transactions) structured to avoid the purposes of this subsection.

(g) Special rule where substantial diminution of risk

(1) In general

If paragraph (2) applies to any property for any period, the running of the period set forth in subsection (f)(1)(C) with respect to such property shall be suspended during such period.

(2) Property to which subsection applies

This paragraph shall apply to any property for any period during which the holder's risk of loss with respect to the property is substantially diminished by--

(A) the holding of a put with respect to such property,

(B) the holding by another person of a right to acquire such property, or

(C) a short sale or any other transaction.

(h) Special rules for foreign real and personal property

For purposes of this section--

(1) Real property

Real property located in the United States and real property located outside the United States are not property of a like kind.

(2) Personal property

(A) In general
Personal property used predominantly within the United States and personal property used predominantly outside the United States are not property of a like kind.

(B) Predominant use
Except as provided in subparagraph \1\ (C) and (D), the predominant use of any property shall be determined based on--
(i) in the case of the property relinquished in the exchange, the 2-year period ending on the date of such relinquishment, and
(ii) in the case of the property acquired in the exchange, the 2-year period beginning on the date of such acquisition.

(C) Property held for less than 2 years
Except in the case of an exchange which is part of a transaction (or series of transactions) structured to avoid the purposes of this subsection--
(i) only the periods the property was held by the person relinquishing the property (or any related person) shall be taken into account under subparagraph (B)(i), and
(ii) only the periods the property was held by the person acquiring the property (or any related person) shall be taken into account under subparagraph (B)(ii).

(D) Special rule for certain property
Property described in any subparagraph of section 168(g)(4) shall be treated as used predominantly in the United States.

Appendix B
Complete Copy of the Regulations
for Section 1031

Regulations for Section 1031

TITLE 26--INTERNAL REVENUE

CHAPTER I--INTERNAL REVENUE SERVICE, DEPARTMENT OF THE TREASURY (CONTINUED)

PART 1--INCOME TAXES--Table of Contents

Sec. 1.1031-0 Table of contents.

This section lists the captions that appear in the regulations under section 1031.

Sec. 1.1031(a)-1 Property held for productive use in a trade or business or for investment.

(a) In general.
(b) Definition of ``like kind."
(c) Examples of exchanges of property of a ``like kind."
(d) Examples of exchanges not solely in kind.
(e) Effective date.

Sec. 1.1031(a)-2 Additional rules for exchanges of personal property.

(a) Introduction.
(b) Depreciable tangible personal property.
(c) Intangible personal property and nondepreciable personal property.

Sec. 1.1031(b)-1 Receipt of other property or money in tax-free exchange.

Sec. 1.1031(b)-2 Safe harbor for qualified intermediaries.

Sec. 1.1031(c)-1 Nonrecognition of loss.

Sec. 1.1031(d)-1 Property acquired upon a tax-free exchange.

Sec. 1.1031(d)-1T Coordination of section 1060 with section 1031 (temporary).

Sec. 1.1031(d)-2 Treatment of assumption of liabilities.

Sec. 1.1031(e)-1 Exchanges of livestock of different sexes.

Sec. 1.1031(j)-1 Exchanges of multiple properties.

    (a) Introduction.
    (b) Computation of gain recognized.
    (c) Computation of basis of properties received.
    (d) Examples.
    (e) Effective date.

Sec. 1.1031(K)-1 Treatment of deferred exchanges.

    (a) Overview.
    (b) Identification and receipt requirements.
    (c) Identification of replacement property before the end of the identification period.
    (d) Receipt of identified replacement property.
    (e) Special rules for identification and receipt of replacement property to be produced.
    (f) Receipt of money or other property.
    (g) Safe harbors.
    (h) Interest and growth factors.
    (i) [Reserved]
    (j) Determination of gain or loss recognized and the basis of property received in a deferred exchange.
    (k) Definition of disqualified person.
    (l) [Reserved]
    (m) Definition of fair market value.
    (n) No inference with respect to actual or constructive receipt rules outside of section 1031.
    (o) Effective date.

TITLE 26--INTERNAL REVENUE

CHAPTER I--INTERNAL REVENUE SERVICE, DEPARTMENT OF THE TREASURY (CONTINUED)

PART 1--INCOME TAXES--Table of Contents

Sec. 1.1031(a)-1 Property held for productive use in trade or business or for investment.

(a) In general--

(1) Exchanges of property solely for property of a like kind. Section 1031(a)(1) provides an exception from the general rule requiring the recognition of gain or loss upon the sale or exchange of property. Under section 1031(a)(1), no gain or loss is recognized if property held for productive use in a trade or business or for investment is exchanged solely for property of a like kind to be held either for productive use in a trade or business or for investment. Under section 1031(a)(1), property held for productive use in a trade or business may be exchanged for property held for investment. Similarly, under section 1031(a)(1), property held for investment may be exchanged for property held for productive use in a trade or business. However, section 1031(a)(2) provides that section 1031(a)(1) does not apply to any exchange of—

(i) Stock in trade or other property held primarily for sale;
(ii) Stocks, bonds, or notes;
(iii) Other securities or evidences of indebtedness or interest;
(iv) Interests in a partnership;
(v) Certificates of trust or beneficial interests; or
(vi) Choses in action.

Section 1031(a)(1) does not apply to any exchange of interests in a partnership regardless of whether the interests exchanged are general or limited partnership interests or are interests in the same partnership or in different partnerships. An interest in a partnership that has in effect a valid election under section 761(a) to be excluded from the application of all of subchapter K is treated as an interest in each of the assets of the partnership and not as an interest in a partnership for purposes of section 1031(a)(2)(D) and paragraph (a)(1)(iv) of this section. An exchange of an interest in such a partnership does not qualify for nonrecognition of gain or loss under section 1031 with respect to any asset of the partnership that is described in section 1031(a)(2) or to the extent the exchange of assets of the partnership does not otherwise satisfy the requirements of section 1031(a).

(2) Exchanges of property not solely for property of a like kind. A transfer is not within the provisions of section 1031(a) if, as part of the consideration, the taxpayer receives money or property which does not meet the requirements of section 1031(a), but the transfer, if otherwise qualified, will be within the provisions of either section 1031 (b) or (c). Similarly, a transfer is not within the provisions of section 1031(a) if, as part of the consideration, the other party to the exchange assumes a liability of the taxpayer (or acquires property from the taxpayer that is subject to a liability), but the transfer, if otherwise qualified, will be within the provisions of either section 1031 (b) or (c). A transfer of property meeting the requirements of section 1031(a) may be within the provisions of section 1031(a) even though the taxpayer transfers in addition property not meeting the requirements of section 1031(a) or money. However, the nonrecognition treatment provided by section 1031(a) does not apply to the property transferred which does not meet the requirements of section 1031(a).

(b) Definition of ``like kind." As used in section 1031(a), the words like kind have reference to the nature or character of the property and not to its grade or quality. One kind or class of property may not, under that section, be exchanged for property of a different kind or class. The fact that any real estate involved is improved or unimproved is not material, for that fact relates only to the grade or quality of the property and not to its kind or class. Unproductive real estate held by one other than a dealer for future use or future realization of the increment in value is held for investment and not primarily for sale. For additional rules for exchanges of personal property, see Sec. 1.1031 (a)-2.

(c) Examples of exchanges of property of a ``like kind." No gain or loss is recognized if (1) a taxpayer exchanges property held for productive use in his trade or business, together with cash, for other property of like kind for the same use, such as a truck for a new truck or a passenger automobile for a new passenger automobile to be used for a like purpose; or (2) a taxpayer who is not a dealer in real estate exchanges city real estate for a ranch or farm, or exchanges a leasehold of a fee with 30 years or more to run for real estate, or exchanges improved real estate for unimproved real estate; or (3) a taxpayer exchanges investment property and cash for investment property of a like kind.

(d) Examples of exchanges not solely in kind. Gain or loss is recognized if, for instance, a taxpayer exchanges (1) Treasury bonds maturing March 15, 1958, for Treasury bonds maturing December 15, 1968, unless section 1037(a) (or so much of section 1031 as relates to section 1037(a)) applies to such exchange, or (2) a real estate mortgage for consolidated farm loan bonds.

(e) Effective date relating to exchanges of partnership interests. The provisions of paragraph (a)(1) of this section relating to exchanges of partnership interests apply to transfers of property made by taxpayers on or after April 25, 1991.

Sec. 1.1031(a)-2 Additional rules for exchanges of personal property.

(a) Introduction. Section 1.1031(a)-1(b) provides that the nonrecognition rules of section 1031 do not apply to an exchange of one kind or class of property for property of a different kind or class. This section contains additional rules for determining whether personal property has been exchanged for property of a like kind or like class. Personal properties of a like class are considered to be of a ``like kind'' for purposes of section 1031. In addition, an exchange of properties of a like kind may qualify under section 1031 regardless of whether the properties are also of a like class. In determining whether exchanged properties are of a like kind, no inference is to be drawn from the fact that the properties are not of a like class. Under paragraph (b) of this section, depreciable tangible personal properties are of a like class if they are either within the same General Asset Class (as defined in paragraph (b)(2) of this section) or within the same Product Class (as defined in paragraph (b)(3) of this section). Paragraph (c) of this section provides rules for exchanges of intangible personal property and nondepreciable personal property.

(b) Depreciable tangible personal property--(1) General rule. Depreciable tangible personal property is exchanged for property of a ``like kind'' under section 1031 if the property is exchanged for property of a like kind or like class. Depreciable tangible personal property is of a like class to other depreciable tangible personal property if the exchanged properties are either within the same General Asset Class or within the same Product Class. A single property may not be classified within more than one General Asset Class or within more than one Product Class. In addition, property classified within any General Asset Class may not be classified within a Product Class. A property's General Asset Class or Product Class is determined as of the date of the exchange.

(2) General Asset Classes. Except as provided in paragraphs (b)(4) and (b)(5) of this section, property within a General Asset Class consists of depreciable tangible personal property described in one of asset classes 00.11 through 00.28 and 00.4 of Rev. Proc. 87-56, 1987-2 C.B. 674. These General Asset Classes describe types of depreciable tangible personal property that frequently are used in many businesses.

The General Asset Classes are as follows:

(i) Office furniture, fixtures, and equipment (asset class 00.11),

(ii) Information systems (computers and peripheral equipment) asset class 00.12),

(iii) Data handling equipment, except computers (asset class 00.13),

(iv) Airplanes (airframes and engines), except those used in commercial or contract carrying of passengers or freight, and all helicopters (airframes and engines) (asset class 00.21),

(v) Automobiles, taxis (asset class 00.22),

(vi) Buses (asset class 00.23),

(vii) Light general purpose trucks (asset class 00.241),

(viii) Heavy general purpose trucks (asset class 00.242),

(ix) Railroad cars and locomotives, except those owned by railroad transportation companies (asset class 00.25),

(x) Tractor units for use over-the-road (asset class 00.26),

(xi) Trailers and trailer-mounted containers (asset class 00.27),

(xii) Vessels, barges, tugs, and similar water-transportation equipment, except those used in marine construction (asset class 00.28), and

(xiii) Industrial steam and electric generation and/or distribution systems (asset class 00.4).

(3) Product Classes. Except as provided in paragraphs (b)(4) and (b)(5) of this section, property within a Product Class consists of depreciable tangible personal property that is listed in a 4-digit product class within Division D of the Standard Industrial Classification codes, set forth in Executive Office of the President, Office of Management and Budget, Standard Industrial Classification Manual (1987) (SIC Manual). Copies of the SIC Manual may be obtained from the National Technical Information Service, an agency of the U.S. Department of Commerce. Division D of the SIC Manual contains a listing of manufactured products and equipment. For this purpose, any 4-digit product class ending in a ``9'' (i.e., a miscellaneous category) will not be considered a Product Class. If a property is listed in more than one product class, the property is treated as listed in any one of those product classes. A property's 4-digit product classification is referred to as the property's ``SIC Code.''

(4) Modifications of Rev. Proc. 87-56 and SIC Manual. The asset classes of Rev. Proc. 87-56 and the product classes of the SIC Manual may be updated or otherwise modified from time to time. In the event Rev. Proc. 87-56 is modified, the General Asset Classes will follow the modification, and the modification will be effective for exchanges occurring on or after the date the modification is published in the Internal Revenue Bulletin, unless otherwise provided. Similarly, in the event the SIC Manual is modified, the Product Classes will follow the

modification, and the modification will be effective for exchanges occurring on or after the effective date of the modification. However, taxpayers may rely on the unmodified SIC Manual for exchanges occurring during the one-year period following the effective date of the modification. The SIC Manual generally is modified every five years, in years ending in a 2 or 7 (e.g., 1987 and 1992). The effective date of the modified SIC Manual is announced in the Federal Register and generally is January 1 of the year the SIC Manual is modified.

(5) Modified classification through published guidance. The Commissioner may, by guidance published in the Internal Revenue Bulletin, supplement the guidance provided in this section relating to classification of properties. For example, the Commissioner may determine not to follow, in whole or in part, any modification of Rev. Proc. 87-56 or the SIC Manual. The Commissioner may also determine that two types of property that are listed in separate product classes each ending in a ``9'' are of a like class, or that a type of property that has a SIC Code is of a like class to a type of property that does not have a SIC Code.

(6) No inference outside of section 1031. The rules provided in this section concerning the use of Rev. Proc. 87-56 and the SIC Manual are limited to exchanges under section 1031. No inference is intended with respect to the classification of property for other purposes, such as depreciation.

(7) Examples. The application of this paragraph (b) may be illustrated by the following examples:

Example 1. Taxpayer A transfers a personal computer (asset class 00.12) to B in exchange for a printer (asset class 00.12). With respect to A, the properties exchanged are within the same General Asset Class and therefore are of a like class.

Example 2. Taxpayer C transfers an airplane (asset class 00.21) to D in exchange for a heavy general purpose truck (asset class 00.242). The properties exchanged are not of a like class because they are within different General Asset Classes. Because each of the properties is within a General Asset Class, the properties may not be classified within a Product Class. The airplane and heavy general purpose truck are also not of a like kind. Therefore, the exchange does not qualify for nonrecognition of gain or loss under section 1031.

Example 3. Taxpayer E transfers a grader to F in exchange for a scraper. Neither property is within any of the General Asset Classes, and both properties are within the same Product Class (SIC Code 3533).

With respect to E, therefore, the properties exchanged are of a like class.

Example 4. Taxpayer G transfers a personal computer (asset class 00.12), an airplane (asset class 00.21) and a sanding machine (SIC Code 3553), to H in exchange for a printer (asset class 00.12), a heavy general purpose truck (asset class 00.242) and a lathe (SIC Code 3553). The personal computer and the printer are of a like class because they are within the same General Asset Class; the sanding machine and the lathe are of a like class because neither property is within any of the General Asset Classes and they are within the same Product Class. The airplane and the heavy general purpose truck are neither within the same General Asset Class nor within the same Product Class, and are not of a like kind.

(c) Intangible personal property and nondepreciable personal property--(1) General rule. An exchange of intangible personal property of nondepreciable personal property qualifies for nonrecognition of gain or loss under section 1031 only if the exchanged properties are of a like kind. No like classes are provided for these properties. Whether intangible personal property is of a like kind to other intangible personal property generally depends on the nature or character of the rights involved (e.g., a patent or a copyright) and also on the nature or character of the underlying property to which the intangible personal property relates.

(2) Goodwill and going concern value. The goodwill or going concern value of a business is not of a like kind to the goodwill or going concern value of another business.

(3) Examples. The application of this paragraph (c) may be illustrated by the following examples:

Example 1. Taxpayer K exchanges a copyright on a novel for a copyright on a different novel. The properties exchanged are of a like kind.

Example 2. Taxpayer J exchanges a copyright on a novel for a copyright on a song. The properties exchanged are not of a like kind.

(d) Effective date. Section 1.1031(a)-2 is effective for exchanges occurring on or after April 11, 1991.

Sec. 1.1031(b)-1 Receipt of other property or money in tax-free exchange.

(a) If the taxpayer receives other property (in addition to property permitted to be received without recognition of gain) or money--

(1) In an exchange described in section 1031(a) of property held for investment or productive use in trade or business for property of like kind to be held either for productive use or for investment,

(2) In an exchange described in section 1035(a) of insurance policies or annuity contracts,

(3) In an exchange described in section 1036(a) of common stock for common stock, or preferred stock for preferred stock, in the same corporation and not in connection with a corporate reorganization, or

(4) In an exchange described in section 1037(a) of obligations of the United States, issued under the Second Liberty Bond Act (31 U.S.C. 774 (2)), solely for other obligations issued under such Act, the gain, if any, to the taxpayer will be recognized under section 1031(b) in an amount not in excess of the sum of the money and the fair market value of the other property, but the loss, if any, to the taxpayer from such an exchange will not be recognized under section 1031(c) to any extent.

(b) The application of this section may be illustrated by the following examples:

Example 1. A, who is not a dealer in real estate, in 1954 exchanges real estate held for investment, which he purchased in 1940 for $5,000, for other real estate (to be held for productive use in trade or business) which has a fair market value of $6,000, and $2,000 in cash. The gain from the transaction is $3,000, but is recognized only to the extent of the cash received of $2,000.

Example 2. (a) B, who uses the cash receipts and disbursements method of accounting and the calendar year as his taxable year, has never elected under section 454(a) to include in gross income currently the annual increase in the redemption price of non-interest-bearing obligations issued at a discount. In 1943, for $750 each, B purchased four $1,000 series E U.S. savings bonds bearing an issue date of March 1, 1943.

(b) On October 1, 1963, the redemption value of each such bond was $1,396, and the total redemption value of the four bonds was $5,584. On that date B submitted the four $1,000 series E bonds to the United States in a transaction in which one of such $1,000 bonds was reissued by issuing four $100 series E U.S. savings bonds bearing an issue date of March 1, 1943, and by considering six $100 series E bonds bearing an issue date of March 1, 1943, to have been issued. The redemption value of each such $100 series E bond was $139.60 on October 1, 1963. Then, as part of the transaction, the six $100 series E bonds so considered to have been issued and the three $1,000 series E bonds were exchanged, in an exchange qualifying under section 1037(a), for five $1,000 series H U.S. savings bonds plus

$25.60 in cash.

(c) The gain realized on the exchange qualifying under section 1037(a) is $2,325.60, determined as follows:

Amount realized:

Par value of five series H bonds	$5,000.00
Cash received	25.60
Total realized...	5,025.60

Less: Adjusted basis of series E bonds surrendered in the exchange:

Three $1,000 series E bonds	$2,250.00
Six $100 series E bonds at $75 each	450.00
	2,700.00
Gain realized...	2,325.60

(d) Pursuant to section 1031(b), only $25.60 (the money received) of the total gain of $2,325.60 realized on the exchange is recognized at the time of exchange and must be included in B's gross income for 1963. The $2,300 balance of the gain ($2,325.60 less $25.60) must be included in B's gross income for the taxable year in which the series H bonds are redeemed or disposed of, or reach final maturity, whichever is earlier, as provided in paragraph (c) of Sec. 1.454-1.

(e) The gain on the four $100 series E bonds, determined by using $75 as a basis for each such bond, must be included in B's gross income for the taxable year in which such bonds are redeemed or disposed of, or reach final maturity, whichever is earlier.

Example 3. (a) The facts are the same as in example (2), except that, as part of the transaction, the $1,000 series E bond is reissued by considering ten $100 series E bonds bearing an issue date of March 1,1943, to have been issued. Six of the $100 series E bonds so considered to have been issued are surrendered to the United States as part of the exchange qualifying under section 1037(a) and the other four are immediately redeemed.

(b) Pursuant to section 1031(b), only $25.60 (the money received) of the total gain of $2,325.60 realized on the exchange qualifying under section 1037(a) is recognized at the time of the exchange and must be included in B's gross income for 1963. The $2,300 balance of the gain ($2,325.60 less $25.60) realized on such exchange must be included in B's gross income for the taxable year in which the series H bonds are redeemed or disposed of, or reach final maturity, whichever is earlier, as provided in paragraph (c) of Sec. 1.454-1.

(c) The redemption on October 1, 1963, of the four $100 series E bonds considered to have been issued at such time results in gain of $258.40, which is then recognized and must be included in B's gross income for 1963. This gain of $258.40 is the difference between the $558.40 redemption value of such bonds on the date of the exchange and

the $300 (4x$75) paid for such series E bonds in 1943.

Example 4. On November 1, 1963, C purchased for $91 a marketable U.S. bond which was originally issued at its par value of $100 under the Second Liberty Bond Act. On February 1, 1964, in an exchange qualifying under section 1037(a), C surrendered the bond to the United States for another marketable U.S. bond, which then had a fair market value of $92, and $1.85 in cash, $0.85 of which was interest. The $0.85 interest received is includible in gross income for the taxable year of the exchange, but the $2 gain ($93 less $91) realized on the exchange is recognized for such year under section 1031(b) to the extent of $1 (the money received). Under section 1031(d), C's basis in the bond received in exchange is $91 (his basis of $91 in the bond surrendered, reduced by the $1 money received and increased by the $1 gain recognized).

(c) Consideration received in the form of an assumption of liabilities (or a transfer subject to a liability) is to be treated as other property or money for the purposes of section 1031(b). Where, on an exchange described in section 1031(b), each party to the exchange either assumes a liability of the other party or acquires property subject to a liability, then, in determining the amount of other property or money for purposes of section 1031(b), consideration given in the form of an assumption of liabilities (or a receipt of property subject to a liability) shall be offset against consideration received in the form of an assumption of liabilities (or a transfer subject to a liability). See Sec. 1.1031(d)-2, examples (1) and (2).

Sec. 1.1031(b)-2 Safe harbor for qualified intermediaries.

(a) In the case of simultaneous transfers of like-kind properties involving a qualified intermediary (as defined in Sec. 1.1031(k)-1(g)(4)(iii)), the qualified intermediary is not considered the agent of the taxpayer for purposes of section 1031(a). In such a case, the transfer and receipt of property by the taxpayer is treated as an exchange.

(b) In the case of simultaneous exchanges of like-kind properties involving a qualified intermediary (as defined in Sec. 1.1031(k)-

1(g)(4)(iii)), the receipt by the taxpayer of an evidence of indebtedness of the transferee of the qualified intermediary is treated as the receipt of an evidence of indebtedness of the person acquiring property from the taxpayer for purposes of section 453 and Sec. 15a.453-1(b)(3)(i) of this chapter.

(c) Paragraph (a) of this section applies to transfers of property made by taxpayers on or after June 10, 1991.

(d) Paragraph (b) of this section applies to transfers of property made by taxpayers on or after April 20, 1994. A taxpayer may choose to apply paragraph (b) of this section to transfers of property made on or after June 10, 1991.

Sec. 1.1031(c)-1 Nonrecognition of loss.

Section 1031(c) provides that a loss shall not be recognized from an exchange of property described in section 1031(a), 1035(a), 1036(a), or 1037(a) where there is received in the exchange other property or money in addition to property permitted to be received without recognition of gain or loss. See example (4) of paragraph (a)(3) of Sec. 1.1037-1 for an illustration of the application of this section in the case of an exchange of U.S. obligations described in section 1037(a).

Sec. 1.1031(d)-1 Property acquired upon a tax-free exchange.

(a)If, in an exchange of property solely of the type described in section 1031, section 1035(a), section 1036(a), or section 1037(a), no part of the gain or loss was recognized under the law applicable to the year in which the exchange was made, the basis of the property acquired is the same as the basis of the property transferred by the taxpayer with proper adjustments to the date of the exchange. If additional consideration is given by the taxpayer in the exchange, the basis of the property acquired shall be the same as the property transferred increased by the amount of additional consideration given (see section 1016 and the regulations thereunder).

(b) If, in an exchange of properties of the type indicated in section 1031, section 1035(a), section 1036(a), or section 1037(a), gain to the taxpayer was recognized under the provisions of section 1031(b)or a similar provision of a prior revenue law, on account of the receipt of money in the transaction, the basis of the property acquired is the basis of the property transferred (adjusted to the date of the exchange), decreased by the amount of money received and increased by the amount of gain recognized on the exchange. The application of this paragaph may be illustrated by the following example:

Example: A, an individual in the moving and storage business, in 1954 transfers one of his moving trucks with an adjusted basis in his hands of $2,500 to B in exchange for a truck (to be used in A's business) with a fair market value of $2,400 and $200 in cash. A realizes a gain of $100 upon the exchange, all of which is recognized under section 1031(b). The basis of the truck acquired by A is determined as follows:

Adjusted basis of A's former truck..................	$2,500
Less: Amount of money received.......................	200

Difference..	2,300
Plus: Amount of gain recognized......................	100

Basis of truck acquired by A......................	2,400

(c) If, upon an exchange of properties of the type described in section 1031, section 1035(a), section 1036(a), or section 1037(a), the taxpayer received other property (not permitted to be received without the recognition of gain) and gain from the transaction was recognized as required under section 1031(b), or a similar provision of a prior revenue law, the basis (adjusted to the date of the exchange) of the property transferred by the taxpayer, decreased by the amount of any money received and increased by the amount of gain recognized, must be allocated to and is the basis of the properties (other than money) received on the exchange. For the purpose of the allocation of the basis of the properties received, there must be assigned to such other property an amount equivalent to its fair market value at the date of the exchange. The application of this paragraph may be illustrated by the following example:

Example: A, who is not a dealer in real estate, in 1954 transfers real estate held for investment which he purchased in 1940 for $10,000 in exchange for other real estate (to be held for investment) which has a fair market value of $9,000, an automobile which has a fair market value of $2,000, and $1,500 in cash. A realizes a gain of $2,500, all of which is recognized under section 1031(b). The basis of the property received in exchange is the basis of the real estate A transfers ($10,000) decreased by the amount of money received ($1,500) and increased in the amount of gain that was recognized ($2,500), which results in a basis for the property received of $11,000. This basis of $11,000 is allocated between the automobile and the real estate received by A, the basis of the automobile being its fair market value at the date of the exchange, $2,000, and the basis of the real estate received being the remainder, $9,000.

(d) Section 1031(c) and, with respect to section 1031 and section 1036(a), similar provisions of prior revenue laws provide that no loss may be recognized on an exchange of properties of a type described in section 1031, section 1035(a), section 1036(a), or section 1037(a), although the taxpayer receives other property or money from the transaction. However, the basis of the property or properties (other than money) received by the taxpayer is the basis (adjusted to the date of the exchange) of the property transferred, decreased by the amount of money received. This basis must be allocated to the properties received, and for this purpose there must be allocated to such other property an amount of such basis equivalent to its fair market value at the date of the exchange.

(e) If, upon an exchange of properties of the type described in section 1031, section 1035(a), section 1036(a), or section 1037(a), the taxpayer also exchanged other property (not permitted to be transferred without the recognition of gain or loss) and gain or loss from the transaction is recognized under section 1002 or a similar provision of a prior revenue law, the basis of the property acquired is the total basis of the properties transferred (adjusted to the date of the exchange) increased by the amount of gain and decreased by the amount of loss recognized on the other property. For purposes of this rule, the taxpayer is deemed to have received in exchange for such other property an amount equal to its fair market value on the date of the exchange. The application of this paragraph may be illustrated by the following example:

Example: A exchanges real estate held for investment plus stock for real estate to be held for investment. The real estate transferred has an adjusted basis of $10,000 and a fair market value of $11,000. The stock transferred has an adjusted basis of $4,000 and a fair market value of $2,000. The real estate acquired has a fair market value of $13,000. A is deemed to have received a $2,000 portion of the acquired real estate in exchange for the stock, since $2,000 is the fair market value of the stock at the time of the exchange. A $2,000 loss is recognized under section 1002 on the exchange of the stock for real estate. No gain or loss is recognized on the exchange of the real estate since the property received is of the type permitted to be received without recognition of gain or loss. The basis of the real estate acquired by A is determined as follows:

Adjusted basis of real estate transferred.......... $10,000
Adjusted basis of stock transferred................   4,000

                                                              14,000

Less: Loss recognized on transfer of stock...............................	2,000
Basis of real estate acquired upon the exchange	12,000

Sec. 1.1031(d)-1T Coordination of section 1060 with section 1031 (temporary).

If the properties exchanged under section 1031 are part of a group of assets which constitute a trade or business under section 1060, the like-kind property and other property or money which are treated as transferred in exchange for the like-kind property shall be excluded from the allocation rules of section 1060. However, section 1060 shall apply to property which is not like-kind property or other property or money which is treated as transferred in exchange for the like-kind property. For application of the section 1060 allocation rules to property which is not part of the like-kind exchange, see Sec. 1.1060-1(b), (c), and (d) Example 1 in Sec. 1.338-6(b), to which reference is made by Sec. 1.1060-1(c)(2).

Sec. 1.1031(d)-2 Treatment of assumption of liabilities.

For the purposes of section 1031(d), the amount of any liabilities of the taxpayer assumed by the other party to the exchange (or of any liabilities to which the property exchanged by the taxpayer is subject) is to be treated as money received by the taxpayer upon the exchange, whether or not the assumption resulted in a recognition of gain or loss to the taxpayer under the law applicable to the year in which the exchange was made. The application of this section may be illustrated by the following examples:

Example 1. B, an individual, owns an apartment house which has an adjusted basis in his hands of $500,000, but which is subject to a mortgage of $150,000. On September 1, 1954, he transfers the apartment house to C, receiving in exchange therefor $50,000 in cash and another apartment house with a fair market value on that date of $600,000. The transfer to C is made subject to the $150,000 mortgage. B realizes a gain of $300,000 on the exchange, computed as follows:

Value of property received..	$600,000
Cash..	50,000
Liabilities subject to which old property was transferred...	150,000
Total consideration received..	800,000
Less: Adjusted basis of property transferred......................	500,000
Gain realized...	300,000

Under section 1031(b), $200,000 of the $300,000 gain is recognized. The basis of the apartment house acquired by B upon the exchange is $500,000, computed as follows:

Adjusted basis of property transferred.....................	500,000
Less: Amount of money received:	
Cash..	$50,000
Amount of liabilities subject to which	
property was transferred..................................	150,000
	200,000
Difference.................................	.300,000
Plus: Amount of gain recognized upon the exchange..........	
	200,000
Basis of property acquired upon the exchange.....	500,000

Example 2. (a) D, an individual, owns an apartment house. On December 1, 1955, the apartment house owned by D has an adjusted basis in his hands of $100,000, a fair market value of $220,000, but is subject to a mortgage of $80,000. E, an individual, also owns an apartment house. On December 1, 1955, the apartment house owned by E has an adjusted basis of $175,000, a fair market value of $250,000, but is subject to a mortgage of $150,000. On December 1, 1955, D transfers his apartment house to E, receiving in exchange therefore $40,000 in cash and the apartment house owned by E. Each apartment house is transferred subject to the mortgage on it.

(b) D realizes a gain of $120,000 on the exchange, computed as follows:

Value of property received......................	$250,000
Cash...	40,000
Liabilities subject to which old property was transferred...	
	80,000
Total consideration received...........................	370,000
Less:	
Adjusted basis of property transferred........	$100,000
Liabilities to which new property is subject..	150,000
	250,000

Gain realized... 120,000

For purposes of section 1031(b), the amount of other property or money received by D is $40,000. (Consideration received by D in the form of a transfer subject to a liability of $80,000 is offset by consideration given in the form of a receipt of property subject to a $150,000 liability. Thus, only the consideration received in the form of cash, $40,000, is treated as other property or money for purposes of section 1031(b).) Accordingly, under section 1031(b), $40,000 of the $120,000 gain is recognized. The basis of the apartment house acquired by D is $170,000, computed as follows:

Adjusted basis of property transferred............	$100,000
Liabilities to which new property is subject......	150,000
Total...	250,000
Less: Amount of money received: Cash...	$40,000
Amount of liabilities subject to which property was transferred...	80,000
	120,000
Difference...	130,000
Plus: Amount of gain recognized upon the exchange.	40,000
Basis of property acquired upon the exchange..	170,000

(c) E realizes a gain of $75,000 on the exchange, computed as follows:

Value of property received.........................	$220,000
Liabilities subject to which old property was transferred......................................	150,000
Total consideration received..................	370,000
Less:	
Adjusted basis of property transferred..............	$175,000
Cash..	40,000
Liabilities to which new property is subject...........................	80,000

```
                                    --------
                                    295,000
                                  ----------------
```

Gain realized................................   75,000

For purposes of section 1031(b), the amount of other property or money received by E is $30,000. (Consideration received by E in the form of a transfer subject to a liability of $150,000 is offset by consideration given in the form of a receipt of property subject to an $80,000 liability and by the $40,000 cash paid by E. Although consideration received in the form of cash or other property is not offset by consideration given in the form of an assumption of liabilities or a receipt of property subject to a liability, consideration given in the form of cash or other property is offset against consideration received in the form of an assumption of liabilities or a transfer of property subject to a liability.) Accordingly, under section 1031(b), $30,000 of the $75,000 gain is recognized. The basis of the apartment house acquired by E is $175,000, computed as follows:

Adjusted basis of property transferred............	$175,000
Cash..	40,000
Liabilities to which new property is subject......	80,000
Total..	295,000
Less: Amount of money received: Amount of liabilities subject to which property was transferred................	$150,000
	150,000
Difference....................................	145,000
Plus: Amount of gain recognized upon the exchange.	30,000
Basis of property acquired upon the exchange..	175,000

Sec. 1.1031(e)-1 Exchange of livestock of different sexes.

Section 1031(e) provides that livestock of different sexes are not property of like kind. Section 1031(e) and this section are applicable to taxable years to which the Internal Revenue Code of 1954 applies.

Sec. 1.1031(j)-1 Exchanges of multiple properties.

(a) Introduction--(1) Overview. As a general rule, the application of section 1031 requires a property-by-property comparison for computing the gain recognized and basis of property received in a like-kind exchange. This section provides an exception to this general rule in the case of an exchange of multiple properties. An exchange is an exchange of multiple properties if, under paragraph (b)(2) of this section, more than one exchange group is created. In addition, an exchange is an exchange of multiple properties if only one exchange group is created but there is more than one property being transferred or received within that exchange group. Paragraph (b) of this section provides rules for computing the amount of gain recognized in an exchange of multiple properties qualifying for nonrecognition of gain or loss under section 1031. Paragraph (c) of this section provides rules for computing the basis of properties received in an exchange of multiple properties qualifying for nonrecognition of gain or loss under section 1031.

(2) General approach. (i) In general, the amount of gain recognized in an exchange of multiple properties is computed by first separating the properties transferred and the properties received by the taxpayer in the exchange into exchange groups in the manner described in paragraph (b)(2) of this section. The separation of the properties transferred and the properties received in the exchange into exchange groups involves matching up properties of a like kind of like class to the extent possible. Next, all liabilities assumed by the taxpayer as part of the transaction are offset by all liabilities of which the taxpayer is relieved as part of the transaction, with the excess liabilities assumed or relieved allocated in accordance with paragraph (b)(2)(ii) of this section. Then, the rules of section 1031 and the regulations thereunder are applied separately to each exchange group to determine the amount of gain recognized in the exchange. See Secs. 1.1031(b)-1 and 1.1031(c)-1. Finally, the rules of section 1031 and the regulations thereunder are applied separately to each exchange group to determine the basis of the properties received in the exchange. See Secs. 1.1031(d)-1 and 1.1031(d)-2.

(ii) For purposes of this section, the exchanges are assumed to be made at arms' length, so that the aggregate fair market value of the property received in the exchange equals the aggregate fair market value of the property transferred. Thus, the amount realized with respect to the properties transferred in each exchange group is assumed to equal their aggregate fair market value.

(b) Computation of gain recognized--(1) In general. In computing the amount of gain recognized in an exchange of multiple properties, the fair market value must be determined for each property transferred and for each property received by the taxpayer in the exchange. In addition, the adjusted basis must be determined for each property transferred by the taxpayer in the exchange.

(2) Exchange groups and residual group. The properties transferred and the properties received by the taxpayer in the exchange are separated into exchange groups and a residual group tothe extent provided in this paragraph (b)(2).

(i) Exchange groups. Each exchange group consists of the properties transferred and received in the exchange, all of which are of a like kind or like class. If a property could be included in more than one exchange group, the taxpayer may include the property in any of those exchange groups. Property eligible for inclusion within an exchange group does not include money or property described in section 1031(a)(2) (i.e., stock in trade or other property held primarily for sale, stocks, bonds, notes, other securities or evidences of indebtedness or interest, interests in a partnership, certificates of trust or beneficial interests, or choses in action). For example, an exchange group may consist of all exchanged properties that are within the same General Asset Class or within the same Product Class (as defined in Sec. 1.1031(a)-2(b)). Each exchange group must consist of at least one property transferred and at least one property received in the exchange.

(ii) Treatment of liabilities. (A) All liabilities assumed by the taxpayer as part of the exchange are offset against all liabilities of which the taxpayer is relieved as part of the exchange, regardless of whether the liabilities are recourse or nonrecourse and regardless of whether the liabilities are secured by or otherwise relate to specific property transferred or received as part of the exchange. See Secs. 1.1031 (b)-1(c) and 1.1031(d)-2. For purposes of this section, liabilities assumed by the taxpayer as part of the exchange consist of liabilities of the other party to the exchange assumed by the taxpayer and liabilities subject to which the other party's property is transferred in the exchange. Similarly, liabilities of which the taxpayer is relieved as part of the exchange consist of liabilities of the taxpayer assumed by the other party to the exchange and liabilities subject to which the taxpayer's property is transferred.

(B) If there are excess liabilities assumed by the taxpayer as part of the exchange (i.e., the amount of liabilities assumed by the taxpayer exceeds the amount of liabilities of which the taxpayer is relieved), the excess is allocated among the exchange groups (but not to the residual group) in proportion to the aggregate fair market value of the properties received by the taxpayer in the exchange groups. The amount of excess liabilities assumed by the taxpayer that are allocated to each exchange group may not exceed the aggregate fair market value of the properties received in the exchange group.

(C) If there are excess liabilities of which the taxpayer is relieved as part of the exchange (i.e., the amount of liabilities of which the taxpayer is relieved exceeds the amount of liabilities assumed by the taxpayer), the excess is treated as a Class I asset for purposes of making allocations to the residual group under paragraph (b)(2)(iii)of this section.

(D) Paragraphs (b)(2)(ii) (A), (B), and (C) of this section are applied in the same manner even if section 1031 and this section apply to only a portion of a larger transaction (such as a transaction described in section 1060(c) and Sec. 1.1060-1T(b)). In that event, the amount of excess liabilities assumed by the taxpayer or the amount of excess liabilities of which the taxpayer is relieved is determined based on all liabilities assumed by the taxpayer and all liabilities of which the taxpayer is relieve as part of the larger transaction.

(iii) Residual group. If the aggregate fair market value of the properties transferred in all of the exchange groups differs from the aggregate fair market value of the properties received in all of the exchange groups (taking liabilities into account in the manner described in paragraph (b)(2)(ii) of this section), a residual group is created. The residual group consists of an amount of money or other property having an aggregate fair market value equal to that difference. The residual group consists of either money or other property transferred in the exchange or money or other property received in the exchange, but not both. For this purpose, other property includes property described in section 1031(a)(2) (i.e., stock in trade or other property held primarily for sale, stocks, bonds, notes, other securities or evidences of indebtedness or interest, interests in a partnership, certificates of trust or beneficial interests, or choses in action), property transferred that is not of a like kind or like class with any property received, and property received that is not of a like kind or like class with any property transferred. The money and properties that are allocated to the residual group are considered to come from the following assets in the following order: first from Class I assets, then from Class II assets, then from Class III assets, and then from Class IV assets. The terms Class I assets, Class II assets, Class III assets, and Class IV assets have the same meanings as in Sec. 1.338-6(b), to which reference is made by Sec. 1.1060-1(c)(2). Within each Class, taxpayers may choose which properties are allocated to the residual group.

(iv) Exchange group surplus and deficiency. For each of the exchange groups described in this section, an ``exchange group surplus'' or ``exchange group deficiency,'' if any, must be determined. An exchange group surplus is the excess of the aggregate fair market value of the properties received (less the amount of any excess liabilities assumed by the taxpayer that are allocated to that exchange group), in an exchange group over the aggregate fair market value of the properties transferred in that exchange group. An exchange group deficiency is the excess of the aggregate fair market value of the properties transferred in an exchange group over the aggregate fair market value of the properties received (less the amount of any excess liabilities assumed by the taxpayer that are allocated to that exchange group) in that exchange group.

(3) Amount of gain recognized. (i) For purposes of this section, the amount of gain or loss realized with respect to each exchange group and the residual group is the difference between the aggregate fair market value of the properties transferred in that exchange group or residual group and the properties' aggregate adjusted basis. The gain realized with respect to each exchange group is recognized to the extent of the lesser of the gain realized and the amount of the exchange group deficiency, if any. Losses realized with respect to an exchange group are not recognized. See section 1031 (a) and (c). The total amount of gain recognized under section 1031 in the exchange is the sum of the amount of gain recognized with respect to each exchange group. With respect to the residual group, the gain or loss realized (as determined under this section) is recognized as provided in section 1001 or other applicable provision of the Code.

(ii) The amount of gain or loss realized and recognized with respect to properties transferred by the taxpayer that are not within any exchange group or the residual group is determined under section 1001 and other applicable provisions of the Code, with proper adjustments made for all liabilities not allocated to the exchange groups or the residual group.

(c) Computation of basis of properties received. In an exchange of multiple properties qualifying for nonrecognition of gain or loss under section 1031 and this section, the aggregate basis of properties received in each of the exchange groups is the aggregate adjusted basis of the properties transferred by the taxpayer within that exchange group, increased by the amount of gain recognized by the taxpayer with respect to that exchange group, increased by the amount of the exchange group surplus or decreased by the amount of the exchange group deficiency, and increased by the amount, if any, of excess liabilities assumed by the taxpayer that are allocated to that exchange group. The resulting aggregate basis of each exchange group is allocated proportionately to each property received in the exchange group in accordance with its fair market value. The basis of each property received within the residual group (other than money) is equal to its fair market value.

(d) Examples. The application of this section may be illustrated by the following examples:

Example 1. (i) K exchanges computer A (asset class 00.12) and automobile A (asset class 00.22), both of which were held by K for productive use in its business, with W for printer B (asset class 00.12) and automobile B (asset class 00.22), both of which will be held by K for productive use in its business. K's adjusted basis and the fair market value of the exchanged properties are as follows:

	Adjusted basis	Fair market value
Computer A............................	$375	$1,000

[[Page 91]]

Automobile A............................	1,500	4,000
Printer B............................		2,050
Automobile B............................		2,950

(ii) Under paragraph (b)(2) of this section, the properties exchanged are separated into exchange groups as follows:

(A) The first exchange group consists of computer A and printer B (both are within the same General Asset Class) and, as to K, has an exchange group surplus of $1050 because the fair market value of printer B ($2050) exceeds the fair market value of computer A ($1000) by that amount.

(B) The second exchange group consists of automobile A and automobile B (both are within the same General Asset Class) and, as to K, has an exchange group deficiency of $1050 because the fair market value of automobile A ($4000) exceeds the fair market value of automobile B ($2950) by that amount.

(iii) K recognizes gain on the exchange as follows:

(A) With respect to the first exchange group, the amount of gain realized is the excess of the fair market value of computer A ($1000) over its adjusted basis ($375), or $625. The amount of gain recognized is the lesser of the gain realized ($625) and the exchange group deficiency ($0), or $0.

(B) With respect to the second exchange group, the amount of gain realized is the excess of the fair market value of automobile A ($4000) over its adjusted basis ($1500), or $2500. The amount of gain recognized is the lesser of the gain realized ($2500) and the exchange group deficiency ($1050), or $1050.

(iv) The total amount of gain recognized by K in the exchange is the sum of the gains recognized with respect to both exchange groups ($0 + $1050), or $1050.

(v) The bases of the property received by K in the exchange, printer B and automobile B, are determined in the following manner:

(A) The basis of the property received in the first exchange group is the adjusted basis of the property transferred within the exchange group ($375), increased by the amount of gain recognized with respect to that exchange group ($0), increased by the amount of the exchange group surplus ($1050), and increased by the amount of excess liabilities assumed allocated to that exchange group ($0), or $1425. Because printer B was the only property received within the first exchange group, the entire basis of $1425 is allocated to printer B.

(B) The basis of the property received in the second exchange group is the adjusted basis of the property transferred within that exchange group ($1500), increased by the amount of gain recognized with respect to that exchange group ($1050), decreased by the amount of the exchange group deficiency ($1050), and increased by the amount of excess liabilities assumed allocated to that exchange group ($0), or $1500. Because automobile B was the only property received within the second exchange group, the entire basis of $1500 is allocated to automobile B.

Example 2. (i) F exchanges computer A (asset class 00.12) and automobile A (asset class 00.22), both of which were held by F for productive use in its business, with G for printer B (asset class 00.12)and automobile B (asset class 00.22), both of which will be held by F for productive use in its business, and corporate stock and $500 cash.

The adjusted basis and fair market value of the properties are as follows:

	Adjusted basis	Fair market value
Computer A.............................	$375	$1,000
Automobile A...........................	3,500	4,000
Printer B.................................		800
Automobile B...........................		2,95
Corporate stock.......................		750
Cash.......................................		500

(ii) Under paragraph (b)(2) of this section, the properties exchanged are separated into exchange groups as follows:

(A) The first exchange group consists of computer A and printer B (both are within the same General Asset Class) and, as to F, has an exchange group deficiency of $200 because the fair market value of computer A ($1000) exceeds the fair market value of printer B ($800) by that amount.

(B) The second exchange group consists of automobile A and automobile B (both are within the same General Asset Class) and, as to F, has an exchange group deficiency of $1050 because the fair market value of automobile A ($4000) exceeds the fair market value of automobile B ($2950) by that amount.

(C) Because the aggregate fair market value of the properties transferred by F in the exchange groups ($5,000) exceeds the aggregate fair market value of the properties received by F in the exchange groups ($3750) by $1250, there is a residual group in that amount consisting of the $500 cash and the $750 worth of corporate stock.

(iii) F recognizes gain on the exchange as follows:

(A) With respect to the first exchange group, the amount of gain realized is the excess of the fair market value of computer A ($1000) over its adjusted basis ($375), or $625. The amount of gain recognized is the lesser of the gain realized ($625) and the exchange group deficiency ($200), or $200.

(B) With respect to the second exchange group, the amount of gain realized is the excess of the fair market value of automobile A ($4000) over its adjusted basis ($3500), or $500. The amount of gain recognized is the lesser of the gain realized ($500) and the exchange group deficiency ($1050), or $500.

(C) No property transferred by F was allocated to the residual group. Therefore, F does not recognize gain or loss with respect to the residual group.

(iv) The total amount of gain recognized by F in the exchange is the sum of the gains recognized with respect to both exchange groups ($200 + $500), or $700.

(v) The bases of the properties received by F in the exchange (printer B, automobile B, and the corporate stock) are determined in the following manner:

(A) The basis of the property received in the first exchange group is the adjusted basis of the property transferred within that exchange group ($375), increased by the amount of gain recognized with respect to that exchange group ($200), decreased by the amount of the exchange group deficiency ($200), and increased by the amount of excess liabilities assumed allocated to that exchange group ($0), or $375.

Because printer B was the only property received within the first exchange group, the entire basis of $375 is allocated to printer B.

(B) The basis of the property received in the second exchange group is the adjusted basis of the property transferred within that exchange group ($3500), increased by the amount of gain recognized with respect to that exchange group ($500), decreased by the amount of the exchange group deficiency ($1050), and increased by the amount of excess liabilites assumed allocated to that exchange group ($0), or $2950. Because automobile B was the only property received within the second exchange group, the entire basis of $2950 is allocated to automobile B.

(C) The basis of the property received within the residual group (the corporate stock) is equal to its fair market value or $750. Cash of $500 is also received within the residual group.

Example 3. (i) J and H enter into an exchange of the following properties. All of the property (except for the inventory) transferred by J was held for productive use in J's business. All of the property received by J will be held by J for productive use in its business.

J Transfers:			H Transfers:	
Property	Adjusted basis	Fair market value	Property	Fair market value
Computer A...........$1,500		$5,000	Computer Z...........4,500	
Computer B.............. 500		3,000	Printer Y.................2,500	
Printer C.................2,000		1,500	Real Estate X......... 1,000	
Real Estate D...........1,200		2,000	Real Estate W........ 4,000	
Real Estate E...................0		1,800	Grader V................ 2,000	
Scraper F................ 3,300		2,500	Truck T.................. 1,700	
Inventory.................1,000		1,700	Cash....................... 1,800	
Total...........9,500		17,500	17,500	

(ii) Under paragraph (b)(2) of this section, the properties exchanged are separated into exchange groups as follows:

(A) The first exchange group consists of computer A, computer B, printer C, computer Z, and printer Y (all are within the same General Asset Class) and, as to J, has an exchange group deficiency of $2500 (($5000 + $3000 + $1500) - ($4500 + $2500)).

(B) The second exchange group consists of real estate D, E, X and W (all are of a like kind) and, as to J, has an exchange group surplus of $1200 (($1000 + $4000) - ($2000 + $1800)).

(C) The third exchange group consists of scraper F and grader V (both are within the same Product Class (SIC Code 3531)) and, as to J, has an exchange group deficiency of $500 ($2500 - $2000).

(D) Because the aggregate fair market value of the properties transferred by J in the exchange groups ($15,800) exceeds the aggregate fair market value of the properties received by J in the exchange groups ($14,000) by $1800, there is a residual group in that amount consisting of the $1800 cash (a Class I asset).

(E) The transaction also includes a taxable exchange of inventory (which is property described in section 1031 (a)(2)) for truck T (which is not of a like kind or like class to any property transferred in the exchange).

(iii) J recognizes gain on the transaction as follows:

(A) With respect to the first exchange group, the amount of gain realized is the excess of the aggregate fair market value of the properties transferred in the exchange group ($9500) over the aggregate adjusted basis ($4000), or $5500. The amount of gain recognized is the lesser of the gain realized ($5500) and the exchange group deficiency ($2500), or $2500.

(B) With respect to the second exchange group, the amount of gain realized is the excess of the aggregate fair market value of the properties transferred in the exchange group ($3800) over the aggregate adjusted basis ($1200), or $2600. The amount of gain recognized is the lesser of the gain realized ($2600) and the exchange group deficiency ($0), or $0.

(C) With respect to the third exchange group, a loss is realized in the amount of $800 because the fair market value of the property transferred in the exchange group ($2500) is less than its adjusted basis ($3300). Although a loss of $800 was realized, under section 1031 (a) and (c) losses are not recognized.

(D) No property transferred by J was allocated to the residual group. Therefore, J does not recognize gain or loss with respect to the residual group.

(E) With respect to the taxable exchange of inventory for truck T, gain of $700 is realized and recognized by J (amount realized of $1700 (the fair market value of truck T) less the adjusted basis of the inventory ($1000)).

(iv) The total amount of gain recognized by J in the transaction is the sum of the gains recognized under section 1031 with respect to each exchange group ($2500 + $0 + $0) and any gain recognized outside of section 1031 ($700), or $3200.

(v) The bases of the property received by J in the exchange are determined in the following manner:

(A) The aggregate basis of the properties received in the first exchange group is the adjusted basis of the properties transferred within that exchange group ($4000), increased by the amount of gain recognized with respect to that exchange group ($2500), decreased by the amount of the exchange group deficiency ($2500), and increased by the amount of excess liabilities assumed allocated to that exchange group ($0), or $4000. This $4000 of basis is allocated proportionately among the assets received within the first exchange group in accordance with their fair market values: Computer Z's basis is $2571 ($4000 x $4500/$7000); printer Y's basis is $1429 ($4000 x $2500/$7000).

(B) The aggregate basis of the properties received in the second exchange group is the adjusted basis of the properties transferred within that exchange group ($1200), increased by the amount of gain recognized with respect to that exchange group ($0), increased by the amount of the exchange group surplus ($1200), and increased by the amount of excess liabilities assumed allocated to that exchange group ($0), or $2400. This $2400 of basis is allocated proportionately among the assets received within the second exchange group in accordance with their fair market values: Real estate X's basis is $480 ($2400 x $1000/$5000); real estate W's basis is $1920 ($2400 x $4000/$5000).

(C) The basis of the property received in the third exchange group is the adjusted basis of the property transferred within that exchange group ($3300), increased by the amount of gain recognized with respect to that exchange group ($0), decreased by the amount of the exchange group deficiency ($500), and increased by the amount of excess liabilities assumed allocated to that exchange group ($0), or $2800. Because grader V was the only property received within the third exchange group, the entire basis of $2800 is allocated to grader V.

(D) Cash of $1800 is received within the residual group.

(E) The basis of the property received in the taxable exchange (truck T) is equal to its cost of $1700.

Example 4. (i) B exchanges computer A (asset class 00.12), automobile A (asset class 00.22) and truck A (asset class 00.241), with C for computer R (asset class 00.12), automobile R (asset class 00.22), truck R (asset class 00.241) and $400 cash. All properties transferred by either B or C were held for productive use in the respective transferor's business. Similarly, all properties to be received by either B or C will be held for productive use in the respective recipient's business. Automobile A, automobile R and truck R are each secured by a nonrecourse liability and are transferred subject to such liability. The adjusted basis, fair market value, and liability secured by each property, if any, are as follows:

	Adjusted basis	Fair market value	Liability
B transfers:			
Computer A..........................	$800	$1,500	$0
Automobile A.........................	900	2,500	500
Truck A.............................	700	2,000	0
C transfers:			
Computer R..........................	1,100	1,600	0
Automobile R.........................	2,100	3,100	750
Truck R.............................	600	1,400	250
Cash............................... .	....	400	....

(ii) The tax treatment to B is as follows:

(A)(1) The first exchange group consists of computers A and R (both are within the same General Asset Class).

(2) The second exchange group consists of automobiles A and R (both are within the same General Asset Class).

(3) The third exchange group consists of trucks A and R (both are in the same General Asset Class).

(B) Under paragraph (b)(2)(ii) of this section, all liabilities assumed by B ($1000) are offset by all liabilities of which B is relieved ($500), resulting in excess liabilities assumed of $500. The excess liabilities assumed of $500 is allocated among the exchange groups in proportion to the fair market value of the properties received by B in the exchange groups as follows:

(1) $131 of excess liabilities assumed ($500 x $1600/$6100) is allocated to the first exchange group. The first exchange group has an exchange group deficiency of $31 because the fair market value of computer A ($1500) exceeds the fair market value of computer R less the excess liabilities assumed allocated to the exchange group ($1600-$131) by that amount.

(2) $254 of excess liabilities assumed ($500 x $3100/$6100) is allocated to the second exchange group. The second exchange group has an exchange group surplus of $346 because the fair market value of automobile R less the excess liabilities assumed allocated to the exchange group ($3100-$254) exceeds the fair market value of automobile A ($2500) by that amount.

(3) $115 of excess liabilities assumed ($500 x $1400/$6100) is allocated to the third exchange group. The third exchange group has an exchange group deficiency of $715 because the fair market value of truck A ($2000) exceeds the fair market value of truck R less the excess liabilities assumed allocated to the exchange group ($1400-$115) by that amount.

(4) The difference between the aggregate fair market value of the properties transferred in all of the exchange groups, $6000, and the aggregate fair market value of the properties received in all of the exchange groups (taking excess liabilities assumed into account), $5600, is $400. Therefore there is a residual group in that amount consisting of $400 cash received.

(C) B recognizes gain on the exchange as follows:
(1) With respect to the first exchange group, the amount of gain realized is the excess of the fair market value of computer A ($1500) over its adjusted basis ($800), or $700. The amount of gain recognized is the lesser of the gain realized ($700) and the exchange group deficiency ($31), or $31.
(2) With respect to the second exchange group, the amount of gain realized is the excess of the fair market value of automobile A ($2500) over its adjusted basis ($900), or $1600. The amount of gain recognized is the lesser of the gain realized ($1600) and the exchange group deficiency ($0), or $0.
(3) With respect to the third exchange group, the amount of gain realized is the excess of the fair market value of truck A ($2000) over its adjusted basis ($700), or $1300. The amount of gain recognized is the lesser of gain realized ($1300) and the exchange group deficiency ($715), or $715.
(4) No property transferred by B was allocated to the residual group. Therefore, B does not recognize gain or loss with respect to the residual group.

(D) The total amount of gain recognized by B in the exchange is the sum of the gains recognized under section 1031 with respect to each exchange group ($31 + $0 +$715), or $746.

(E) the bases of the property received by B in the exchange (computer R, automobile R, and truck R) are determined in the following manner:
(1) The basis of the property received in the first exchange group is the adjusted basis of the property transferred within that exchange group ($800), increased by the amount of gain recognized with respect to that exchange group ($31), decreased by the amount of the exchange group deficiency ($31), and increased by the amount of excess liabilities assumed allocated to that exchange group ($131), or $931. Because computer R was the only property received within the first exchange group, the entire basis of $931 is allocated to computer R.
(2) The basis of the property received in the second exchange group is the adjusted basis of the property transferred within that exchange group ($900), increased by the amount of gain recognized with respect to that exchange group ($0), increased by the amount of

the exchange group surplus ($346), and increased by the amount of excess liabilities assumed allocated to that exchange group ($254), or $1500. Because automobile R was the only property received within the second exchange group, the entire basis of $1500 is allocated to automobile R.

(3) The basis of the property received in the third exchange group is the adjusted basis of the property transferred within that exchange group ($700), increased by the amount of gain recognized with respect to that exchange group ($715), decreased by the amount of the exchange group deficiency ($715), and increased by the amount of excess liabilities assumed allocated to that exchange group ($115), or $815. Because truck R was the only property received within the third exchange group, the entire basis of $815 is allocated to truck R.

(F) Cash of $400 is also received by B.

(iii) The tax treatment to C is as follows:
(A) (1) The first exchange group consists of computers R and A (both are within the same General Asset Class).
(2) The second exchange group consists of automobiles R and A (both are within the same General Asset Class).
(3) The third exchange group consists of trucks R and A (both are in the same General Asset Class).
(B) Under paragraph (b)(2)(ii) of this section, all liabilities of which C is relieved ($1000) are offset by all liabilities assumed by C ($500), resulting in excess liabilities relieved of $500. This excess liabilities relieved is treated as cash received by C.
(1) The first exchange group has an exchange group deficiency of $100 because the fair market value of computer R ($1600) exceeds the fair market value of computer A ($1500) by that amount.
(2) The second exchange group has an exchange group deficiency of $600 because the fair market value of automobile R ($3100) exceeds the fair market value of automobile A ($2500) by that amount.
(3) The third exchange group has an exchange group surplus of $600 because the fair market value of truck A ($2000) exceeds the fair market value of truck R ($1400) by that amount.
(4) The difference between the aggregate fair market value of the properties transferred by C in all of the exchange groups, $6100, and the aggregate fair market value of the properties received by C in all of the exchange groups, $6000, is $100. Therefore, there is a residual group in that amount, consisting of excess liabilities relieved of $100, which is treated as cash received by C.
(5) The $400 cash paid by C and $400 of the excess liabilities relieved which is treated as cash received by C are not within the exchange groups of the residual group.
(C) C recognizes gain on the exchange as follows:

(1) With respect to the first exchange group, the amount of gain realized is the excess of the fair market value of computer R ($1600) over its adjusted basis ($1100), or $500. The amount of gain recognized is the lesser of the gain realized ($500) and the exchange group deficiency ($100), or $100.

(2) With respect to the second exchange group, the amount of gain realized is the excess of the fair market value of automobile R ($3100) over its adjusted basis ($2100), or $1000. The amount of gain recognized is the lesser of the gain realized ($1000) and the exchange group deficiency ($600), or $600.

(3) With respect to the third exchange group, the amount of gain realized is the excess of the fair market value of truck R ($1400) over its adjusted basis ($600), or $800. The amount of gain recognized is the lesser of gain realized ($800) and the exchange group deficiency ($0), or $0.

(4) No property transferred by C was allocated to the residual group. Therefore, C does not recognize any gain with respect to the residual group.

(D) The total amount of gain recognized by C in the exchange is the sum of the gains recognized under section 1031 with respect to each exchange group ($100+$600+$0), or $700.

(E) The bases of the properties received by C in the exchange (computer A, automobile A, and truck A) are determined in the following manner:

(1) The basis of the property received in the first exchange group is the adjusted basis of the property transferred within that exchange group ($1100), increased by the amount of gain recognized with respect to that exchange group ($100), decreased by the amount of the exchange group deficiency ($100), and increased by the amount of excess liabilities assumed allocated to that exchange group ($0), or $1100. Because computer A was the only property received within the first exchange group, the entire basis of $1100 is allocated to computer A.

(2) The basis of the property received in the second exchange group is the adjusted basis of the property transferred within that exchange group ($2100), increased by the amount of gain recognized with respect to that exchange group ($600), decreased by the amount of the exchange group deficiency ($600), and increased by the amount of excess liabilities assumed allocated to that exchange group ($0), or $2100. Because automobile A was the only property received within the second exchange group, the entire basis of $2100 is allocated to automobile A.

(3) The basis of the property received in the third exchange group is the adjusted basis of the property transferred within that exchange group ($600), increased by the amount of gain recognized with respect to that exchange group ($0), increased by the amount of the exchange group surplus ($600), and increased by the amount of

excess liabilities
assumed allocated to that exchange group ($0), or $1200. Because
truck A was the only property received within the third exchange
group, the
entire basis of $1200 is allocated to truck A.

Example 5. (i) U exchanges real estate A, real estate B, and grader
A (SIC Code 3531) with V for real estate R and railroad car R (General
Asset Class 00.25). All properties transferred by either U or V were
held for productive use in the respective transferor's business.
Similarly, all properties to be received by either U or V will be held
for productive use in the respective recipient's business. Real estate R
is secured by a recourse liability and is transferred subject to that
liability. The adjusted basis, fair market value, and liability secured
by each property, if any, are as follows:

	Adjusted basis	Fair market value	Liability
U transfers:			
Real Estate A............................	2,000	$5,000	
Real Estate B........................	8,000	13,500	500
Grader A..............................	500	2,000	
C transfers:			
Real Estate R............................	20,000	26,500	$7000
Railroad car R..........................	1,200	1,000	

(ii) The tax treatment to U is as follows:

(A) The exchange group consists of real estate A, real estate B,
and real estate R.

(B) Under paragraph (b)(2)(ii) of this section, all liabilities
assumed by U ($7000) are excess liabilities assumed. The excess
liabilities assumed of $7000 is allocated to the exchange group.
(1) The exchange group has an exchange group surplus of $1000
because the fair market value of real estate R less the excess
liabilities assumed allocated to the exchange group ($26,500-$7000)
exceeds the aggregate fair market value of real estate A and B
($18,500) by that amount.
(2) The difference between the aggregate fair market value of the
properties received in the exchange group (taking excess liabilities
assumed into account), $19,500, and the aggregate fair market value
of the properties transferred in the exchange group, $18,500, is $1000.

Therefore, there is a residual group in that amount consisting of $1000 (or 50 percent of the fair market value) of grader A.

(3) The transaction also includes a taxable exchange of the 50 percent portion of grader A not allocated to the residual group (which is not of a like kind or like class to any property received by U in the exchange) for railroad car R (which is not of a like kind or like class to any property transferred by U in the exchange).

(C) U recognizes gain on the exchange as follows:

(1) With respect to the exchange group, the amount of the gain realized is the excess of the aggregate fair market value of real estate A and B ($18,500) over the aggregate adjusted basis ($10,000), or $8500. The amount of the gain recognized is the lesser of the gain realized ($8500) and the exchange group deficiency ($0), or $0.

(2) With respect to the residual group, the amount of gain realized and recognized is the excess of the fair market value of the 50 percent portion of grader A that is allocated to the residual group ($1000) over its adjusted basis ($250), or $750.

(3) With respect to the taxable exchange of the 50 percent portion of grader A not allocated to the residual group for railroad car R, gain of $750 is realized and recognized by U (amount realized of $1000 (the fair market value of railroad car R) less the adjusted basis of the 50 percent portion of grader A not allocated to the residual group ($250)).

(D) The total amount of gain recognized by U in the transaction is the sum of the gain recognized under section 1031 with respect to the exchange group ($0), any gain recognized with respect to the residual group ($750), and any gain recognized with respect to property transferred that is not in the exchange group or the residual group ($750), or $1500.

(E) The bases of the property received by U in the exchange (real estate R and railroad car R) are determined in the following manner:

(1) The basis of the property received in the exchange group is the aggregate adjusted basis of the property transferred within that exchange group ($10,000), increased by the amount of gain recognized with respect to that exchange group ($0), increased by the amount of the exchange group surplus ($1000), and increased by the amount of excess liabilities assumed allocated to that exchange group ($7000), or $18,000. Because real estate R is the only property received within the exchange group, the entire basis of $18,000 is allocated to real estate R.

(2) The basis of railroad car R is equal to its cost of $1000.

(iii) The tax treatment to V is as follows:

(A) The exchange group consists of real estate R, real estate A, and real estate B.

(B) Under paragraph (b)(2)(ii) of this section, the liabilities of which V is relieved ($7000) results in excess liabilities relieved of $7000 and is treated as cash received by V.

(1) The exchange group has an exchange group deficiency of $8000 because the fair market value of real estate R ($26,500) exceeds the aggregate fair market value of real estate A and B ($18,500) by that amount.

(2) The difference between the aggregate fair market value of the properties transferred by V in the exchange group, $26,500, and the aggregate fair market value of the properties received by V in the exchange group, $18,500, is $8000. Therefore, there is a residual group in that amount, consisting of the excess liabilities relieved of $7000, which is treated as cash received by V, and $1000 (or 50 percent of the fair market value) of grader A.

(3) The transaction also includes a taxable exchange of railroad car R (which is not of a like kind or like class to any property received by V in the exchange) for the 50 percent portion of grader A (which is not of a like kind or like class to any property transferred by V in the exchange) not allocated to the residual group.

(C) V recognizes gain on the exchange as follows:

(1) With respect to the exchange group, the amount of the gain realized is the excess of the fair market value of real estate R ($26,500) over its adjusted basis ($20,000), or $6500. The amount of the gain recognized is the lesser of the gain realized ($6500) and the exchange group deficiency ($8000), or $6500.

(2) No property transferred by V was allocated to the residual group. Therefore, V does not recognize gain or loss with respect to the residual group.

(3) With respect to the taxable exchange of railroad car R for the 50 percent portion of grader A not allocated to the exchange group or the residual group, a loss is realized and recognized in the amount of $200 (the excess of the $1200 adjusted basis of railroad car R over the amount realized of $1000 (fair market value of the 50 percent portion of grader A)).

(D) The basis of the property received by V in the exchange (real estate A, real estate B, and grader A) are determined in the following manner:

(1) The basis of the property received in the exchange group is the adjusted basis of the property transferred within that exchange group ($20,000), increased by the amount of gain recognized with respect to that exchange group ($6500), and decreased by the amount of the exchange group deficiency ($8000), or $18,500. This $18,500 of basis is allocated proportionately among the assets received within the exchange group in accordance with their fair market values: real estate A's basis is $5000 ($18,500 x $5000/$18,500); real estate B's basis is $13,500 ($18,500 x $13,500/$18,500).

(2) The basis of grader A is $2000.

Sec. 1.1031(k)-1 Treatment of deferred exchanges.

(a) Overview. This section provides rules for the application of section 1031 and the regulations thereunder in the case of a ``deferred exchange.'' For purposes of section 1031 and this section, a deferred exchange is defined as an exchange in which, pursuant to an agreement, the taxpayer transfers property held for productive use in a trade or business or for investment (the ``relinquished property'') and subsequently receives property to be held either for productive use in a trade or business or for investment (the ``replacement property''). In the case of a deferred exchange, if the requirements set forth in paragraphs (b), (c), and (d) of this section (relating to identification and receipt of replacement property) are not satisfied, the replacement property received by the taxpayer will be treated as property which is not of a like kind to the relinquished property. In order to constitute a deferred exchange, the transaction must be an exchange (i.e., a transfer of property for property, as distinguished from a transfer of property for money). For example, a sale of property followed by a purchase of property of a like kind does not qualify for nonrecognition of gain or loss under section 1031 regardless of whether the identification and receipt requirements of section 1031(a)(3) and paragraphs (b), (c), and (d) of this section are satisfied. The transfer of relinquished property in a deferred exchange is not within the provisions of section 1031(a) if, as part of the consideration, the taxpayer receives money or property which does not meet the requirements of section 1031(a), but the transfer, if otherwise qualified, will be within the provisions of either section 1031 (b) or (c). See Sec. 1.1031(a)-1(a)(2). In addition, in the case of a transfer of relinquished property in a deferred exchange, gain or loss may be recognized if the taxpayer actually or constructively receives money or property which does not meet the requirements of section 1031(a) before the taxpayer actually receives like-kind replacement property. If the taxpayer actually or constructively receives money or property which does not meet the requirements of section 1031(a) in the full amount of the consideration for the relinquished property, the transaction will constitute a sale, and not a deferred exchange, even though the taxpayer may ultimately receive like-kind replacement property. For purposes of this section, property which does not meet the requirements of section 1031(a) (whether by being described in section 1031(a)(2) or otherwise) is referred to as ``other property.'' For rules regarding actual and constructive receipt, and safe harbors therefrom, see paragraphs (f) and (g), respectively, of this section. For rules regarding the determination of gain or loss recognized and the basis of property received in a deferred exchange, see paragraph (j) of this section.

(b) Identification and receipt requirements--(1) In general. In the case of a deferred exchange, any replacement property received by the taxpayer will be treated as property which is not of a like kind to the relinquished property if--

(i) The replacement property is not ``identified'' before the end of the ``identification period,'' or

(ii) The identified replacement property is not received before the end of the ``exchange period.''

(2) Identification period and exchange period. (i) The identification period begins on the date the taxpayer transfers the relinquished property and ends at midnight on the 45th day thereafter.

(ii) The exchange period begins on the date the taxpayer transfers the relinquished property and ends at midnight on the earlier of the 180th day thereafter or the due date (including extensions) for the taxpayer's return of the tax imposed by chapter 1 of subtitle A of the Code for the taxable year in which the transfer of the relinquished property occurs.

(iii) If, as part of the same deferred exchange, the taxpayer transfers more than one relinquished property and the relinquished properties are transferred on different dates, the identification period and the exchange period are determined by reference to the earliest date on which any of the properties are transferred.

(iv) For purposes of this paragraph (b)(2), property is transferred when the property is disposed of within the meaning of section 1001(a).

(3) Example. This paragraph (b) may be illustrated by the following example.

Example: (i) M is a corporation that files its Federal income tax return on a calendar year basis. M and C enter into an agreement for an exchange of property that requires M to transfer property X to C. Under the agreement, M is to identify like-kind replacement property which C is required to purchase and to transfer to M. M transfers property X to C on November 16, 1992.

(ii) The identification period ends at midnight on December 31, 1992, the day which is 45 days after the date of transfer of property X. The exchange period ends at midnight on March 15, 1993, the due date for M's Federal income tax return for the taxable year in which M transferred property X. However, if M is allowed the automatic six-month extension for filing its tax return, the exchange period ends at midnight on May 15, 1993, the day which is 180 days after the date of transfer of property X.

(c) Identification of replacement property before the end of the identification period--(1) In general. For purposes of paragraph (b)(1)(i) of this section (relating to the identification requirement), replacement property is identified before the end of the identification period only if the requirements of this paragraph (c) are satisfied with respect to the replacement property. However, any replacement property that is received by the taxpayer before the end of the identification period will in all events be treated as identified before the end of the identification period.

(2) Manner of identifying replacement property. Replacement property is identified only if it is designated as replacement property in a written document signed by the taxpayer and hand delivered, mailed, telecopied, or otherwise sent before the end of the identification period to either--

(i) The person obligated to transfer the replacement property to the taxpayer (regardless of whether that person is a disqualified person as defined in paragraph (k) of this section); or

(ii) Any other person involved in the exchange other than the taxpayer or a disqualified person (as defined in paragraph (k) of this section).

Examples of persons involved in the exchange include any of the parties to the exchange, an intermediary, an escrow agent, and a title company. An identification of replacement property made in a written agreement for the exchange of properties signed by all parties thereto before the end of the identification period will be treated as satisfying the requirements of this paragraph (c)(2).

(3) Description of replacement property. Replacement property is identified only if it is unambiguously described in the written document or agreement. Real property generally is unambiguously described if it is described by a legal description, street address, or distinguishable name (e.g., the Mayfair Apartment Building). Personal property generally is unambiguously described if it is described by a specific description of the particular type of property. For example, a truck generally is unambigously described if it is described by a specific make, model, and year.

(4) Alternative and multiple properties. (i) The taxpayer may identify more than one replacement property. Regardless of the number of relinguished properties transferred by the taxpayer as part of the same deferred exchange, the maximum number of replacement properties that the taxpayer may identify is--

(A) Three properties without regard to the fair market values of the properties (the ``3-property rule"), or

(B) Any number of properties as long as their aggregate fair market value as of the end of the identification period does not exceed 200 percent of the aggregate fair market value of all the relinguished properties as of the date the relinguished properties were transferred by the taxpayer (the "200-percent rule").

(ii) If, as of the end of the identification period, the taxpayer has identified more properties as replacement properties than permitted by paragraph (c)(4)(i) of this section, the taxpayer is treated as if no replacement property had been identified. The preceding sentence will not apply, however, and an identification satisfying the requirements of paragraph (c)(4)(i) of this section will be considered made, with respect to—

(A) Any replacement property received by the taxpayer before the end of the identification period, and

(B) Any replacement property identified before the end of the identification period and received before the end of the exchange period, but only if the taxpayer receives before the end of the exchange period identified replacement property the fair market vlaue of which is at least 95 percent of the aggregate fair market value of all identified replacement properties (the ``95-percent rule").

For this purpose, the fair market value of each identified replacement property is determined as of the earlier of the date the property is received by the taxpayer or the last day of the exchange period.

(iii) For purposes of applying the 3-property rule, the 200-percent rule, and the 95-percent rule, all identifications of replacement property, other than identifications of replacement property that have been revoked in the manner provided in paragraph (c)(6) of this section, are taken into account. For example, if, in a deferred exchange, B transfers property X with a fair market value of $100,000 to C and B receives like-kind property Y with a fair market value of $50,000 before the end of the identification period, under paragraph (c)(1) of this section, property Y is treated as identified by reason of being received before the end of the identification period. Thus, under paragraph (c)(4)(i) of this section, B may identify either two additional replacement properties of any fair market value or any number of additional replacement properties as long as the aggregate fair market value of the additional replacement properties does not exceed $150,000.

(5) Incidental property disregarded. (i) Solely for purposes of applying this paragraph (c), property that is incidental to a larger item of property is not treated as property that is separate from the larger item of property. Property is incidental to a larger item of property if--

(A) In standard commercial transactions, the property is typically transferred together with the larger item of property, and

(B) The aggregate fair market value of all of the incidental property does not exceed 15 percent of the aggregate fair market value of the larger item of property.

(ii) This paragraph (c)(5) may be illustrated by the following examples.

Example 1. For purposes of paragraph (c) of this section, a spare tire and tool kit will not be treated as separate property from a truck with a fair market value of $10,000, if the aggregate fair market value of the spare tire and tool kit does not exceed $1,500. For purposes of the 3-property rule, the truck, spare tire, and tool kit are treated as 1 property. Moreover, for purposes of paragraph (c)(3) of this section (relating to the description of replacement property), the truck, spare tire, and tool kit are all considered to be unambiguously described if the make, model, and year of the truck are specified, even if no reference is made to the spare tire and tool kit.

Example 2. For purposes of paragraph (c) of this section, furniture, laundry machines, and other miscellaneous items of personal property will not be treated as separate property from an apartment building with a fair market value of $1,000,000, if the aggregate fair market value of the furniture, laundry machines, and other personal property does not exceed $150,000. For purposes of the 3-property rule, the apartment building, furniture, laundry machines, and other personal property are treated as 1 property. Moreover, for purposes of paragraph (c)(3) of this section (relating to the description of replacement property), the apartment building, furniture, laundry machines, and other personal property are all considered to be unambiguously described if the legal description, street address, or distinguishable name of the apartment building is specified, even if no reference is made to the furniture, laundry machines, and other personal property.

(6) Revocation of identification. An identification of replacement property may be revoked at any time before the end of the identification period. An identification of replacement property is revoked only if the revocation is made in a written document signed by the taxpayer and hand delivered, mailed, telecopied, or othewise sent before the end of the identification period to the person to whom the identification of the replacement property was sent. An identification of replacement property that is made in a written agreement for the exchange of properties is treated as revoked only if the revocation is made in a written amendment to the agreement or in a written document signed by the taxpayer and hand delivered, mailed, telecopied, or othewise sent before the end of the identification period to all of the parties to the agreement.

(7) Examples. This paragraph (c) may be illustrated by the following examples. Unless otherwise provided in an example, the following facts are assumed: B, a calendar year taxpayer, and C agree to enter into a deferred exchange. Pursuant to their agreement, B

transfers real property X to C on May 17, 1991. Real property X, which has been held by B for investment, is unencumbered and has a fair market value on May 17,1991, of $100,000. On or before July 1, 1991 (the end of the identification period), B is to identify replacement property that is of a like kind to real property X. On or before November 13, 1991 (the end of the exchange period), C is required to purchase the property identified by B and to transfer that property to B. To the extent the fair market value of the replacement property transferred to B is greater or less than the fair market value of real property X, either B or C, as applicable, will make up the difference by paying cash to the other party after the date the replacement property is received by B. No replacement property is identified in the agreement. When subsequently identified, the replacement property is described by legal description and is of a like kind to real property X (determined without regard to section 1031(a)(3) and this section). B intends to hold the replacement property received for investment.

Example 1. (i) On July 2, 1991, B identifies real property E as replacement property by designating real property E as replacement property in a written document signed by B and personally delivered to
C.

(ii) Because the identification was made after the end of the identification period, pursuant to paragraph (b)(1)(i) of this section (relating to the identification requirement), real property E is treated as property which is not of a like kind to real property X.

Example 2. (i) C is a corporation of which 20 percent of the outstanding stock is owned by B. On July 1, 1991, B identifies real property F as replacement property by designating real property F as replacement property in a written document signed by B and mailed to C.

(ii) Because C is the person obligated to transfer the replacement property to B, real property F is identified before the end of the identification period. The fact that C is a ``disqualified person" as defined in paragraph (k) of this section does not change this result.

(iii) Real property F would also have been treated as identified before the end of the identification period if, instead of sending the identification to C, B had designated real property F as replacement property in a written agreement for the exchange of properties signed by all parties thereto on or before July 1, 1991.

Example 3. (i) On June 3, 1991, B identifies the replacement property as ``unimproved land located in Hood County with a fair market value not to exceed $100,000." The designation is made in a written document signed by B and personally delivered to C. On July

8, 1991, B and C agree that real property G is the property described in the June 3, 1991 document.

(ii) Because real property G was not unambiguously described before the end of the identification period, no replacement property is identified before the end of the identification period.

Example 4. (i) On June 28, 1991, B identifies real properties H, J, and K as replacement properties by designating these properties as replacement properties in a written document signed by B and personally delivered to C. The written document provides that by August 1, 1991, B will orally inform C which of the identified properties C is to transfer to B. As of July 1, 1991, the fair market values of real properties H, J, and K are $75,000, $100,000, and $125,000, respectively.

(ii) Because B did not identify more than three properties as replacement properties, the requirements of the 3-property rule are satisfied, and real properties H, J, and K are all identified before the end of the identification period.

Example 5. (i) On May 17, 1991, B identifies real properties L, M, N, and P as replacement properties by designating these properties as replacement properties in a written document signed by B and personally delivered to C. The written document provides that by July 2, 1991, B will orally inform C which of the identified properties C is to transfer to B. As of July 1, 1991, the fair market values of real properties L, M, N, and P are $30,000, $40,000, $50,000, and $60,000, respectively.

(ii) Although B identified more than three properties as replacement properties, the aggregate fair market value of the identified properties as of the end of the identification period ($180,000) did not exceed 200 percent of the aggregate fair market value of real property X (200% x $100,000 = $200,000). Therefore, the requirements of the 200-percent rule are satisfied, and real properties L, M, N, and P are all identified before the end of the identification period.

Example 6. (i) On June 21, 1991, B identifies real properties Q, R, and S as replacement properties by designating these properties as replacement properties in a written document signed by B and mailed to C. On June 24, 1991, B identifies real properties T and U as replacement properties in a written document signed by B and mailed to C. On June 28, 1991, B revokes the identification of real properties Q and R in a written document signed by B and personally delivered to C.

(ii) B has revoked the identification of real properties Q and R in the manner provided by paragraph (c)(6) of this section.

Identifications of replacement property that have been revoked in the manner provided by paragraph (c)(6) of this section are not taken into account for purposes of applying the 3-property rule. Thus, as of June 28, 1991, B has identified only replacement properties S, T, and U for purposes of the 3-property rule. Because B did not identify more than three properties as replacement properties for purposes of the 3-property rule, the requirements of that rule are satisfied, and real properties S, T, and U are all identified before the end of the identification period.

Example 7. (i) On May 20, 1991, B identifies real properties V and W as replacement properties by designating these properties as replacement properties in a written document signed by B and personally delivered to C. On June 4, 1991, B identifies real properties Y and Z as replacement properties in the same manner. On June 5, 1991, B telephones C and orally revokes the identification of real properties V and W. As of July 1, 1991, the fair market values of real properties V, W, Y, and Z are $50,000, $70,000, $90,000, and $100,000, respectively. On July 31, 1991, C purchases real property Y and Z and transfers them to B.

(ii) Pursuant to paragraph (c)(6) of this section (relating to revocation of identification), the oral revocation of the identification of real properties V and W is invalid. Thus, the identification of real properties V and W is taken into account for purposes of determining whether the requirements of paragraph (c)(4) of this section (relating to the identification of alternative and multiple properties) are satisfied. Because B identified more than three properties and the aggregate fair market value of the identified properties as of the end of the identification period ($310,000) exceeds 200 percent of the fair market value of real property X (200% x $100,000 = $200,000), the requirements of paragraph (c)(4) of this section are not satisfied, and B is treated as if B did not identify any replacement property.

(d) Receipt of identified replacement property--(1) In general. For purposes of paragraph (b)(1)(ii) of this section (relating to the receipt requirement), the identified replacement property is received before the end of the exchange period only if the requriements of this paragraph (d) are satisfied with respect to the replacement property. In the case of a deferred exchange, the identified replacement property is received before the end of the exchange period if--

(i) The taxpayer receives the replacement property before the end of the exchange period, and

(ii) The replacement property received is substantially the same property as identified.

If the taxpayer has identified more than one replacement property, section 1031(a)(3)(B) and this paragraph (d) are applied separately to each replacement property.

(2) Examples. This paragraph (d) may be illustrated by the following examples. The following facts are assumed: B, a calendar year taxpayer, and C agree to enter into a deferred exchange. Pursuant to their agreement, B transfers real property X to C on May 17, 1991. Real property X, which has been held by B for investment, is unencumbered and has a fair market value on May 17, 1991, of $100,000. On or before July 1, 1991 (the end of the identification period), B is to identify replacement property that is of a like kind to real property X. On or before November 13, 1991 (the end of the exchange period), C is required to purchase the property identified by B and to transfer that property to B. To the extent the fair market value of the replacement property transferred to B is greater or less than the fair market value of real property X, either B or C, as applicable, will make up the difference by paying cash to the other party after the date the replacement property is received by B. The replacement property is identified in a manner that satisfies paragraph (c) of this section (relating to identification of replacement property) and is of a like kind to real property X (determined without regard to section 1031(a)(3) and this section). B intends to hold any replacement property received for investment.

Example 1. (i) In the agreement, B identifies real properties J, K, and L as replacement properties. The agreement provides that by July 26, 1991, B will orally inform C which of the properties C is to transfer to B.

(ii) As of July 1, 1991, the fair market values of real properties J, K, and L are $75,000, $100,000, and $125,000, respectively. On July 26, 1991, B instructs C to acquire real property K. On October 31, 1991, C purchases real property K for $100,000 and transfers the property to B.

(iii) Because real property K was identified before the end of the identification period and was received before the end of the exchange period, the identification and receipt requirements of section 1031(a)(3) and this section are satisfied with respect to real property K.

Example 2. (i) In the agreement, B identifies real property P as replacement property. Real property P consists of two acres of unimproved land. On October 15, 1991, the owner of real property P erects a fence on the property. On November 1, 1991, C purchases real property P and transfers it to B.

(ii) The erection of the fence on real property P subsequent to its identification did not alter the basic nature or character of real property P as unimproved land. B is considered to have received substantially the same property as identified.

Example 3. (i) In the agreement, B identifies real property Q as replacement property. Real property Q consists of a barn on two acres of land and has a fair market value of $250,000 ($187,500 for the barn and underlying land and $87,500 for the remaining land). As of July 26, 1991, real property Q remains unchanged and has a fair market value of $250,000. On that date, at B's direction, C purchases the barn and underlying land for $187,500 and transfers it to B, and B pays $87,500 to C.

(ii) The barn and underlying land differ in basic nature or character from real property Q as a whole, B is not considered to have received substantially the same property as identified.

Example 4. (i) In the agreement, B identifies real property R as replacement property. Real property R consists of two acres of unimproved land and has a fair market value of $250,000. As of October 3, 1991, real property R remains unimproved and has a fair market value of $250,000. On that date, at B's direction, C purchases 1\1/2\ acres of real property R for $187,500 and transfers it to B, and B pays $87,500 to C.

(ii) The portion of real property R that B received does not differ from the basic nature or character of real property R as a whole. Moreover, the fair market value of the portion of real property R that B received ($187,500) is 75 percent of the fair market value of real property R as of the date of receipt. Accordingly, B is considered to have received substantially the same property as identified.

(e) Special rules for identification and receipt of replacement property to be produced--(1) In general. A transfer of relinquished property in a deferred exchange will not fail to qualify for nonrecognition of gain or loss under section 1031 merely because the replacement property is not in existence or is being produced at the time the property is identified as replacement property. For purposes of this paragraph (e), the terms ``produced" and ``production" have the same meanings as provided in section 263A(g)(1) and the regulations
thereunder.

(2) Identification of replacement property to be produced. (i) In the case of replacement property that is to be produced, the replacement property must be identified as provided in paragraph (c) of this section (relating to identification of replacement property). For example, if the identified replacement property consists of improved real property where the improvements are to be constructed, the description of the replacement property satisfies the requirements of paragraph (c)(3) of this section (relating to description of replacement property) if a legal description is provided for the underlying land and as much detail is provided regarding construction of the improvements as is practicable at the time the identification is made.

(ii) For purposes of paragraphs (c)(4)(i)(B) and (c)(5) of this section (relating to the 200-percent rule and incidental property), the fair market value of replacement property that is to be produced is its estimated fair market value as of the date it is expected to be received by the taxpayer.

(3) Receipt of replacement property to be produced. (i) For purposes of paragraph (d)(1)(ii) of this section (relating to receipt of the identified replacement property), in determining whether the replacement property received by the taxpayer is substantially the same property as identified where the identified replacement property is property to be produced, variations due to usual or typical production changes are not taken into account. However, if substantial changes are made in the property to be produced, the replacement property received will not be considered to be substantially the same property as identified.

(ii) If the identified replacement property is personal property to be produced, the replacement property received will not be considered to be substantially the same property as identified unless production of the replacement property received is completed on or before the date the property is received by the taxpayer.

(iii) If the identified replacement property is real property to be produced and the production of the property is not completed on or before the date the taxpayer receives the property, the property received will be considered to be substantially the same property as identified only if, had production been completed on or before the date the taxpayer receives the replacement property, the property received would have been considered to be substantially the same property as identified. Even so, the property received is considered to be substantially the same property as identified only to the extent the property received constitutes real property under local law.

(4) Additional rules. The transfer of relinquished property is not within the provisions of section 1031(a) if the relinquished property is transferred in exchange for services (including production services). Thus, any additional production occurring with respect to the replacement property after the property is received by the taxpayer will not be treated as the receipt of property of a like kind.

(5) Example. This paragraph (e) may be illustrated by the following example.

Example: (i) B, a calendar year taxpayer, and C agree to enter into a deferred exchange. Pursuant to their agreement, B transfers improved real property X and personal property Y to C on May 17, 1991. On or before November 13, 1991 (the end of the exchange period), C is required to transfer to B real property M, on which C is constructing improvements, and personal property N, which C is producing. C is obligated to complete the improvements and production regardless of when properties M and N are transferred to B. Properties M and N are identified in a manner that satisfies paragraphs (c) (relating to identification of replacement property) and (e)(2) of this section. In addition, properties M and N are of a like kind, respectively, to real property X and personal property Y (determined without regard to section 1031(a)(3) and this section). On November 13, 1991, when construction of the improvements to property M is 20 percent completed and the production of property N is 90 percent completed, C transfers to B property M and property N. If construction of the improvements had been completed, property M would have been considered to be substantially the same property as identified. Under local law, property M constitutes real property to the extent of the underlying land and the 20 percent of the construction that is completed.

(ii) Because property N is personal property to be produced and production of property N is not completed before the date the property is received by B, property N is not considered to be substantially the same property as identified and is treated as property which is not of a like kind to property Y.

(iii) Property M is considered to be substantially the same property as identified to the extent of the underlying land and the 20 percent of the construction that is completed when property M is received by B. However, any additional construction performed by C with respect to property M after November 13, 1991, is not treated as the receipt of property of a like kind.

(f) Receipt of money or other property--(1) In general. A transfer of relinquished property in a deferred exchange is not within the provisions of section 1031(a) if, as part of the consideration, the taxpayer receives money or other property. However, such a transfer, if otherwise qualified, will be within the provisions of either section 1031 (b) or (c). See Sec. 1.1031(a)-1(a)(2). In addition, in the case of a transfer of relinquished property in a deferred exchange, gain or loss may be recognized if the taxpayer actually or constructively receives money or other property before the taxpayer actually receives like-kind replacement property. If the taxpayer actually or constructively receives money or other property in the full amount of the consideration for the relinquished property before the taxpayer actually receives like-kind replacement property, the transaction will constitute a sale and not a deferred exchange, even though the taxpayer may ultimately receive like-kind replacement property.

(2) Actual and constructive receipt. Except as provided in paragraph (g) of this section (relating to safe harbors), for purposes of section 1031 and this section, the determination of whether (or the extent to which) the taxpayer is in actual or constructive receipt of

money or other property before the taxpayer actually receives like-kind replacement property is made under the general rules concerning actual and constructive receipt and without regard to the taxpayer's method of accounting. The taxpayer is in actual receipt of money or property at the time the taxpayer actually receives the money or property or receives the economic benefit of the money or property. The taxpayer is in constructive receipt of money or property at the time the money or property is credited to the taxpayer's account, set apart for the taxpayer, or otherwise made available so that the taxpayer may draw upon it at any time or so that the taxpayer can draw upon it if notice of intention to draw is given. Although the taxpayer is not in constructive receipt of money or property if the taxpayer's control of its receipt is subject to substantial limitations or restrictions, the taxpayer is in constructive receipt of the money or property at the time the limitations or restrictions lapse, expire, or are waived. In addition, actual or constructive receipt of money or property by an agent of the taxpayer (determined without regard to paragraph (k) of this section) is actual or constructive receipt by the taxpayer.

(3) Example. This paragraph (f) may be illustrated by the following example.

Example: (i) B, a calendar year taxpayer, and C agree to enter into a deferred exchange. Pursuant to the agreement, on May 17, 1991, B transfers real property X to C. Real property X, which has been held by B for investment, is unencumbered and has a fair market value on May 17, 1991, of $100,000. On or before July 1, 1991 (the end of the identification period), B is to identify replacement property that is of a like kind to real property X. On or before November 13, 1991 (the end of the exchange period), C is required to purchase the property identified by B and to transfer that property to B. At any time after May 17, 1991, and before C has purchased the replacement property, B has the right, upon notice, to demand that C pay $100,000 in lieu of acquiring and transferring the replacement property. Pursuant to the agreement, B identifies replacement property, and C purchases the replacement property and transfers it to B.

(ii) Under the agreement, B has the unrestricted right to demand the payment of $100,000 as of May 17, 1991. B is therefore in constructive receipt of $100,000 on that date. Because B is in constructive receipt of money in the full amount of the consideration for the relinquished property before B actually receives the like-kind replacement property, the transaction constitutes a sale, and the transfer of real property X does not qualify for nonrecognition of gain or loss under section 1031. B is treated as if B received the $100,000 in consideration for the sale of real property X and then purchased the like-kind replacement property.

(iii) If B's right to demand payment of the $100,000 were subject to a substantial limitation or restriction (e.g., the agreement provided that B had no right to demand payment before November 14, 1991 (the end of the exchange period)), then, for purposes of this section, B would not be in actual or constructive receipt of the money unless (or until) the limitation or restriction lapsed, expired, or was waived.

(g) Safe harbors--(1) In general. Paragraphs (g)(2) through (g)(5) of this section set forth four safe harbors the use of which will result in a determination that the taxpayer is not in actual or constructive receipt of money or other property for purposes of section 1031 and this section. More than one safe harbor can be used in the same deferred exchange, but the terms and conditions of each must be separately satisfied. For purposes of the safe harbor rules, the term ``taxpayer'' does not include a person or entity utilized in a safe harbor (e.g., a qualified intermediary). See paragraph (g)(8), Example 3(v), of this section.

(2) Security or guarantee arrangements. (i) In the case of a deferred exchange, the determination of whether the taxpayer is in actual or constructive receipt of money or other property before the taxpayer actually receives like-kind replacement property will be made without regard to the fact that the obligation of the taxpayer's transferee to transfer the replacement property to the taxpayer is or may be secured or guaranteed by one or more of the following--

(A) A mortgage, deed of trust, or other security interest in property (other than cash or a cash equivalent),

(B) A standby letter of credit which satisfies all of the requirements of Sec. 15A.453-1 (b)(3)(iii) and which may not be drawn upon in the absence of a default of the transferee's obligation to transfer like-kind replacement property to the taxpayer, or

(C) A guarantee of a third party.

(ii) Paragraph (g)(2)(i) of this section ceases to apply at the time the taxpayer has an immediate ability or unrestricted right to receive money or other property pursuant to the security or guarantee arrangement.

(3) Qualified escrow accounts and qualified trusts. (i) In the case of a deferred exchange, the determination of whether the taxpayer is in actual or constructive receipt of money or other property before the taxpayer actually receives like-kind replacement property will be made without regard to the fact that the obligation of the taxpayer's transferee to transfer the replacement property to the taxpayer is or may be secured by cash or a cash equivalent if the cash or cash equivalent is held in a qualified escrow account or in a qualified trust.

(ii) A qualified escrow account is an escrow account wherein--

(A) The escrow holder is not the taxpayer or a disqualified person (as defined in paragraph (k) of this section), and

(B) The escrow agreement expressly limits the taxpayer's rights to receive, pledge, borrow, or otherwise obtain the benefits of the cash or cash equivalent held in the escrow account as provided in paragraph (g)(6) of this section.

(iii) A qualified trust is a trust wherein--

(A) The trustee is not the taxpayer or a disqualified person (as defined in paragraph (k) of this section, except that for this purpose the relationship between the taxpayer and the trustee created by the qualified trust will not be considered a relationship under section 267(b)), and   (B) The trust agreement expressly limits the taxpayer's rights to receive, pledge, borrow, or otherwise obtain the benefits of the cash or cash equivalent held by the trustee as provided in paragraph (g)(6) of this section.

(iv) Paragraph (g)(3)(i) of this section ceases to apply at the time the taxpayer has an immediate ability or unrestricted right to receive, pledge, borrow, or otherwise obtain the benefits of the cash or cash equivalent held in the qualified escrow account or qualified trust. Rights conferred upon the taxpayer under state law to terminate or dismiss the escrow holder of a qualified escrow account or the trustee of a qualified trust are disregarded for this purpose.

(v) A taxpayer may receive money or other property directly from a party to the exchange, but not from a qualified escrow account or a qualified trust, without affecting the application of paragraph (g)(3)(i) of this section.

(4) Qualified intermediaries. (i) In the case of a taxpayer's transfer of relinquished property involving a qualified intermediary, the qualified intermediary is not considered the agent of the taxpayer for purposes of section 1031(a). In such a case, the taxpayer's transfer of relinquished property and subsequent receipt of like-kind replacement property is treated as an exchange, and the determination of whether the taxpayer is in actual or constructive receipt of money or other property before the taxpayer actually receives like-kind replacement property is made as if the qualified intermediary is not the agent of the taxpayer.

(ii) Paragraph (g)(4)(i) of this section applies only if the agreement between the taxpayer and the qualified intermediary expressly limits the taxpayer's rights to receive, pledge, borrow, or otherwise obtain the benefits of money or other property held by the qualified intermediary as provided in paragraph (g)(6) of this section.

(iii) A qualified intermediary is a person who--

(A) Is not the taxpayer or a disqualified person (as defined in paragraph (k) of this section), and

(B) Enters into a written agreement with the taxpayer (the ``exchange agreement'') and, as required by the exchange agreement, acquires the relinquished property from the taxpayer, transfers the relinquished property, acquires the replacement property, and transfers the replacement property to the taxpayer.

(iv) Regardless of whether an intermediary acquires and transfers property under general tax principals, solely for purposes of paragraph (g)(4)(iii)(B) of this section--

(A) An intermediary is treated as acquiring and transferring property if the intermediary acquires and transfers legal title to that property,

(B) An intermediary is treated as acquiring and transferring the relinquished property if the intermediary (either on its own behalf or as the agent of any party to the transaction) enters into an agreement with a person other than the taxpayer for the transfer of the relinquished property to that person and, pursuant to that agreement, the relinquished property is transferred to that person, and

(C) An intermediary is treated as acquiring and transferring replacement property if the intermediary (either on its own behalf or as the agent of any party to the transaction) enters into an agreement with the owner of the replacement property for the transfer of that property and, pursuant to that agreement, the replacement property is transferred to the taxpayer.

(v) Solely for purposes of paragraphs (g)(4)(iii) and (g)(4)(iv) of this section, an intermediary is treated as entering into an agreement if the rights of a party to the agreement are assigned to the intermediary and all parties to that agreement are notified in writing of the assignment on or before the date of the relevent transfer of property. For example, if a taxpayer enters into an agreement for the transfer of relinquished property and thereafter assigns its rights in that agreement to an intermediary and all parties to that agreement are notified in writing of the assignment on or before the date of the transfer of the relinquished property, the intermediary is treated as entering into that agreement. If the relinquished property is transferred pursuant to that agreement, the intermediary is treated as having acquired and transferred the relinquished property.

(vi) Paragraph (g)(4)(i) of this section ceases to apply at the time the taxpayer has an immediate ability or unrestricted right to receive, pledge, borrow, or otherwise obtain the benefits of money or other property held by the qualified intermediary. Rights conferred upon the taxpayer under state law to terminate or dismiss the qualified intermediary are disregarded for this purpose.

(vii) A taxpayer may receive money or other property directly from a party to the transaction other than the qualified intermediary without affecting the application of paragraph (g)(4)(i) of this section.

(5) Interest and growth factors. In the case of a deferred exchange, the determination of whether the taxpayer is in actual or constructive receipt of money or other property before the taxpayer actually receives the like-kind replacement property will be made without

regard to the fact that the taxpayer is or may be entitled to receive any interest or growth factor with respect to the deferred exchange. The preceding sentence applies only if the agreement pursuant to which the taxpayer is or may be entitled to the interest or growth factor expressly limits the taxpayer's rights to receive the interest or growth factor as provided in paragragh (g)(6) of this section. For additional rules concerning interest or growth factors, see paragraph (h) of this section.

(6) Additional restrictions on safe harbors under paragraphs (g)(3) through (g)(5). (i) An agreement limits a taxpayer's rights as provided in this paragraph (g)(6) only if the agreement provides that the taxpayer has no rights, except as provided in paragraph (g)(6)(ii) and (g)(6)(iii) of this section, to receive, pledge, borrow, or otherwise obtain the benefits of money or other property before the end of the exchange period.

(ii) The agreement may provide that if the taxpayer has not identified replacement property by the end of the identification period, the taxpayer may have rights to receive, pledge, borrow, or othewise obtain the benefits of money or other property at any time after the end of the identification period.

(iii) The agreement may provide that if the taxpayer has identified replacement property, the taxpayer may have rights to receive, pledge, borrow, or otherwise obtain the benefits of money or other property upon or after--

(A) The receipt by the taxpayer of all of the replacement property to which the taxpayer is entitled under the exchange agreement, or

(B) The occurrence after the end of the identification period of a material and substantial contingency that--

(1) Relates to the deferred exchange,

(2) Is provided for in writing, and

(3) Is beyond the control of the taxpayer and of any disqualified person (as defined in paragraph (k) of this section), other than the person obligated to transfer the replacement property to the taxpayer.

(7) Items disregarded in applying safe harbors under paragraphs (g)(3) through (g)(5). In determining whether a safe harbor under paragraphs (g)(3) through (g)(5) of this section ceases to apply and whether the taxpayer's rights to receive, pledge, borrow, or otherwise obtain the benefits of money or other property are expressly limited as provided in paragraph (g)(6) of this section, the taxpayer's receipt of or right to receive any of the following items will be disregarded--

(i) Items that a seller may receive as a consequence of the disposition of property and that are not included in the amount realized from the disposition of property (e.g., prorated rents), and

(ii) Transactional items that relate to the disposition of the relinquished property or to the acquisition of the replacement property and appear under local standards in the typical closing statements as the responsibility of a buyer or seller (e.g., commissions, prorated taxes, recording or transfer taxes, and title company fees).

(8) Examples. This paragraph (g) may be illustrated by the following examples. Unless otherwise provided in an example, the following facts are assumed: B, a calendar year taxpayer, and C agree to enter into a deferred exchange. Pursuant to their agreement, B is to transfer real property X to C on May 17, 1991. Real property X, which has been held by B for investment, is unencumbered and has a fair market value on May 17, 1991, of $100,000. On or before July 1, 1991 (the end of the identification period), B is to identify replacement property that is of a like kind to real property X. On or before November 13, 1991 (the end of the exchange period), C is required to purchase the property identified by B and to transfer that property to B. To the extent the fair market value of the replacement property transferred to B is greater or less than the fair market value property X, either B or C, as applicable, will make up the difference by paying cash to the other party after the date the replacement property is received by B. The replacement property is identified as provided in paragraph (c) of this section (relating to identification of replacement property) and is of a like kind to real property X (determined without regard to section 1031(a)(3) and this section). B intends to hold any replacement property received for investment.

Example 1. (i) On May 17, 1991, B transfers real property X to C. On the same day, C pays $10,000 to B and deposits $90,000 in escrow as security for C's obligation to perform under the agreement. The escrow agreement provides that B has no rights to receive, pledge, borrow, or otherwise obtain the benefits of the money in escrow before November 14, 1991, except that:

(A) if B fails to identify replacement property on or before July 1, 1991, B may demand the funds in escrow at any time after July 1, 1991; and

(B) if B identifies and receives replacement property, then B may demand the balance of the remaining funds in escrow at any time after B has received the replacement property.

The funds in escrow may be used to purchase the replacement property. The escrow holder is not a disqualified person as defined in paragraph (k) of this section. Pursuant to the terms of the agreement, B identifies replacement property, and C purchases the replacement property using the funds in escrow and tranfers the replacement property to B.

(ii) C's obligation to transfer the replacement property to B was secured by cash held in a qualified escrow account because the escrow holder was not a disqualified person and the escrow agreement expressly limited B's rights to receive, pledge, borrow, or otherwise obtain the benefits of the money in escrow as provided in paragraph (g)(6) of this section. In addition, B did not have the immediate ability or unrestricted right to receive money or other property in escrow before B actually received the like-kind replacement property. Therefore, for purposes of section 1031 and this section, B is determined not to be in actual or constructive receipt of the $90,000 held in escrow before B received the like-kind replacement property. The transfer of real property X by B and B's acquisition of the replacement property qualify as an exchange under section 1031. See paragraph (j) of this section for determining the amount of gain or loss recognized.

Example 2. (i) On May 17, 1991, B transfers real property X to C, and C deposits $100,000 in escrow as security for C's obligation to perform under the agreement. Also on May 17, B identifies real property J as replacement property. The escrow agreement provides that no funds may be paid out without prior written approval of both B and C. The escrow agreement also provides that B has no rights to receive, pledge, borrow, or otherwise obtain the benefits of the money in escrow before November 14, 1991, except that:

(A) B may demand the funds in escrow at any time after the later of July 1, 1991, and the occurrence of any of the following events--

(1) real property J is destroyed, seized, requisitioned, or condemned, or

(2) a determination is made that the regulatory approval necessary for the transfer of real property J cannot be obtained in time for real property J to be transferred to B before the end of the exchange period;

(B) B may demand the funds in escrow at any time after August 14, 1991, if real property J has not been rezoned from residential to commercial use by that date; and

(C) B may demand the funds in escrow at the time B receives real property J or any time thereafter.

Otherwise, B is entitled to all funds in escrow after November 13, 1991. The funds in escrow may be used to purchase the replacement property. The escrow holder is not a disqualified person as described in paragraph (k) of this section. Real property J is not rezoned from residential to commercial use on or before August 14, 1991.

(ii) C's obligation to transfer the replacement property to B was secured by cash held in a qualified escrow account because the escrow holder was not a disqualified person and the escrow agreement expressly limited B's rights to receive, pledge, borrow, or otherwise obtain the benefits of the money in escrow as provided in paragraph (g)(6) of this section. From May 17, 1991, until August 15, 1991, B did not have the immediate ability or unrestricted right to receive money or other property before B actually received the like-kind replacement property. Therefore, for purposes of section 1031 and this section, B is determined not to be in actual or constructive receipt of the $100,000 in escrow from May 17, 1991, until August 15, 1991. However, on August 15, 1991, B had the unrestricted right, upon notice, to draw upon the $100,000 held in escrow. Thus, the safe harbor ceased to apply and B was in constructive receipt of the funds held in escrow. Because B constructively received the full amount of the consideration ($100,000) before B actually received the like-kind replacement property, the transaction is treated as a sale and not as a deferred exchange. The result does not change even if B chose not to demand the funds in escrow and continued to attempt to have real property J rezoned and to receive the property on or before November 13, 1991.

(iii) If real property J had been rezoned on or before August 14, 1991, and C had purchased real property J and transferred it to B on or before November 13, 1991, the transaction would have qualified for nonrecognition of gain or loss under section 1031(a).

Example 3. (i) On May 1, 1991, D offers to purchase real property X for $100,000. However, D is unwilling to participate in a like-kind exchange. B thus enters into an exchange agreement with C whereby B retains C to facilitate an exchange with respect to real property X. C is not a disqualified person as described in paragraph (k) of this section. The exchange agreement between B and C provides that B is to execute and deliver a deed conveying real property X to C who, in turn, is to execute and deliver a deed conveying real property X to D. The exchange agreement expressly limits B's rights to receive, pledge, borrow, or otherwise obtain the benefits of money or other property held by C as provided in paragraph (g)(6) of this section. On May 3, 1991, C enters into an agreement with D to transfer real property X to D for $100,000. On May 17, 1991, B executes and delivers to C a deed conveying real property X to C. On the same date, C executes and delivers to D a deed conveying real property X to D, and D deposits $100,000 in escrow. The escrow holder is not a disqualified person as defined in paragraph (k) of this section and the escrow agreement expressly limits B's rights to receive, pledge, borrow, or otherwise obtain the benefits of money or other property in escrow as provided in paragraph (g)(6) of this section. However, the escrow agreement provides that the money in escrow may be used to purchase replacement property. On June 3, 1991, B identifies real property K as replacement property. On August 9, 1991, E executes and delivers to C a deed conveying real property K to C and $80,000 is released from the escrow and paid to E. On the same date, C executes and delivers to B a deed conveying real property K to B, and the escrow holder pays B $20,000, the balance of the $100,000 sale price of real property X remaining after the purchase of real property K for $80,000.

(ii) B and C entered into an exchange agreement that satisfied the requirements of paragraph (g)(4)(iii)(B) of this section. Regardless of whether C may have acquired and transferred real property X under general tax principles, C is treated as having acquired and transferred real property X because C acquired and transferred legal title to real property X. Similarly, C is treated as having acquired and transferred real property K because C acquired and transferred legal title to real property K. Thus, C was a qualified intermediary. This result is reached for purposes of this section regardless of whether C was B's agent under state law.

(iii) Because the escrow holder was not a disqualified person and the escrow agreement expressly limited B's rights to receive, pledge, borrow, or otherwise obtain the benefits of money or other property in escrow as provided in paragraph (g)(6) of this section, the escrow account was a qualified escrow account. For purposes of section 1031 and this section, therefore, B is determined not to be in actual or constructive receipt of the funds in escrow before B received real property K.

(iv) The exchange agreement between B and C expressly limited B's rights to receive, pledge, borrow, or otherwise obtain the benefits of any money held by C as provided in paragraph (g)(6) of this section. Because C was a qualified intermediary, for purposes of section 1031 and this section B is determined not to be in actual or constructive receipt of any funds held by C before B received real property K. In addition, B's transfer of real property X and acquisition of real property K qualify as an exchange under section 1031. See paragraph (j) of this section for determining the amount of gain or loss recognized.

(v) If the escrow agreement had expressly limited C's rights to receive, pledge, borrow, or otherwise obtain the benefits of money or other property in escrow as provided in paragraph (g)(6) of this section, but had not expressly limited B's rights to receive, pledge, borrow, or otherwise obtain the benefits of that money or other property, the escrow account would not have been a qualified escrow account. Consequently, paragraph (g)(3)(i) of this section would not have been applicable in determining whether B was in actual or constructive receipt of that money or other property before B received real property K.

Example 4. (i) On May 1, 1991, B enters into an agreement to sell real property X to D for $100,000 on May 17, 1991. However, D is unwilling to participate in a like-kind exchange. B thus enters into an exchange agreement with C whereby B retains C to facilitate an exchange with respect to real property X. C is not a disqualified person as described in paragraph (k) of this section. In the exchange agreement between B and C, B assigns to C all of B's rights in the agreement with D. The exchange agreement expressly limits B's rights to receive, pledge, borrow, or otherwise obtain the benefits of money or other property held by C as provided in paragraph (g)(6) of this section. On May 17, 1991, B notifies D in writing of the assignment. On the same date, B executes and delivers to D a deed conveying real property X to D. D pays $10,000 to B and $90,000 to C. On June 1, 1991, B identifies real property L as replacement property. On July 5, 1991, B enters into an agreement to purchase real property L from E for $90,000, assigns its rights in that agreement to C, and notifies E in writing of the assignment. On August 9, 1991, C pays $90,000 to E, and E executes and delivers to B a deed conveying real property L to B.

(ii) The exchange agreement entered into by B and C satisfied the requirements of paragraph (g)(4)(iii)(B) of this section. Because B's rights in its agreements with D and E were assigned to C, and D and E were notified in writing of the assignment on or before the transfer of real properties X and L, respectively, C is treated as entering into those agreements. Because C is treated as entering into an agreement with D for the transfer of real property X and, pursuant to that agreement, real property X was transferred to D, C is treated as acquiring and transferring real property X. Similarly, because C is treated as entering into an agreement with E for the transfer of real property K and, pursuant to that agreement, real property K was transferred to B, C is treated as acquiring and transferring real property K. This result is reached for purposes of this section regardless of whether C was B's agent under state law and regardless of whether C is considered, under general tax principles, to have acquired title or beneficial ownership of the properties. Thus, C was a qualified intermediary.

(iii) The exchange agreement between B and C expressly limited B's rights to receive, pledge, borrow, or otherwise obtain the benefits of the money held by C as provided in paragraph (g)(6) of this section. Thus, B did not have the immediate ability or unrestricted right to receive money or other property held by C before B received real property L. For purposes of section 1031 and this section, therefore, B is determined not to be in actual or constructive receipt of the $90,000 held by C before B received real property L. In addition, the transfer of real property X by B and B's acquisition of real property L qualify as an exchange under section 1031. See paragraph (j) of this section for determining the amount of gain or loss recognized.

Example 5. (i) On May 1, 1991, B enters into an agreement to sell real property X to D for $100,000. However, D is unwilling to participate in a like-kind exchange. B thus enters into an agreement with C whereby B retains C to facilitate an exchange with respect to real property X. C is not a disqualified person as described in paragraph (k) of this section. The agreement between B and C expressly limits B's rights to receive, pledge, borrow, or otherwise obtain the benefits of money or other property held by C as provided in paragraph (g)(6) of this section. C neither enters into an agreement with D to transfer real property X to D nor is assigned B's rights in B's agreement to sell real property X to D. On May 17, 1991, B transfers real property X to D and instructs D to transfer the $100,000 to C. On June 1, 1991, B identifies real property M as replacement property. On August 9, 1991, C purchases real property L from E for $100,000, and E executes and delivers to C a deed conveying real property M to C. On the same date, C executes and delivers to B a deed conveying real property M to B.

(ii) Because B transferred real property X directly to D under B's agreement with D, C did not acquire real property X from B and transfer real property X to D. Moreover, because C did not acquire legal title to real property X, did not enter into an agreement with D to transfer real property X to D, and was not assigned B's rights in B's agreement to sell real property X to D, C is not treated as acquiring and transferring real property X. Thus, C was not a qualified intermediary and paragraph (g)(4))(i) of this section does not apply.

(iii) B did not exchange real property X for real property M. Rather, B sold real property X to D and purchased, through C, real property M. Therefore, the transfer of real property X does not qualify for nonrecognition of gain or loss under section 1031.

(h) Interest and growth factors--(1) In general. For purposes of this section, the taxpayer is treated as being entitled to receive interest or a growth factor with respect to a deferred exchange if the amount of money or property the taxpayer is entitled to receive depends upon the length of time elapsed between transfer of the relinquished property and receipt of the replacement property.

(2) Treatment as interest. If, as part of a deferred exchange, the taxpayer receives interest or a growth factor, the interest or growth factor will be treated as interest, regardless of whether it is paid to the taxpayer in cash or in property (including property of a like kind). The taxpayer must include the interest or growth factor in income according to the taxpayer's method of accounting.

(i) [Reserved]

(j) Determination of gain or loss recognized and the basis of property received in a deferred exchange--(1) In general. Except as otherwise provided, the amount of gain or loss recognized and the basis of property received in a deferred exchange is determined by applying the rules of section 1031 and the regulations thereunder. See Secs. 1.1031(b)-1, 1.1031(c)-1, 1.1031(d)-1, 1.1031(d)-1T, 1.1031(d)-2, and 1.1031(j)-1.

(2) Coordination with section 453--(i) Qualified escrow accounts and qualified trusts. Subject to the limitations of paragraphs (j)(2) (iv) and (v) of this section, in the case of a taxpayer's transfer of relinquished property in which the obligation of the taxpayer's transferee to transfer replacement property to the taxpayer is or may

be secured by cash or a cash equivalent, the determination of whether the taxpayer has received a payment for purposes of section 453 and Sec. 15a.453-1(b)(3)(i) of this chapter will be made without regard to the fact that the obligation is or may be so secured if the cash or cash equivalent is held in a qualified escrow account or a qualified trust. This paragraph (j)(2)(i) ceases to apply at the earlier of--

(A) The time described in paragraph (g)(3)(iv) of this section; or

(B) The end of the exchange period.

(ii) Qualified intermediaries. Subject to the limitations of paragraphs (j)(2) (iv) and (v) of this section, in the case of a taxpayer's transfer of relinquished property involving a qualified intermediary, the determination of whether the taxpayer has received a payment for purposes of section 453 and Sec. 15a.453-1(b)(3)(i) of this chapter is made as if the qualified intermediary is not the agent of the taxpayer. For purposes of this paragraph (j)(2)(ii), a person who otherwise satisfies the definition of a qualified intermediary is treated as a qualified intermediary even though that person ultimately fails to acquire identified replacement property and transfer it to the taxpayer. This paragraph (j)(2)(ii) ceases to apply at the earlier of--

(A) The time described in paragraph (g)(4)(vi) of this section; or

(B) The end of the exchange period.

(iii) Transferee indebtedness. In the case of a transaction described in paragraph (j)(2)(ii) of this section, the receipt by the taxpayer of an evidence of indebtedness of the transferee of the qualified intermediary is treated as the receipt of an evidence of indebtedness of the person acquiring property from the taxpayer for purposes of section 453 and Sec. 15a.453-1(b)(3)(i) of this chapter.

(iv) Bona fide intent requirement. The provisions of paragraphs (j)(2) (i) and (ii) of this section do not apply unless the taxpayer has a bona fide intent to enter into a deferred exchange at the beginning of the exchange period. A taxpayer will be treated as having a bona fide intent only if it is reasonable to believe, based on all the facts and circumstances as of the beginning of the exchange period, that like-kind replacement property will be acquired before the end of the exchange period.

(v) Disqualified property. The provisions of paragraphs (j)(2) (i) and (ii) of this section do not apply if the relinquished property is disqualified property. For purposes of this paragraph (j)(2), disqualified property means property that is not held for productive use in a trade or business or for investment or is property described in section 1031(a)(2).

(vi) Examples. This paragraph (j)(2) may be illustrated by the following examples. Unless otherwise provided in an example, the following facts are assumed: B is a calendar year taxpayer who agrees to enter into a deferred exchange. Pursuant to the agreement, B is to transfer real property X. Real property X, which has been held by B for investment, is unencumbered and has a fair market value of

$100,000 at the time of transfer. B's adjusted basis in real property X at that time is $60,000. B identifies a single like-kind replacement property before the end of the identification period, and B receives the replacement property before the end of the exchange period. The transaction qualifies as a like-kind exchange under section 1031.

Example 1. (i) On September 22, 1994, B transfers real property X to C and C agrees to acquire like-kind property and deliver it to B. On that date B has a bona fide intent to enter into a deferred exchange. C's obligation, which is not payable on demand or readily tradable, is secured by $100,000 in cash. The $100,000 is deposited by C in an escrow account that is a qualified escrow account under paragraph (g)(3) of this section. The escrow agreement provides that B has no rights to receive, pledge, borrow, or otherwise obtain the benefits of the cash deposited in the escrow account until the earlier of the date the replacement property is delivered to B or the end of the exchange period. On March 11, 1995, C acquires replacement property having a fair market value of $80,000 and delivers the replacement property to B. The $20,000 in cash remaining in the qualified escrow account is distributed to B at that time.

(ii) Under section 1031(b), B recognizes gain to the extent of the $20,000 in cash that B receives in the exchange. Under paragraph (j)(2)(i) of this section, the qualified escrow account is disregarded for purposes of section 453 and Sec. 15a.453-1(b)(3)(i) of this chapter in determining whether B is in receipt of payment. Accordingly, B's receipt of C's obligation on September 22, 1994, does not constitute a payment. Instead, B is treated as receiving payment on March 11, 1995, on receipt of the $20,000 in cash from the qualified escrow account. Subject to the other requirements of sections 453 and 453A, B may report the $20,000 gain in 1995 under the installment method. See section 453(f)(6) for special rules for determining total contract price and gross profit in the case of an exchange described in section 1031(b).

Example 2. (i) D offers to purchase real property X but is unwilling to participate in a like-kind exchange. B thus enters into an exchange agreement with C whereby B retains C to facilitate an exchange with respect to real property X. On September 22, 1994, pursuant to the agreement, B transfers real property X to C who transfers it to D for $100,000 in cash. On that date B has a bona fide intent to enter into a deferred exchange. C is a qualified intermediary under paragraph (g)(4) of this section. The exchange agreement provides that B has no rights to receive, pledge, borrow, or otherwise obtain the benefits of the money held by C until the earlier of the date the replacement property is delivered to B or the end of the exchange period. On March 11, 1995, C acquires replacement property having a fair market value of $80,000 and delivers it, along with the remaining $20,000 from the transfer of real property X to B.

(ii) Under section 1031(b), B recognizes gain to the extent of the $20,000 cash B receives in the exchange. Under paragraph (j)(2)(ii) of this section, any agency relationship between B and C is disregarded for purposes of section 453 and Sec. 15a.453-1(b)(3)(i) of this chapter in determining whether B is in receipt of payment. Accordingly, B is not treated as having received payment on September 22, 1994, on C's receipt of payment from D for the relinquished property. Instead, B is treated as receiving payment on March 11, 1995, on receipt of the $20,000 in cash from C. Subject to the other requirements of sections 453 and 453A, B may report the $20,000 gain in 1995 under the installment method.

Example 3. (i) D offers to purchase real property X but is unwilling to participate in a like-kind exchange. B enters into an exchange agreement with C whereby B retains C as a qualified intermediary to facilitate an exchange with respect to real property X. On December 1, 1994, pursuant to the agreement, B transfers real property X to C who transfers it to D for $100,000 in cash. On that date B has a bona fide intent to enter into a deferred exchange. The exchange agreement provides that B has no rights to receive, pledge, borrow, or otherwise obtain the benefits of the cash held by C until the earliest of the end of the identification period if B has not identified replacement property, the date the replacement property is delivered to B, or the end of the exchange period. Although B has a bona fide intent to enter into a deferred exchange at the beginning of the exchange period, B does not identify or acquire any replacement property. In 1995, at the end of the identification period, C delivers the entire $100,000 from the sale of real property X to B.

(ii) Under section 1001, B realizes gain to the extent of the amount realized ($100,000) over the adjusted basis in real property X ($60,000), or $40,000. Because B has a bona fide intent at the beginning of the exchange period to enter into a deferred exchange, paragraph (j)(2)(iv) of this section does not make paragraph (j)(2)(ii) of this section inapplicable even though B fails to acquire replacement property. Further, under paragraph (j)(2)(ii) of this section, C is a qualified intermediary even though C does not acquire and transfer replacement property to B. Thus, any agency relationship between B and C is disregarded for purposes of section 453 and Sec. 15a.453-1(b)(3)(i) of this chapter in determining whether B is in receipt of payment. Accordingly, B is not treated as having received payment on December 1, 1994, on C's receipt of payment from D for the relinquished property. Instead, B is treated as receiving payment at the end of the identification period in 1995 on receipt of the $100,000 in cash from C. Subject to the other requirements of sections 453 and 453A, B may report the $40,000 gain in 1995 under the installment method.

Example 4. (i) D offers to purchase real property X but is unwilling to participate in a like-kind exchange. B thus enters into an exchange agreement with C whereby B retains C to facilitate an exchange with respect to real property X. C is a qualified intermediary under paragraph (g)(4) of this section. On September 22, 1994, pursuant to the agreement, B transfers real property X to C who then transfers it to D for $80,000 in cash and D's 10-year installment obligation for $20,000. On that date B has a bona fide intent to enter into a deferred exchange. The exchange agreement provides that B has no rights to receive, pledge, borrow, or otherwise obtain the benefits of the money or other property held by C until the earlier of the date the replacement property is delivered to B or the end of the exchange period. D's obligation bears adequate stated interest and is not payable on demand or readily tradable. On March 11, 1995, C acquires replacement property having a fair market value of $80,000 and delivers it, along with the $20,000 installment obligation, to B.

(ii) Under section 1031(b), $20,000 of B's gain (i.e., the amount of the installment obligation B receives in the exchange) does not qualify for nonrecognition under section 1031(a). Under paragraphs (j)(2) (ii) and (iii) of this section, B's receipt of D's obligation is treated as the receipt of an obligation of the person acquiring the property for purposes of section 453 and Sec. 15a.453-1(b)(3)(i) of this chapter in determining whether B is in receipt of payment. Accordingly, B's receipt of the obligation is not treated as a payment. Subject to the other requirements of sections 453 and 453A, B may report the $20,000 gain under the installment method on receiving payments from D on the obligation.

Example 5. (i) B is a corporation that has held real property X to expand its manufacturing operations. However, at a meeting in November 1994, B's directors decide that real property X is not suitable for the planned expansion, and authorize a like-kind exchange of this property for property that would be suitable for the planned expansion. B enters into an exchange agreement with C whereby B retains C as a qualified intermediary to facilitate an exchange with respect to real property X. On November 28, 1994, pursuant to the agreement, B transfers real property X to C, who then transfers it to D for $100,000 in cash. The exchange agreement does not include any limitations or conditions that make it unreasonable to believe that like-kind replacement property will be acquired before the end of the exchange period. The exchange agreement provides that B has no rights to receive, pledge, borrow, or otherwise obtain the benefits of the cash held by C until the earliest of the end of the identification period, if B has not identified replacement property, the date the replacement property is delivered to B, or the end of the exchange period. In early January 1995, B's directors meet and decide that it is not feasible to proceed with the planned expansion due to a business downturn reflected in B's preliminary financial reports for the last quarter of 1994. Thus, B's directors instruct C to stop seeking replacement property. C delivers the $100,000 cash to B on January

12, 1995, at the end of the identification period. Both the decision to exchange real property X for other property and the decision to cease seeking replacement property because of B's business downturn are recorded in the minutes of the directors' meetings. There are no other facts or circumstances that would indicate whether, on November 28, 1994, B had a bona fide intent to enter into a deferred like-kind exchange.

(ii) Under section 1001, B realizes gain to the extent of the amount realized ($100,000) over the adjusted basis of real property X ($60,000), or $40,000. The directors' authorization of a like-kind exchange, the terms of the exchange agreement with C, and the absence of other relevant facts, indicate that B had a bona fide intent at the beginning of the exchange period to enter into a deferred like-kind exchange. Thus, paragraph (j)(2)(iv) of this section does not make paragraph (j)(2)(ii) of this section inapplicable, even though B fails to acquire replacement property. Further, under paragraph (j)(2)(ii) of this section, C is a qualified intermediary, even though C does not transfer replacement property to B. Thus, any agency relationship between B and C is disregarded for purposes of section 453 and Sec. 15a.453-1(b)(3)(i) of this chapter in determining whether B is in receipt of payment. Accordingly, B is not treated as having received payment until January 12, 1995, on receipt of the $100,000 cash from C. Subject to the other requirements of sections 453 and 453A, B may report the $40,000 gain in 1995 under the installment method.

Example 6. (i) B has held real property X for use in its trade or business, but decides to transfer that property because it is no longer suitable for B's planned expansion of its commercial enterprise. B and D agree to enter into a deferred exchange. Pursuant to their agreement, B transfers real property X to D on September 22, 1994, and D deposits $100,000 cash in a qualified escrow account as security for D's obligation under the agreement to transfer replacement property to B before the end of the exchange period. D's obligation is not payable on demand or readily tradable. The agreement provides that B is not required to accept any property that is not zoned for commercial use. Before the end of the identification period, B identifies real properties J, K, and L, all zoned for residential use, as replacement properties. Any one of these properties, rezoned for commercial use, would be suitable for B's planned expansion. In recent years, the zoning board with jurisdiction over properties J, K, and L has rezoned similar properties for commercial use. The escrow agreement provides that B has no rights to receive, pledge, borrow, or otherwise obtain the benefits of the money in the escrow account until the earlier of the time that the zoning board determines, after the end of the identification period, that it will not rezone the properties for commercial use or the end of the exchange period. On January 5, 1995, the zoning board decides that none of the properties will be rezoned for commercial use. Pursuant to the exchange agreement, B receives the $100,000 cash from the escrow on January 5, 1995. There are no other facts or circumstances that would indicate whether, on September 22, 1994, B had a bona fide intent to enter into a deferred like-kind exchange.

(ii) Under section 1001, B realizes gain to the extent of the amount realized ($100,000) over the adjusted basis of real property X ($60,000), or $40,000. The terms of the exchange agreement with D, the identification of properties J, K, and L, the efforts to have those properties rezoned for commercial purposes, and the absence of other relevant facts, indicate that B had a bona fide intent at the beginning of the exchange period to enter into a deferred exchange. Moreover, the limitations imposed in the exchange agreement on acceptable replacement property do not make it unreasonable to believe that like-kind replacement property would be acquired before the end of the exchange period. Therefore, paragraph (j)(2)(iv) of this section does not make paragraph (j)(2)(i) of this section inapplicable even though B fails to acquire replacement property. Thus, for purposes of section 453 and Sec. 15a.453-1(b)(3)(i) of this chapter, the qualified escrow account is disregarded in determining whether B is in receipt of payment. Accordingly, B is not treated as having received payment on September 22, 1994, on D's deposit of the $100,000 cash into the qualified escrow account. Instead, B is treated as receiving payment on January 5, 1995. Subject to the other requirements of sections 453 and 453A, B may report the $40,000 gain in 1995 under the installment method.

(vii) Effective date. This paragraph (j)(2) is effective for transfers of property occurring on or after April 20, 1994. Taxpayers may apply this paragraph (j)(2) to transfers of property occurring before April 20, 1994, but on or after June 10, 1991, if those transfers otherwise meet the requirements of Sec. 1.1031(k)-1. In addition, taxpayers may apply this paragraph (j)(2) to transfers of property occurring before June 10, 1991, but on or after May 16, 1990, if those transfers otherwise meet the requirements of Sec. 1.1031(k)-1 or follow the guidance of IA-237-84 published in 1990-1, C.B. See Sec. 601.601(d)(2)(ii)(b) of this chapter.

(3) Examples. This paragraph (j) may be illustrated by the following examples. Unless otherwise provided in an example, the following facts are assumed: B, a calendar year taxpayer, and C agree to enter into a deferred exchange. Pursuant to their agreement, B is to transfer real property X to C on May 17, 1991. Real property X, which has been held by B for investment, is unencumbered and has a fair market value on May 17, 1991, of $100,000. B's adjusted basis in real property X is $40,000. On or before July 1, 1991 (the end of the identification period), B is to identify replacement property that is of a

like kind to real property X. On or before November 13, 1991 (the end of the exchange period), C is required to purchase the property identified by B and to transfer that property to B. To the extent the fair market value of the replacement property transferred to B is greater or less than the fair market value of real property X, either B or C, as applicable, will make up the difference by paying cash to the other party after the date the replacement property is received. The replacement property is identified as provided in paragraph (c) of this section and is of a like kind to real property X (determined without regard to section 1031(a)(3) and this section). B intends to hold any replacement property received for investment.

Example 1. (i) On May 17, 1991, B transfers real property X to C and identifies real property R as replacement property. On June 3, 1991, C transfers $10,000 to B. On September 4, 1991, C purchases real property R for $90,000 and transfers real property R to B.

(ii) The $10,000 received by B is ``money or other property'' for purposes of section 1031 and the regulations thereunder. Under section 1031(b), B recognizes gain in the amount of $10,000. Under section 1031(d), B's basis in real property R is $40,000 (i.e., B's basis in real property X ($40,000), decreased in the amount of money received ($10,000), and increased in the amount of gain recognized ($10,000) in the deferred exchange).

Example 2. (i) On May 17, 1991, B transfers real property X to C and identifies real property S as replacement property, and C transfers $10,000 to B. On September 4, 1991, C purchases real property S for $100,000 and transfers real property S to B. On the same day, B transfers $10,000 to C.

(ii) The $10,000 received by B is ``money or other property'' for purposes of section 1031 and the regulations thereunder. Under section 1031(b), B recognizes gain in the amount of $10,000. Under section 1031(d), B's basis in real property S is $50,000 (i.e., B's basis in real property X ($40,000), decreased in the amount of money received ($10,000), increased in the amount of gain recognized ($10,000), and increased in the amount of the additional consideration paid by B ($10,000) in the deferred exchange).

Example 3. (i) Under the exchange agreement, B has the right at all times to demand $100,000 in cash in lieu of replacement property. On May 17, 1991, B transfers real property X to C and identifies real property T as replacement property. On September 4, 1991, C purchases real property T for $100,000 and transfers real property T to B.

(ii) Because B has the right on May 17, 1991, to demand $100,000 in cash in lieu of replacement property, B is in constructive receipt of the $100,000 on that date. Thus, the transaction is a sale and not an exchange, and the $60,000 gain realized by B in the transaction (i.e., $100,000 amount realized less $40,000 adjusted basis) is recognized.

Under section 1031(d), B's basis in real property T is $100,000.

Example 4. (i) Under the exchange agreement, B has the right at all times to demand up to $30,000 in cash and the balance in replacement propertry instead of receiving replacement property in the amount of $100,000. On May 17, 1991, B transfers real property X to C and identifies real property U as replacement property. On September 4, 1991, C purchases real property U for $100,000 and transfers real property U to B.

(ii) The transaction qualifies as a deferred exchange under section 1031 and this section. However, because B had the right on May 17, 1991, to demand up to $30,000 in cash, B is in constructive receipt of $30,000 on that date. Under section 1031(b), B recognizes gain in the amount of $30,000. Under section 1031(d), B's basis in real property U is $70,000 (i.e., B's basis in real property X ($40,000), decreased in the amount of money that B received ($30,000), increased in the amount of gain recognized ($30,000), and increased in the amount of additional consideration paid by B ($30,000) in the deferred exchange).

Example 5. (i) Assume real property X is encumbered by a mortgage of $30,000. On May 17, 1991, B transfers real property X to C and identifies real property V as replacement property, and C assumes the $30,000 mortgage on real property X. Real property V is encumbered by a $20,000 mortgage. On July 5, 1991, C purchases real property V for $90,000 by paying $70,000 and assuming the mortgage and transfers real property V to B with B assuming the mortgage.

(ii) The consideration received by B in the form of the liability assumed by C ($30,000) is offset by the consideration given by B in the form of the liability assumed by B ($20,000). The excess of the liability assumed by C over the liability assumed by B, $10,000, is treated as ``money or other property." See Sec. 1.1031(b)-1(c). Thus, B recognizes gain under section 1031(b) in the amount of $10,000. Under section 1031(d), B's basis in real property V is $40,000 (i.e., B's basis in real property X ($40,000), decreased in the amount of money that B is treated as receiving in the form of the liability assumed by C ($30,000), increased in the amount of money that B is treated as paying in the form of the liability assumed by B ($20,000), and increased in the amount of the gain recognized ($10,000) in the deferred exchange).

(k) Definition of disqualified person. (1) For purposes of this section, a disqualified person is a person described in paragraph (k)(2), (k)(3), or (k)(4) of this section.

(2) The person is the agent of the taxpayer at the time of the transaction. For this purpose, a person who has acted as the taxpayer's employee, attorney, accountant, investment banker or broker, or real estate agent or broker within the 2-year period ending on the date of the transfer of the first of the relinquished properties is

treated as an agent of the taxpayer at the time of the transaction. Solely for purposes of this paragraph (k)(2), performance of the following services will not be taken into account--

(i) Services for the taxpayer with respect to exchanges of property intended to qualify for nonrecognition of gain or loss under section 1031; and

(ii) Routine financial, title insurance, escrow, or trust services for the taxpayer by a financial institution, title insurance company, or escrow company.

(3) The person and the taxpayer bear a relationship described in either section 267(b) or section 707(b) (determined by substituting in each section ``10 percent'' for ``50 percent'' each place it appears).

(4)(i) Except as provided in paragraph (k)(4)(ii) of this section, the person and a person described in paragraph (k)(2) of this section bear a relationship described in either section 267(b) or 707(b) (determined by substituting in each section ``10 percent'' for ``50 percent'' each place it appears).

(ii) In the case of a transfer of relinquished property made by a taxpayer on or after January 17, 2001, paragraph (k)(4)(i) of this section does not apply to a bank (as defined in section 581) or a bank affiliate if, but for this paragraph (k)(4)(ii), the bank or bank affiliate would be a disqualified person under paragraph (k)(4)(i) of this section solely because it is a member of the same controlled group (as determined under section 267(f)(1), substituting ``10 percent'' for ``50 percent' where it appears) as a person that has provided investment banking or brokerage services to the taxpayer within the 2-year period described in paragraph (k)(2) of this section. For purposes of this paragraph (k)(4)(ii), a bank affiliate is a corporation whose principal activity is rendering services to facilitate exchanges of property intended to qualify for nonrecognition of gain under section 1031 and all of whose stock is owned by either a bank or a bank holding company (within the meaning of section 2(a) of the Bank Holding Company Act of 1956 (12 U.S.C. 1841(a)).

(5) This paragraph (k) may be illustrated by the following examples. Unless otherwise provided, the following facts are assumed: On May 1, 1991, B enters into an exchange agreement (as defined in paragraph (g)(4)(iii)(B) of this section) with C whereby B retains C to facilitate an exchange with respect to real property X. On May 17, 1991, pursuant to the agreement, B executes and delivers to C a deed conveying real property X to C. C has no relationship to B described in paragraph (k)(2), (k)(3), or (k)(4) of this section.

Example 1. (i) C is B's accountant and has rendered accounting services to B within the 2-year period ending on May 17, 1991, other than with respect to exchanges of property intended to qualify for nonrecognition of gain or loss under section 1031.

(ii) C is a disqualified person because C has acted as B's

accountant within the 2-year period ending on May 17, 1991.

(iii) If C had not acted as B's accountant within the 2-year period ending on May 17, 1991, or if C had acted as B's accountant within that period only with respect to exchanges intended to qualify for nonrecognition of gain or loss under section 1031, C would not have been a disqualified person.

Example 2. (i) C, which is engaged in the trade or business of acting as an intermediary to facilitate deferred exchanges, is a wholly owned subsidiary of an escrow company that has performed routine escrow services for B in the past. C has previously been retained by B to act as an intermediary in prior section 1031 exchanges.

(ii) C is not a disqualified person notwithstanding the intermediary services previously provided by C to B (see paragraph (k)(2)(i) of this section) and notwithstanding the combination of C's relationship to the escrow company and the escrow services previously provided by the escrow company to B (see paragraph (k)(2)(ii) of this section).

Example 3. (i) C is a corporation that is only engaged in the trade or business of acting as an intermediary to facilitate deferred exchanges. Each of 10 law firms owns 10 percent of the outstanding stock of C. One of the 10 law firms that owns 10 percent of C is M. J is the managing partner of M and is the president of C. J, in his capacity as a partner in M, has also rendered legal advice to B within the 2-year period ending on May 17, 1991, on matters other than exchanges intended to qualify for nonrecognition of gain or loss under section 1031.

(ii) J and M are disqualified persons. C, however, is not a disqualified person because neither J nor M own, directly or indirectly, more than 10 percent of the stock of C. Similarly, J's participation in the management of C does not make C a disqualified person.

(l) [Reserved]

(m) Definition of fair market value. For purposes of this section, the fair market value of property means the fair market value of the property without regard to any liabilities secured by the property.

(n) No inference with respect to actual or constructive receipt rules outside of section 1031. The rules provided in this section relating to actual or constructive receipt are intended to be rules for determining whether there is actual or constructive receipt in the case of a deferred exchange. No inference is intended regarding the application of these rules for purposes of determining whether actual or constructive receipt exists for any other purpose.

(o) Effective date. This section applies to transfers of property made by a taxpayer on or after June 10, 1991. However, a transfer of property made by a taxpayer on or after May 16, 1990, but before June 10, 1991, will be treated as complying with section 1031 (a)(3) and this section if the deferred exchange satisfies either the provision of this section or the provisions of the notice of proposed rulemaking published in the Federal Register on May 16, 1990 (55 FR 20278).

About the Author

Gary Gorman is a retired CPA who has a history of teaching. He has taught national tax classes for both Arthur Andersen & Co. and for Price Waterhouse & Co. and has taught numerous undergraduate tax classes at Oregon State University.

Since 1994 he has educated realtors, investors, CPAs and attorneys throughout the United States and Mexico on the intricacies of 1031 Exchanges. He has a national reputation for making complicated tax concepts seem logical and understandable and is sought after as a speaker at conferences and real estate symposiums.

Gary is also a renowned author of articles dealing with real estate investments and 1031 Exchanges. He has written an extensive array of nationally published articles and has been quoted in a number of national publications, including "Forbes" and "Bloomberg's Wealth Manager." An archive of his articles can be found online at http://www.1031expert.com/1031facts/articles/index.html.

As a Qualified Intermediary, Gary has been involved in more than 30,000 1031 Exchange transactions since 1994. He is the owner and managing partner of the national firm, **1031 Exchange Experts, LLC**, which has headquarters in Denver, Colorado and offices in Arizona, Colorado, Connecticut and Florida.

Gary is dedicated to leading the improvement of the 1031 industry and has developed a number of revolutionary Exchange systems such as the "1031 TouchPoints System™," a system designed to keep clients informed about the status of their Exchange; "1031 Access™," which allows clients to see the details of their separate Exchange accounts online, 24/7; "TeeShots™," which is a periodical e-mail notification tool designed to keep recipients notified of hot topics such as new rulings and court cases; and "1031 TaxPak™," a tool to help clients report their Exchanges on their income tax returns.

About the 1031 Exchange Experts, LLC

Gary Gorman is the founder and managing partner of 1031 Exchange Experts, LLC, a Qualified Intermediary firm structured differently from other Intermediaries in a number of ways:

First, and most importantly, 1031 Exchange Experts is a national group of CPAs and attorneys dedicated to treating each client as if he or she is the firm's only (and therefore most important) client. Their clients have nearly unlimited consultation with the firm, and are available to their clients 24 hours a day, 7 days a week.

1031 Exchange Experts, LLC is renowned in the Exchange industry for its development of several revolutionary Exchange systems:

1031SafeGuards™ – Recognizing that the protection of each client's Exchange proceeds is its most important responsibility, the firm developed 1031SafeGuards™ to ensure that every dollar of client proceeds is protected.

Disaster Protection – All of the firm's computer files and banking records are transferred off-site nightly to the custody of one of the world's top disaster protection companies. If disaster does strike, the firm can be back in business in less than 24 hours.

Bonding – Every Exchange is protected by a multi-million dollar bond. 1031 Exchange Experts is one of the few Intermediary firms in the country that is so bonded.

Separate Accounts – Each client's Exchange proceeds are maintained in a separate, FDIC-insured account and never commingled with any other client's funds. Each client receives the interest on his or her account directly from the bank.

1031Access™ – Each client can view his or her separate account online any time he or she wishes using the firm's state of the art program called 1031Access™. This is a secure, password protected Web portal that allows clients to view the status and history of their accounts, at the bank, whenever they wish. They can see what funds have been deposited to their accounts, what funds have been transferred out, how much interest they've earned and the daily interest rate being paid by the bank.

1031TouchPoints™ – This unique program enables the firm to coordinate all the parties to the exchange, and to inform them of the status of their Exchanges at critical points throughout the Exchange process.

1031TaxPak™ – At the end of the year, each client receives a packet that includes copies of all of the documents from their Exchange that they will need in order to file their tax return. In addition, each client receives a copy of the 1031TaxPak™ Guide Book, which explains line by line how to complete the tax return. Included in the packet are passwords to a part of the Web site that is dedicated to current tax updates about filing tax returns and reporting Exchanges.

TEE-Shots™ – Tips from the Exchange Experts are short, concise, periodic e-mails designed to provide updates on the latest in 1031 laws and cases. It is a service provided free of charge by the company to any who sign up for it on their Web site at: http://www.1031expert.com/1031education/teeshots/subscribe.html.

Web Site – The Web site is easy to navigate and has a substantial, searchable library of articles published throughout the country by or about the firm. It also has numerous downloadable documents and brochures. Pictures and biographies of the staff are also accessible. The site can be accessed at www.1031expert.com. The complete Web site is also viewable in Spanish.

How Can I Protect My Real Estate Assets?

For more information on forming limited liability companies and limited partnerships to protect your real estate holdings in all 50 states, as well as useful tips and strategies, visit Nevada Corporate Center's Web site at www.nevadacorporate.com or call toll-free 1.877.683.9343.

Special Offer: Mention this book and receive a 5% discount on the basic formation fee.

Where Can I Receive More Free Entrepreneur Information?

Sign up to receive SuccessDNA's FREE e-newsletter featuring useful articles and entrepreneur resources. Visit www.successdna.com for more details.

SUCCESS DNA